Scuttle Your Ships
Before Advancing

Scuttle Your Ships Before Advancing

And Other Lessons from History on Leadership and Change for Today's Managers

RICHARD A. LUECKE

OXFORD UNIVERSITY PRESS

For my parents

Oxford University Press

Oxford   New York
Athens   Auckland   Bangkok   Bombay
Calcutta   Cape Town   Dar es Salaam   Delhi
Florence   Hong Kong   Istanbul   Karachi
Kuala Lumpur   Madras   Madrid   Melbourne
Mexico City   Nairobi   Paris   Singapore
Taipei   Tokyo   Toronto

and associated companies in
Berlin   Ibadan

First published in 1994 by Oxford University Press, Inc.,
200 Madison Avenue, New York, New York 10016

First issued as an Oxford University Press paperback, 1995

Library of Congress Cataloging-in-Publication Data
Luecke, Richard A.
Scuttle your ships before advancing: and other lessons
from history on leadership and change
for today's managers / Richard A. Luecke.
p.   cm.   Includes bibliographical references and index.
ISBN 0-19-508408-X
ISBN 0-19-509642-8 (pbk.)
1. Management—History.
2. Management—Case studies.
I. Title.
HD30.5.L83   1994
658—dc20   93-12859

2 4 6 8 10 9 7 5 3 1
Printed in the United States of America

Preface

This book contains a number of historical episodes involving conflict, planning, leadership, and change from which the modern executive may draw useful lessons. The episodes document situations faced by some of history's most intriguing leaders, draw parallels to circumstances faced by modern executives, and illuminate these situations with insights and important scholarship from the literature of contemporary management. They are intended to help readers see business problems of today with new eyes, particularly with respect to the management of change, the power of ideas in shaping enterprise, and the revitalization of organizations through innovation.

History has a great deal to teach us about human foibles and the problems that challenge leaders of organizations in every age. Not so long ago it was fashionable to think otherwise. When I was in college during the 1960s my peers declared history to be irrelevant—perhaps it is irrelevant to twenty-year olds. But no one stays twenty forever (regrettably). As we grow older and gain experience, the relevance of history only becomes more apparent.

The idea of developing this book came in 1988, shortly after the publication of *The Classic Touch: Lessons in Leadership from Homer to Hemingway* by John Clemens and Douglas Mayer (Dow Jones-Irwin, 1987). Clemens and Mayer used great literature to focus on the problems of business leadership. This approach was both original and useful, and Professor Clemens has subsequently developed it into an interesting new method for business school education at Hartwick College's Humanities in Management Institute. Art, after all, mirrors life's important conflicts and challenges, and the artist is free to draw in the bolder strokes that enable us to appreciate them more completely.

The idea of substituting real people and real events for those drawn from literature, however, seemed to me both logical and potentially effective. History and story, after all, share the same Latin root *(historia)*, and in their earliest traditions were practically identical. Further, the historical record is as rich in dramatic situations and memorable characters as the collective imagination of the world's greatest fiction writers. Simply put, true tales of princes, generals, reformers, and adventurers have much to offer the modern executive—as examples, inspirations, and cautions. A number of these tales are offered here in the hope that the reader will find them both relevant and engaging.

Salem, Mass.   R. A. L.
April 1993

Acknowledgments

As a business book editor, it has been my good fortune to have worked closely with dozens of truly top-notch business scholars, economists, consultants, and executives. All have been generous in sharing their ideas about the problems that confront modern managers, and many have encouraged me to complete this work. Several of those individuals have been kind enough to read and comment on parts of the manuscript.

Ben C. Ball, Jr., took time from his world-ranging consulting practice to offer advice on two chapters—advice that really helped me to see the issues addressed in those chapters with new eyes.

Gregory Watson of Xerox Corporation straightened me out on several aspects of statistical process control and the quality movement. Work conducted with Greg on a related project further enriched some of the text in this volume.

Brian L. Joiner, CEO of Joiner Associates, also provide advice in the quality area.

Joe Pine of IBM offered dozens of helpful suggestions for improvement to the chapters he read.

Roy C. Smith of New York University's Stern School of Management gave what may have been the best advice of all, "let the history tell its own story" and keep the "B-School" interpretation to a minimum.

David Meerschwan, now of Goldman Sachs, International, offered a number of valued ideas.

Jim Utterback of MIT, with whom I have worked on another project over the past year, has been a continuing source of support, encouragement, and fresh ideas that no amount of thanks can repay.

Special thanks must go to Herb Addison and his colleagues at Oxford University Press for their encouragement, editing, and suggestions for improvement.

Contents

. . . whoever wishes to foresee the future must consult the past; for human events ever resemble those of preceding times. This arises from the fact that they are produced by men who ever have been, and ever will be, animated by the same passions, and thus they necessarily have the same result.

Machiavelli, *Discourses*

1

Introduction

Life can only be understood backwards; but it must be lived forwards.

Soren Kierkegaard

Several years ago, Robert Hayes of the Harvard Business School wrote an article on *The Timeless Secrets of Industrial Success*. "Business pundits," he wrote, "seem to be forever rediscovering the truths known to those who lived two generations earlier. . . ." He considered calling this phenomenon Hayes's Law of Circular Progress until an erudite British businessman referred him to an 1843 edition of the *Edinburgh Review* that proposed a similar idea: "In the pure and in the Physical Sciences, each generation inherits the conquests made by its predecessors . . . But in the moral sciences . . . particularly the arts of administration . . . the ground seems never to be incontestably won." That each generation receives the hard sciences intact but must ever *relearn* the moral sciences explains, perhaps, why we have succeeded in putting people on the moon while failing to resolve fundamental problems in education, employment, and international peace.

The moral sciences and the arts of administration are the stuff of management, leadership, negotiation, and diplomacy. They contain lessons that must be learned in dealing with people and with difficult and ambiguous situations. Because they are not amenable to codification or formulas, as are the physical and natural sciences, and because they never appear in exactly the same guise twice, they are lessons more difficult to learn and understand than are the behaviors of falling objects and refracted light.

3

The amazing progress made in the hard sciences over the past four hundred years has been made possible by the fact that the discoveries of one scientist can be recorded and distributed in written form across time and space to other scientists, who can pick up the first scientist's trail and advance knowledge still further before passing on their enhanced knowledge to others. Each generation of scientists stands, as Newton put it, on the shoulders of giants: Galileo, Kepler, Pasteur, Einstein, and thousands of others. Every scientist has the opportunity to absorb the experience of his or her predecessors, as apprentices absorb the knowledge and skills of their masters, and then push the boundaries of knowledge still farther. This methodology has eluded practitioners of the moral sciences and administrative arts. In management, the school of hard knocks—direct personal experience—continues to function as the de facto finishing school for executives.

Today, our ability to lead others in important undertakings, to manage organizations, to deal with human conflict and change, and to avoid repeating the foolish mistakes of our predecessors is probably no greater than was that of people who lived hundreds—or thousands—of years ago. While science and medicine race forward, the people-related disciplines seem to go around in circles. The reason for this disappointing state of affairs may be the fact that the skills of leadership, of managing, of interpersonal relations are not easily taught in textbooks or in the classroom, but must be gained instead by individuals through their own experience.

It is this approach to learning—experience—that this book hopes to advance through a number of historical episodes from which men and women who lead and manage can derive useful lessons. Personal ambition, the impact of random events on strategies, the power of ideas and technological innovations to create change, and the vexing problem of institutional decline are among the subjects treated here. At the same time, every effort has been made to create bridges between the issues developed in these episodes from the past and the very pressing problems faced by leaders and managers today.

Experience is highly valued, perhaps because it can only be acquired with patience and effort. Employers pay a premium for the person who has already performed a job over the person who has not. Politicians tout their experience to the voters; job applicants embellish résumés with experiences real and contrived. There are just two ways to gain experience. The first is by trying things out and observing the results. Since we learn from our mistakes, every trial and every error should improve our performance in the next round. The whole notion of the learning curve by which a manufacturer improves efficiency and lowers costs with each successive batch of product run through the factory is based upon this simple idea; in fact, many refer to it as the experience curve. Trial and error is a fine way to learn to ride a bicycle or to improve the quality and throughput of an assembly operation, but it is a terrible way to learn to disarm a bomb. Here, some other way must be found to gain experience.

That other way to gain experience is vicarious (i.e., through the experience of others). Here we step back and review the success or failure of the poor devil who was sent to disarm the bomb! We cannot help but improve our understanding and our performance by being perceptive observers of others—by grasping the lessons of their successes and failures and making them our own.

History is a useful and unexploited tool in this important form of vicarious learning because it provides opportunities to stand aside and observe people in situations that may be analogous to our own, weigh the facts and options involved, and try to make some sense of the outcomes. Historian Joseph Strayer said,

> There will always be familiar elements in a new situation which will aid us in making decisions and in judging what the results of those decisions will be. The wider and deeper our experience the greater our chances of recognizing these familiar elements. . . . We may go wrong in following the clues which [history] offers, but we would be lost without them. . . . History at its best gives us a real chance of reacting sensibly to a new situation. It does not guarantee the correctness of our response, but it should improve the quality of our judgment.[1]

Important lessons can be drawn from the past, from the experience of men and women who have already faced difficult situations in management, in governance, and in leadership that are fundamentally the same as those encountered today. The important corollary that the past is a storehouse of human experience that is ours for the taking can be added to Santayana's adage that "those who cannot remember the past are condemned to repeat it."

Some disagree. Coleridge said that "history is a lantern at the stern of a ship, revealing only where it has been" and casting little light on the course ahead. Some professional historians would argue that past events are unique and cannot be used as guides for future action; we will never find, they would argue, an exact replication of an event such as Chamberlain's famous meeting with

Hitler in Munich. It is true, of course, that the moral sciences lack precision; they cannot conduct controlled experiments or isolate particular variables. Historians cannot conduct a "what if" replay of Munich to see if a hard-line British position would have blunted Nazi aggression. But these objections should not deter us if we proceed with care. We should remember two important things. First, no one doubts that we can learn from our own experiences; this being the case, it logically follows that we can learn from the experiences of others. Second, many of today's challenges are the same as yesterday's—part of the human condition and not unique to any time or place. The confrontation between a man like Neville Chamberlain, who wanted peace at almost any price, and an acquisitive bully like Hitler is a situation we have all seen many times in some fundamental way. Indeed, many were struck by the similarity between Iraq's aggression against Kuwait in 1990 and that of Hitler's invasion of the Sudatenland in 1938. The newsreel image of Chamberlain waving his signed agreement with Hitler, proclaiming "Peace in our time," was surely vivid in the memory of President George Bush, an active participant in the World War II experience, and instrumental in his resolution, "This will not stand."

In the business world, the invasion of established and stable industries by technological innovations has happened so often over the past century that anyone who has studied these invasions can see the patterns that take place in the pace of product and process change, discontinuities in technologies, and desperate attempts of established firms to fight back. These patterns are not much different today than they were in the nineteenth century when Edison's incandescent lamp invaded the market controlled by gas lighting or when the railroads started to elbow out the canal systems. In this sense, history helps us to see the present in a different way.

Many chapters in this book are about leaders. Leaders are by nature at the center of action, where opposing forces collide and where the sparks fly. They are the ones who get things done by pointing the way to others; it is from them that we can learn the most.

There is a great hunger for leadership today, perhaps because we observe it so rarely. In a Charles Addams cartoon published in the *New Yorker* several years ago, an elderly gentleman and a younger colleague were walking past a statue pedestal on top of which a group of stone men were posed in discussion. "There are no great men," the older man advised, "only great committees." That remark captures an unsettling truth about leadership today, particularly in business. In our bones we have a sense that our progress is in the hands of managers and tenders of the organizational machinery, not true leaders: people who know how to keep the trains running on schedule, but who cannot see beyond where the tracks are already laid. We will make no progress without the leaders and the seers who can extend the tracks in new directions, we will merely travel around on the same route.

Human fascination with leaders is long-standing. It finds its first expression in the oral tradition of Homer and his heroes on the shores of Ilium, and in the written epics of Moses, Beowolf, and El Cid. These stories reveal to us the aspects of greatness and frailty that mark leaders as apart from others:

> He ruled lands on all sides.
> Wherever the sea would take them his soldiers sailed,
> And returned with tribute and obedience.
> There was a brave king.
>
> From *Beowolf*

Chroniclers and biographers like Plutarch, Suetonius, Tacitus, Einhardt, and Fulcher of Chartres continued the tradition of literature that focused on leaders as larger-than-life characters. Perhaps the last of this breed was William Prescott, the American scholar of the mid-nineteenth century whose multivolume histories of the conquests of Mexico and Peru, the life and times of Isabella the Catholic, and Emperor Charles V leave us portraits of powerful characters in settings of great drama.

Both the epic storytellers and the old chroniclers share a common approach to the great figures they portray. Heroes and leaders, even great villains, are revealed in terms of their traits: physical stature, keen intellect, craftiness, oratorical powers, ability to inspire, swordsmanship.

> This king Richard Coeur-de-lion was of terrible strength, proven valour and indominable character; he had already gained a reputation. . . . In dignity and power he was inferior to the king of France, but he was richer and was braver.
>
> Beha ed-Din Ibn Shedad, *Life of Saladin*

It should not be surprising, then, that the early formal studies of leadership should focus on the particular traits that leaders share. These have been shown to include:[2]

- above average intelligence
- self-confidence
- social skills
- vision
- creativity
- speaking fluency
- high energy level

Close to three thousand books and articles have been published on the subject of leadership, mostly within the past three decades. Indeed, the youthful sciences of psychology and sociology have found this subject to be a true factory for the production of scholarly articles and theoretical books, mostly written for other scholars and theorists. For the most part, these studies have limited practical value, prompting Warren Bennis, a leading expert in this field, to say, "Never have so many labored so long to say so little."[3] Unlike the old chroniclers and the first generation of researchers, modern scholars tend to focus on what leaders *do*, not on what leaders *are*: They create a vision of the future that others cannot see unaided; their actions are consistent with their values; they act as if failure were impossible; they articulate the deeper feelings of their followers; they develop plans that others can follow.[4]

The trouble with modern scholarship on leadership is that it is so clinical. Like surgeons with a patient, scholars anesthetize their subject, lay it out like a corpse, and probe its recesses with their fine tools. We end up with a lifeless something whose true spirit has gone elsewhere, when it should be alive and speaking for itself. Leadership is an art. Like art, it dies when you cut into it with cold instruments; it does not translate well into words. As Braque said of art, "the only thing that matters in art is the part that cannot be explained." Can the same not be said of leadership and the art of leading people? Neither can art be appreciated secondhand. No one can know the power of Beethoven or appreciate what made his music so remarkable without having heard it performed. Likewise, leadership and the art of managing are only truly understood when we have experienced them in some way—when we are in their presence. That is why this book turns to the record of the past, to real people in real situations.

The other major theme of this book is change. Philosopher Eric Hoffer once wrote a book on the ordeal of change, and many of the chapters here aim at giving a sense of how change creates pain and conflict and how people and institutions react to it, albeit sometimes in self-destructive ways. Some of the best literature on this subject is to be found in the scholarship on technological innovation, and an effort is made to bring this to the work.

In developing this book, I began with my own knowledge of interesting and instructive historical episodes from which people in business and other areas of administration might benefit. To these I added the suggestions of a number of business professors and professional managers. For each episode, the following criteria were applied. Each must:

- provide a useful lesson;
- be sufficiently well documented that the motives and actions of the characters can be vividly and accurately drawn;
- have a high degree of dramatic content;
- avoid events and characters already commonplace to modern readers.

Within these guidelines dozens of potentially instructive historical events and figures were investigated. Many were blind alleys. For some, like Savonarola, the charismatic Renaissance church reformer, sufficient documentation was not readily available (at least not to me). For others, like Gandhi, the story is familiar to contemporary readers and has been well told by others.

There are few business or industrial leaders in this book. That is by design. If readers of this book are anything like me, they have had their fill of discourses on contemporary business leaders, high-stakes takeovers, and all the rest. The focus on today's corporate drama is served up in a steady stream by the business press and need not be augmented here. Many of the best and most interesting lessons for business people are actually found *outside* the corporate domain, in the worlds of generals, clergy, revolutionaries, and adventurers. Among these we find events and human struggles where leadership, daring, and the skills of artful management made a difference, often between life and death. The fact that the stakes were so high makes the lessons that much more vivid.

Plan of the Book

In these chapters we will travel through some nineteen hundred years of human history, making stops at a half-dozen widely separated places where events are promising for our purposes.

In Chapter 2 we follow a small band of sixteenth-century adventurers into the heart of the powerful Aztec empire. Its leader was so confident of success that he had his ships scuttled, making retreat impossible. The Aztec emperor was unnerved by a prophesy of a god who would one day come from the eastern sea to take the throne. This chapter focuses on risk-taking entrepreneurs and the personality of Hernán Cortés as pursuer of opportunities and decisive leader. He is juxtaposed to the fatalistic and indecisive Moctezuma.

Chapter 3 introduces France's Louis XI—the Spider King—a modern-thinking man coming of age in the closing decades of the Middle Ages. He had a vision of a well-managed nation-state, but his resources were so pitifully meager that he had to develop the cunning and subtlety of the spider to survive the violence and shifting alliances around him. Centuries of inertia and a feudal aristocracy that despised him and his new ideas stood against him. We draw lessons from this chapter on how those who challenge the status quo must, like King Louis, exercise patience and cunning. For example, how the Japanese successfully challenged American industrial dominance is discussed.

Nothing is more powerful than an idea whose time has come. Chapter 4 focuses on two individuals who created change through their ideas: Martin Luther, the religious reformer, and W. Edwards Deming, the missionary of industrial quality. The relationship between ideas and the circumstances that make their acceptance possible are explored. Contributions from sociological research on the diffusion of innovation and the role of change agents are brought into the discussion.

At the beginning of World War II Japan had a strategic plan for achieving hegemony in the western Pacific, and, by spring 1942, everything had gone according to plan. One final step remained: The Japanese had to lure the remnants of the U.S. Pacific Fleet into a trap where the knockout punch would be delivered. Admiral Yamamoto's strategic plan was more elaborate than anything attempted by any navy in history. It would work wonderfully if everyone, including the Americans, would do his part. Chapter 5 considers the Battle of Midway and the roles that random events and complex planning had on its outcome. Like military strategies, business strategies are constructed on assumptions about the future and are vulnerable to unforeseen circumstances. The chapter discusses the pitfalls of great plans and cites scholarship that helps us to think more prudently about planning and accommodating the unexpected.

Chapter 6 examines the Roman Empire of the early second

century A.D., which had by then pushed past the limits of its resources. Conquest and annexations had made the empire a mosaic of cultures, religions, and languages. Emperor Hadrian assumed the task of consolidating this empire and its many parts, developing a structure for managing and defending it, and making Romans out of its many peoples. As corporations become multinational, and then global, with fading national identities, the Roman model and the later experience of the Roman Catholic church provide useful perspectives on managing and enlisting the allegiance of personnel from around the globe.

Wars are always the result of some prior failure. America's war of revolution was no exception: It represented a failure by colonial leaders and British officialdom to work out a satisfactory relationship for the new circumstances that followed Britain's great victory in the French and Indian War. Chapter 7 is about Thomas Hutchinson of Massachusetts, who represented the king's interests in a colony aflame with the spirit of revolutionary change. Hutchinson was sincere and competent, but he was temperamentally the wrong man to deal with the changes that would overwhelm him and his world. His career provides a striking example of how the leadership qualities that serve organizations well in one era are sometimes inadequate to the challenges of another. In this he provides an interesting contrast to Samuel Adams, who understood the currents of the times and how to manage them for his purposes.

Chapter 8 is about a timeless phenomenon currently on the minds of many in the business world—the seeming inevitability of institutional decline. History records the rise and decline of great nations and empires: all experienced a cycle of energetic expansion, dominance, and eventual decline. Where did their energy come from and where did it go? Corporations and entire industries are subject to this same cycle. Historians can enrich our thinking on this, particularly Toynbee's "challenge-response" theory. Apropos to business is scholarship from MIT on industrial dynamics as well as the invasion of stable markets by radical innovation, which is related here to a dramatic episode from fifteenth-century France.

The final chapter is about the lessons of history—about it limits and the danger of using it carelessly. The failure to see history repeating itself is just one type of error; mistaking present circumstances as a simple repeat of the past is a second type. Lyndon Johnson and his advisers had in mind the Munich experience when they mistakenly saw developments in Vietnam as an analogous situation, and committed the nation to years of futile warfare. Stock market forecasters routinely cite historical analogies to current circumstances—often using the flimsiest evidence—and commit their clients to expensive errors. Chapter 9 acquaints the reader with methods of drawing valid historical analogies. Here, particular attention is given to the contributions of Richard E. Neustad and Ernest R. May, who have done pioneering work in this important area.

It is hoped that these episodes from history will not only entertain but also serve up lessons of enduring value to those men and women in business and public life who will guide our institutions into the next century.

2

Entrepreneurs and Opportunists: Cortés Takes Mexico

An army of lions led by a sheep is no match for an army of sheep lead by a lion.

Winston Churchill

In the summer of 1518 four ships traveled along the Caribbean coast of Yucatán, the large peninsula that forms the southern boundary of modern Mexico. Without maps or pilots to guide them, they stayed within sight of land, hugging the sparkling sand beaches that fringed the lush but monotonous landscape. Unbroken but for an occasional bay, the coastline offered little of interest to the sunburnt crews.

This voyage, the third to these parts by Spanish explorers, had been disappointing. After nearly seven months aboard ship and on the mainland, they had little to show for their time and wounds. Hostile Maya warriors had repulsed one of their most recent landings. Juan de Grijalva, the expedition's commander, lost two teeth during this episode when an arrow struck him in the mouth. Grijalva later attributed this misfortune to God's wrath, as his mouth had been cursing a slow-moving Dominican chaplin just as the missile struck.

Fortunately, receptions elsewhere had been more hospitable. The expedition had been able to barter for a little gold. It was not much, but it was an encouraging sign. The natives had told Grijalva what freebooters everywhere in the New World were told: there was plenty more gold "farther on."

Grijalva was contemplating the end of the expedition when he had an astonishing and cordial encounter with yet another group of natives. About fifty miles south of modern Veracruz, the voyagers were signaled ashore by a group of natives. These were friendly, opulently dressed, and clearly of a different nation than the Maya encountered earlier. They spoke a language that Grijalva's interpreters could not make out. Native priests fumigated the Spaniards with smoking censors, examined their apparel, their steel armor, and their swords. Grijalva offered some paltry glass beads as gifts; in return the leader of the native group lavished him with food, a small fortune in gold artifacts, cloth, and elaborate capes of featherwork and fringe. With communication limited to signs and gestures, Grijalva thanked his generous hosts and did his best to indicate that he and his party would return in the near future.

Thinking himself lucky to be ending his voyage on a positive note, Grijalva weighed anchor and pushed farther up the coast, where he made a final landing at a small island to take on fresh water. A shore party was detailed for this task, and it found something there it had not been seeking. Among the shore detail was Bernal Díaz del Castillo, who left this account in his gripping chronicle, *The True History of the Conquest of New Spain:*

> There we found a prayer house with a huge and ugly idol which they call Tezcatlipoca in the charge of four Indians in black cloaks and hoods, very like those of our Dominicans or canons. These were the priests or *papas*. That day they had sacrificed two boys, cutting open their chests and offering their blood and hearts to that accursed idol.[1]

Disgusted by their discovery, Díaz and his companions hurried back to the ship to relate this grizzly aspect of Mesoamerican religion to their companions. His mission completed, Grijalva set course back to Cuba not realizing that the natives who had feted his party near Veracruz had begun their own journey, traveling inland at the double quick for over two hundred miles through deserts and over mountain passes to the great city of Tenochtitlán. The people Grijalva had met were not coastal Indians, but personal emissaries of the most powerful ruler in the entire Western Hemisphere—the Aztec emperor, Moctezuma.[2]

Reports of Grijalva's landings among the Maya had reached the capital months earlier, creating tremendous interest and appre-

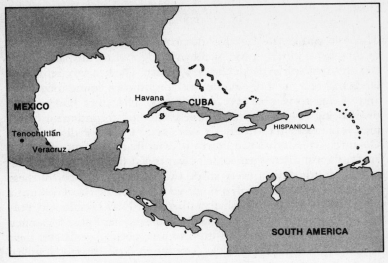

Figure 2.1   Mexico and the Indies

hension at court. Moctezuma wanted to know everything about
these aliens and sent men to watch the coastline for any subsequent landings.

Within a matter of days, the first eyewitnesses arrived at the
palace with news of the meeting near Veracruz. They fell to their
knees before the great emperor, being careful not to look directly
upon his divine person for fear of instant death. They turned over
Grijalva's trinkets and the pictures they had sketched of the strangers;
and they told Moctezuma everything that had happened in the
greatest detail—the amazing rafts with white wings on which they
sailed; the remarkable skin and dress of these aliens; their hairy
faces. What they told Moctezuma confirmed his worst fears—fears
he did not intimate to them.

The emperor told them, "You have traveled far; you are tired.
Rest. What you have shown me is to remain secret. Let no one
speak of it. This has been between you and me only." He told his
council: "See that the shoreline is constantly watched everywhere
. . . wherever the strangers may land."[3] For years the Aztec ruler
and his priesthood had been dreading the prophesized return of
the powerful god, Quetzalcoatl, and their minds were prepared to
accept what they had learned about these strangers on the coast as
evidence that they were, indeed, his advance party.

The Fortune Seekers

The gold and stories Grijalva took back to Cuba stirred the juices in every adventurer on the island and neighboring Hispaniola (today the Dominican Republic and Haiti). These newly settled islands had become a destination for adventurous young men eager and willing to gamble everything for the chance of finding gold or of being rewarded with a large estate and a contingent of Indian serfs. Over the twenty-six years since their first discovery by Columbus, the Indies had been a magnet that drew from Spain its landless sons, discharged soldiers, vagabond hidalgos, and acquisitive ne'er-do-wells of every stripe. A remarkable number of these had come from the thinly populated province of Estremadura, a dusty and sun-bleached tableland between New Castile and Portugal. Arid and rocky, it was—and remains—a hard place to scratch out a living. Its most noted exports have been its sons and their swords. During the late Middle Ages the men of Estremadura filled the ranks of Spain's armies of the *reconquista,* the centuries-long struggle to reclaim the land from Moslem hands. In another century they would troop off to Italy and the Low Countries, or wherever else the Crown was engaged and booty and recognition were to be gained. They tramped through the jungles and mountains of the New World in search of fame, estates, and treasure. Many died there from wounds, disease, and starvation; others returned to Spain broken in spirit and health. A few found what they had come for.

This was Europe's entrepreneurial age of exploration, discovery, and trading. In the fifteenth century the Portugese pushed back the boundaries of the known world, skirting the coast of Africa and beyond to the Asian subcontinent, where they established wildly profitable trading operations. Their success and stories of opulent cities, exotic people, and the fabled kingdom of Prester John circulated through the port cities of the Mediterranean and the Atlantic coast. In the final decade of the century, the newly united kingdom of Spain joined the game when it commissioned Columbus to seek a new route to the Orient by sailing west. The sixteenth century produced another bumper crop of daring explorers: Vasco da Gama, Cabral, Magellan, Coronado, Pizarro, Cabot, Hawkins, and Drake. These were the entrepreneurs of their age. Perhaps none was more single-minded in pursuance of his mission than was Hernán Cortés.

Hernán Cortés was of the tribe of Estremaduran émigrés. The

son of minor gentry in the town of Medellín, his parents sent him to Salamanca at the age of fourteen to study the law, but he lost interest in this and returned home within two years. In 1504, at the age of eighteen, he went to Hispaniola, where he was set up with a modest ranch with Indian workers.

The life of the colonial squire was, for Cortés, pleasant but boring. Like other petty Spanish gentry of the time, he aspired to far greater things: conquest, great deeds and adventures, and the status of a titled nobleman. This was the legacy of the *reconquista*—to carry on the crusade against the unbelievers, and become wealthy and titled at the same time—and this legacy remained potent among those of Cortés's class, who were cleverly parodied in Cervantes's great novel *Don Quixote*. These were men for whom honor and glory were the supreme virtues and worthy of any personal risk.

Apprenticeship for Conquest

In 1509 Cortés had an opportunity to join an expedition bound for Panama in the company of Diego de Nicuesa, where gold had been reported, but he was forced to stay behind for reason of poor health. Years later, his secretary, Gomara, blamed an abscess on his leg for his missing this great adventure; others suggest that he was suffering from a venereal infection. Whatever the case, the affliction probably saved the young adventurer's life as only a handful of the men who sailed off to Panama survived the poison arrows that awaited them.

Another opportunity for Cortés to show his mettle came in 1511 when Diego Velázquez organized an expedition to subdue the nearby island of Cuba. This venture was no great challenge as the natives were few and not especially warlike. Cortés played a minor role in this operation, but was rewarded by Velázquez—now the island's governor—with land and position; however, his ambition remained unfulfilled.

When Grijalva's ships straggled into the port of Havana in the fall of 1518, Hernán Cortés was thirty-two years old, and had been chosen by Governor Velásquez to command the next expedition. Bernal Díaz, who would join this venture, describes Cortés as

> A tall man, well proportioned and robust. . . . He had a deep chest and broad shoulders, was lean and slightly bow-legged. Both as a horseman and

a swordsman he was very skillful. Above all, he had courage and high spirit, which is what matters most. As a youth in Hispaniola he was somewhat dissolute with women, and fought with knives several times with strong and agile men, and he always won.. . . He was very affable to his companions, was a Latin scholar and something of a poet. Every morning he recited prayers from a Book of Hours and heard Mass with devoutness. He was fond of cards and dice and excessively fond of women.[4]

Cortés's aptitude for leadership, management of a large enterprise, and military tactics were unknown and unproven on the eve of his departure for the coast of Mexico. He had been a rancher and town magistrate. He had been on a mission of conquest, but as a bit player. He had made no serious mistakes, but neither had he undertaken any serious initiatives. Governor Velásquez's choice of Cortés for an important venture of exploration and possible conquest would seem, then, to be a poor one. Nothing had prepared him for what might lie ahead. The islands were full of bold and proven captains; indeed, historian Salvador de Madariaga called the Indies "a nest of hawks." Velásquez, however, was fearful of the independence and avarice of these others. Cortés appeared more loyal and reliable, and so he got the job. The governor only discovered the truth about Cortés and his personal ambitions later.

On the eve of their embarcation, Hernán Cortés brought together his companions and delivered a speech. His words tell us much of his mind and values:

Certain it is, my friends and companions, that every good man of spirit desires and strives, by his own effort, to make himself the equal of the excellent men of his day and even those of the past. And so it is that I am embarking upon a great and beautiful enterprise, which will be famous in times to come, because I know in my heart that we shall take vast and wealthy lands, peoples such as have never before been seen, and kingdoms greater than those of our monarchs.. . .

I have assembled ships, arms, horses, and other materials of war, a great stock of provisions, and everything else commonly needed and profitable in conquests. I have spent large sums, for which I have put in pawn my own estate and those of my friends. . . .

. . . if you do not abandon me, as I shall not abandon you, I shall make you in a very short time the richest of all men who have crossed the seas.[5]

With these words Cortés reveals himself as someone willing to put his life and material assets on the line in the hope of great wealth and greater fame.

When his fleet of eleven ships set off from Cuba in February 1519, Hernán Cortés commanded an expedition of 508 soldiers and 100 sailors. His force included sixteen horses, ten bronze cannon, four falconets, and thirteen muskets. Most of the soldiers carried the accoutrements of the age: swords, crossbows, lances, and light armor—which made them only slightly better armed than the native warriors of the region.

Given Spain's resources in the New World at that time, this was a large and well-equipped expedition, but compared with the forces it would soon encounter it was small potatoes.

The Aztec Nation

Moctezuma was about forty years old when Cortés left Cuba. He presided as a godlike figure over the most powerful empire ever organized in the Western Hemisphere up to that time.

The Aztec people, who called themselves the Mexica, were new to the stage of power and hegemony in Mexico. They had wandered into the valley of Mexico in the twelfth century as a tribe of weak and uncultured nomads. Over the course of one century, however, they managed to conquer and dominate all of their more advanced neighbors. At the same time they absorbed the culture and science that had been passed down through the centuries from the Olmecs, the Mayas, the mysterious people of Teotihuacán, and the Toltecs. By 1519, the Aztecs controlled an empire of several million people, extending from the Pacific to the Gulf coast, from central Mexico to what is now Guatamala.

The Aztecs built a capital city called Tenochtitlán in the midst of a broad brackish lake. Some estimates place its population at three hundred thousand. Its ruins today form the foundation of modern Mexico City. Aqueducts brought fresh water into the city; canoes carried food and trade goods into its many markets. Wide earthen and stone causeways radiated outward from Tenochtitlán to the many cities of other tribes that flourished around the shoreline of the lake. The Aztecs dominated these other peoples and their sway extended to distant tribes, who paid heavily in material tribute and human cargo.

The extent of Aztec military power is difficult to know with precision. Eyewitness estimates of the number of Aztec warriors at the time of the conquest are between 150,000 and 300,000. This no doubt included auxilaries supplied by allied tribes. While there is no reason to accept these figures as accurate, we do know that their numbers were vast relative to other powers in the area and that they armed themselves with bows and arrows, spears, darts with fire-hardened tips, and two-handed wooden clubs in whose edges sharp obsidian glass shards were imbedded. The technology for making iron and steel was unknown to the Aztecs and their neighbors. Many wore quilted cotton armor.

The Aztecs had a very gloomy view of life; to them human existence was a continuing tightrope walk between survival and catastrophe. Nature and human affairs were seen in the most unfriendly terms: famine, drought, pestilence, earthquake, and military defeat were always in the realm of immediate possibilities. This gloomy outlook was supported by the tribal experience. We know for a fact that all of these misfortunes had befallen the Aztec people in their remembered history, so the gods who commanded these affairs had to be accommodated if the nation was to survive.

Like other nations of Mesoamerica, the Aztecs had many gods and a priestly caste whose job was to fathom their divine wills. The satisfaction of the gods was so important that religion and government were one. Thus, Moctezuma was both supreme leader and high priest. One of the most important gods was Huitzilopochtli—the Hummingbird of the Left. As god of war, the Hummingbird was the supreme deity of the Aztec nation. He was a bloodthirsty deity, demanding human sacrifice on a regular basis. As the Aztec military machine rolled over its neighbors and then far-distant tribes, temple worship of the Hummingbird was extended.

The ritual of human sacrifice itself was abominable. The victim—usually a captured warrior—was dragged up the stone steps of the god's pyramid temple. At the top he was grabbed by a squad of four priests—one to a limb. While these threw the hapless victim backward over a great stone, a fifth priest plunged an obsidian blade into his chest and yanked out the still beating heart. The victim's remains were pushed down the western slope of the pyramid as if to symbolize the dying sun.[6] Limbs of victims were often eaten by the priests and nobility.

By the early 1500s, the Aztec priests had become obsessed with the need to appease the Hummingbird. His annual feast day demanded hundreds of victims at each of his many temples. At the dedication of the Great Temple in Tenochtitlan, some twenty thousand victims were dispatched by teams of priests.[7] Just where these victims came from and how they were obtained has much to do with the ultimate collapse of the Aztec empire. Since their own people were not anxious to end their lives in this gruesome way, foreigners were the logical choice. The Aztec imperative for conquest and domination is explained in part by the continual need for POWs and sacrificial levies.

Combat was undertaken to capture enemies alive for later sacrifice, not to kill them. When armies went into combat, support troops waited just behind the lines to receive and bind up any enemy warriors unfortunate enough to become captives. Once a tribe had been subjugated by the Aztecs, it was required to send a specified number of annual sacrificial victims to Tenochtitlán, along with the traditional tributes of foodstuffs and treasure.

The Aztecs were so successful militarily that they eventually ran out of enemies to fight, which greatly limited the number of available sacrificial victims. Faced with this vexing problem, Aztec leaders secretly negotiated with chieftains of other tribes for a series of periodic and inconclusive conflicts called The Flower Wars, the sole purpose of which was to give each side an opportunity to obtain fresh captives.

The Legend of Quetzalcoatl

In addition to the Hummingbird, the Aztecs had another important god, who plays a big part in our story, this one borrowed from the earlier Toltec people. He was called Quetzalcoatl—the Feathered Serpent. Unlike the gory Hummingbird, Quetzalcoatl opposed human sacrifice. He was remembered as having fair skin and a beard, and, according to legend, he had been disgraced and driven out of Mexico by another deity in the dim past. He had departed from the eastern coast of Mexico on a raft of entwined serpents, vowing to return in a One Reed year to reclaim his rightful domain. Despite his long absence, the Aztecs and their neighbors regarded the prophesy of his return with the utmost gravity.

Reed years came in regular four-year cycles within the Aztec calendar. The first year of the four was always a time of high anxiety among the priesthood and the people, when every sign on the earth and in the heavens was regarded with care to discern if it were a portent of Quetzalcoatl's apocalyptic return. Ten years before the appearance of Grijalva's party, important signs were observed. Reports were made of a "tongue of fire" that appeared in the night sky. In another year, the Hummingbird's temple quite mysteriously burst into flames. A bright meteor pierced the daylight sky. A three-headed comet appeared. The waters of the lake boiled (probably the result of geothermal activity beneath its surface).

Quite coincidentally the year in which both Grijalva and Cortés appeared on the Gulf shore, 1517, was a One Reed year. These developments seemed to be the fulfillment of the dreadful prophesy to the Aztec priesthood. The ships in which the Spaniards sailed were reminiscent of the mysterious raft on which Quetzalcoatl had departed. Their fair skin and beards were confirming evidence. Moctezuma and his spiritual advisers speculated that the return of Quetzalcoatl was at hand. According to accounts given by Aztecs after the conquest, "Moctezuma had been unable to rest, to sleep or eat. He would speak to no one. He seemed to be in great torment."[8]

The origins of the Quetzalcoatl legend are hard to know. Speculation includes the theory that ancient Egyptians or Phoenicians had found their way to Mexico, where, among other things, they introduced the practice of building pyramids. Others believe that a visit from some group of far-ranging Vikings lies behind the tale of a fair-skinned, bearded god with a serpent raft. Some consider the entire story to be a contrivance—a *post hoc* explanation that the Aztecs used to rationalize their own defeat—but there is little evidence for this view. Whatever the truth about the legend of Quetzalcoatl and his return, the fact remains that the Aztecs were an extremely superstitious people who had given much control of their affairs into the hands of magicians, necromancers, and priests. Their encounter with a people as exotic as the sixteenth-century Spaniards—who had their own considerable superstitions—was bound to result in a showdown at the spiritual level.

From Veracruz to Tenochtitlán

Cortés and his small force landed on the gulf coast near the present site of Veracruz, where they were met and feted by two of Moctezuma's emissaries and their retinue. He told the Mexicans that he was the vassal of Don Carlos, emperor of the Christians, king of Spain, and a great and powerful lord. He also told them that Don Carlos had heard of the great Moctezuma and that it was Cortés's mission to visit and speak with Moctezuma. Cortés did his best to impress the Aztec emissaries, firing the cannons and having his men race their horses—an animal unknown in the Americas—past them. The Aztecs took all of this in, and had their artists make sketches of everything.

One of the emissaries hurried back to the capital to inform Moctezuma of all he had seen and heard. The Aztec leader, we are told, was very frightened and depressed by the news and by the drawings shown to him. These things confirmed his fear that he was dealing with a returning god who would overthrow the existing order and destroy the Aztec people. He resolved to do what he could to keep the strangers away from the capital. He would send them rich gifts and hope that they would go away, and he would enlist all of the magic of his sorcerers to keep the strangers from moving inland.

The emissary returned to the coast with Moctezuma's gifts and told Cortés that he should not attempt to visit the capital. The gifts of gold, silver, and jewelry sent by Moctezuma had quite the opposite effect on the Spaniard, who was now even more encouraged to find the source of such great wealth.

After establishing a fortified base camp, Cortés and some four hundred of his followers prepared to move inland toward the great and forbidding city of Tenochtitlán. First, however, he did something quite remarkable. He sent the presents of Moctezuma to Emperor Charles V in a ship commanded by one of his trusted captains. The Crown was owed only "the royal fifth," but Cortés sent everything in the hope of winning the special favor of the emperor, much to the dismay of his men. Cortés ordered that the compasses and gear of the remaining ships be brought ashore; then he had them all scuttled! There would be no turning back for anyone. Cortés understood what Sun-tzu had postulated long before—an army that lacked an escape route would fight "with the courage of dispair." The outcome for the army would be either victory or death. As Bernal Díaz relates, "[Cortés] said that we could look for no help or assistance except from God for we now had no ships in which to return to Cuba. Therefore we must rely on our own good swords and stout hearts."[9]

Though weak in numbers, the Spanish invaders had two factors working to their advantage. First, Moctezuma's confusion over the divinity of Cortés made him a passive and indecisive opponent, unwilling or unable to unleash the superior forces at his command. Just as valuable to Cortés was his discovery that the Aztec nation had many powerful enemies. Mexico was home to many nations, many of whom had tired of Aztec bullying and were willing to give aid and comfort to whomever would destroy them. The Tlaxcalans, a nation situated between Cortés's base camp and the Aztec capital, were chief among these.

The Tlaxcalans had maintained their independence from Moctezuma over years of perpetual warfare. At first, they contested

Cortés's passage through their territory. Bernal Díaz describes them as furious and competent fighters who attacked in such vast numbers that they nearly overwhelmed the Spaniards. The terror caused by the cannon and the skillful use of manuever saved the tiny group of European adventurers from being smothered beneath a wave of Tlaxcalan warriors. Díaz relates,

> One of our men was killed in the fighting, and sixty wounded. All our horses were wounded also. I too was hit twice, once in the head by a stone, and once in the thigh by an arrow. But this did not prevent me from fighting, performing my watch, and helping our men.[10]

Cortés ultimately prevailed over the Tlaxcalans by making further hostilities futile and costly. When they asked for peace, he was glad to give it. It would be his policy to give his opponents every opportunity to come to terms throughout the conquest. When they did, Cortés praised their valor and welcomed them into the circle of his expanding enterprise. He recognized the value of the Tlaxcalans as allies in the coming confrontation with the Aztecs. Later, he would march with the aid of some 75,000 Tlaxcalan warriors, who were eager to settle old scores with their traditional enemy.

Moctezuma was deeply troubled by the course of events. Neither his magic nor the resistance of the fierce Tlaxcalans had prevented the strangers from moving inland toward the capital. Even at Cholula, their next stop, the Spaniards had foiled a plot to defeat them. The Cholulans, allies of the Aztecs, had invited the Spaniards into their city, where they entertained and fed them in grand style. The Cholulans were conspiring to overwhelm them and sacrifice them to their idols, but Cortés uncovered their plot and, with the aid of the Tlaxcalans, created a great slaughter within the walls of the city. The power of their magic seemed overwhelming.

On November 1, 1519, the little band of adventurers, in the company of a few thousand Tlaxcalan porters, began the final leg of its journey toward Tenochtitlán. Having failed to impede their progress, Moctezuma at last sent his welcome to the approaching god and his companions, who marched from Cholula through mountain passes and into the valley of Mexico, where they saw for the first time the great city that, until then, no European eyes had ever beheld. Bernal Díaz wrote:

> And when we saw all those cities and villages built in the water, and other great towns on dry land, and that straight and level causeway leading to

Mexico, we were astounded. These great towns and *cues* [temples] and buildings rising from the water, all made of stone, seemed like an enchanted vision from the tale of Amadis. Indeed, some of our soldiers asked whether it was not all a dream.[11]

The meeting of Cortés and Moctezuma on November 8, 1519, was a moment of great spectacle. The Spaniards approached the capital city along one of its great causeways, now lined with people. In the vanguard came four riders and a number of hunting dogs. Then came foot soldiers with crossbows, mounted lancers, and a platoon of musketeers. The sight of these aliens and their strange and wonderful beasts added to the excitement of the crowd.

The emperor's approach was from the city in a litter festooned with fine cloth and feathers, flanked by a company of great chieftains and attendants in ornate livery. Moctezuma was magnificently clad, and the chieftains swept the ground and placed cloaks before him when he stepped down from the litter. None of his own people would look directly at him.

When Cortés rode to the head of his column, the representatives of two civilizations—until then unknown to each other—were at last face to face. Cortés dismounted and approached the great emperor as if he were being reunited to a long-lost brother. Gifts and greetings were exchanged. After months on shipboard and in the field, the Spaniards must have been a smelly and motley crew, especially when compared to the elegance of their hosts. But their steel weapons, fierce mastiffs, and horses—all new sights to the Aztecs—must have amazed the crowds that gathered about them.

According to Spanish sources, Moctezuma made a speech in which he invited Cortés and his band to the city that he and his ancestors had been keeping until the day of his [Cortés thought to be Quetzalcoatl] return. "You have come here to sit on your throne, to sit under its canopy. . . . This was foretold by the kings who governed your city, and now it has taken place. You have come back to us. You have come down from the sky." After a terse speech by Cortés, in which he assured Moctezuma and his followers that they had nothing to fear, they all proceeded into the great city amid pomp and nervous celebration.

Moctezuma lodged his guests in the spacious palace of his late father, near the Great Teocalli (the temple of the Hummingbird) and just a short walk from his own residence. There the guests were entertained by the emperor, who came regularly with his lieutenants to converse with the strangers. Despite every indication of welcome and goodwill, Cortés had cannon placed on the walls of the palace and kept guards posted around the clock.

From this guarded base within Tenochtitlán the Spaniards took in the marvels of an exotic and alien culture. Aside from the barbarity of their religious practices, the Aztecs presided over an advanced civilization that counted great achievements in astronomy, engineering, medicine, and the arts. Those Spaniards who had seen the great cities of Europe marveled at the splendor of the capital. In a letter to the emperor, Cortés describes Tenochtitlán as being as large as Seville or Córdoba.

> The city has many open squares in which markets are continously held and the general business of buying and selling proceeds. One square in particular is twice as big as that of Salamanca and completely surrounded by arcades where there are daily more than sixty thousand folk buying and selling. Every kind of merchandise such as may be met with in every land is for sale there.[12]

The rest of this tale is a book unto itself and best told in the lively chronicle of Bernal Díaz, who set down his eyewitness account some forty years after the conquest. During the winter of 1519 and into the following spring, the Aztecs, for all their superstition, came to see the Spaniards for what they really were: mortal men with mortal appetites for food, women, and most of all, for gold. Even Moctezuma, to the last the most gullible of the lot, came to recognize his error. By then, however, he had become a hostage and instrument of Cortés and resigned to his fate. As his power among the people faded, the collective will to cast out the intruders grew stronger and eventually turned to violence. Moctezuma was denounced by his own people as a puppet of Cortés and was fatally stoned while appealing for peace from the parapets of the fortress-palace of his captors. With his death, Cortés lost his wild card.

What followed has come to be known in Spanish history as *la noche triste* (the sad night). Cortés and his followers attempted to fight their way out of the city with as much of Moctezuma's gold as they could carry. They burst from their camp in a fusillade of cannon fire and musketry and charged down one of the long causeways that connected the island city to the shores of the lake and to the open country beyond. Finding the causeway blocked by hordes of angry Aztecs and attacked on their flanks by canoe-borne warriors, many fell from the causeway into the lake, where the weight of the gold stuffed beneath their armor dragged them under. Much of Moctezuma's treasure is said to remain there today. Others were seized and dragged off to the Great Teocalli to be offered up to the Hummingbird. As Bernal Díaz describes it:

> For as we passed along the causeway, charging Mexican bands, the water was on one side of us and flat roofs on the other, and the lake was full of canoes. . . . Moreover, all the muskets and crossbows had been left behind at the bridge, and it was night. What more could we have attempted than we did, which was to charge and deal sword-thrusts at those who tried to seize us, and push ahead till we were off the causeway.[13]

Cortés and those of his followers who survived were a broken force by the time they reached the safety of Tlaxcala. Virtually all were wounded, only a few horses had survived, and their supplies of muskets, powder, cannon, and most of the crossbows had been lost. The advantages they had first carried into the endeavor were gone. What chance could Cortés have now to win land and fame? What also of the Tlaxcalans: Would they hand over the Spaniards as a way of mending fences with the Aztecs? Cortés's streak of luck seemed to have run out.

Most sensible people, as many of his followers now insisted, would have chalked the adventure up to experience and headed back to Veracruz, content to be alive with a little gold and a life-time of tales to tell back in Cuba or Spain. Instead of planning an evacuation, however, Hernán Cortés set himself to the task of pre-paring a new assault on Tenochtitlán. Within twenty-two days, with only modest reinforcements, he was back in the field with the renewed backing of the Tlaxcalans. A newly arrived ship from the Indies brought in fresh troops, horses, and munitions.

In the final episode of this story, which is too long to tell in detail, Cortés returned to the outskirts of the capital where, over a four-month period, he and his Tlaxcalan allies systematically re-duced all the important towns around the lake to his will. With the island city cut off from its supply of fresh food and water, he laid siege, fighting along the causeways that led into the heart of the city.

Cortés and his allies finally prevailed in August 1520. The magnificent city had become a ruin filled with corpses and starving survivors. The gold of the Aztecs had been spirited away in the canoes of its exiles or thrown into the lake's depths and never recovered. In the months that followed the fall of Tenochtitlán, the conquerors destroyed the city's temples and many of its build-ings, using their ruins as fill for the new Spanish city that would rise upon its foundations.

The mines that had produced the silver and gold of Moctezuma's treasure were found and exploited by the Spanish conquerors, using forced Indian labor. These created wealth for Spain and its emperor on a scale never before imagined.

The Heart and Mind of the Entrepreneur

What can we make of a remarkable character like Cortés and his adventure from a distance of more than four centuries? Do we see his like in our own times? Hernán Cortés clearly had a sense of the possible and was not averse to the risks that went with it. He was a true sixteenth-century entrepreneur, willing to put everything on the line for a chance at fame and wealth. Charles Garfield, a psychologist at the University of California and author of *Peak Performers* (Warner Books, 1985), studied the modern equivalent of this personality type and found it to be totally focused upon successful results, never allowing the details of achieving that success to distress or derail them. Jeffry Timmons and his associates have distilled the essential traits of the entrepreneur from dozens of studies. They find that they can be characterized by:

- Total commitment, determination, and perseverence
- A drive to achieve
- A goal orientation
- Persistant problem solving
- Realism and a sense of humor
- Internal focus of control
- Calculated risk taking and risk seeking
- Low need for status and power.[14]

With the exception of the last trait, Cortés fits the profile very well. The best description of his mind and character probaby comes from ninteenth century historian William Prescott:

> The great feature in his character was constancy of purpose; a constancy not to be daunted by danger, nor baffled by disappointment, nor wearied out by impediments and delays.
> He was a knight-errant, in the literal sense of the word. Of all the band of adventurous cavaliers, whom Spain, in the sixteenth century, sent forth on the career of discovery and conquest, there was none more deeply filled with spirit of romantic enterprise than Hernando Cortés. Dangers and difficulties, instead of deterring, seemed to have a charm in his eyes. . . . He conceived, at the first moment of his landing in Mexico, the design of its conquest. When he saw the strength of its civilization, he was not turned from his purpose.[15]

There may be a dark side to people like Cortés and to many of the people we honor today for their entrepreneurial spirit. This is the problem they allegedly have in dealing with situations in which the ability to function in a bureaucractic environment and to accept the authority of a direct superior are important. Manfred Kets de Vries has written that people like this do not accept authority well. Unlike managers who are capable of alternating comfortably between being a boss and being a subordinate, the prototypical entrepreneur cannot play both parts well. Kets de Vries speculates that their inability to submit to the organizational rules is what drives them to create their own environments in the first place.[16] Others dispute these characterizations, finding through their research that entrepreneurs are as well-adjusted as the next person.

Cortés, however, had trouble with authority throughout his career. He cut all ties to the legitimate sponsor of his expedition, Governor Diego Velázquez, as soon as his ships left Cuban waters. Once the conquest was completed, and the Spanish treasury officials, viceroys, and other bureaucracts came in to administer New Spain, Cortés was suddenly a fish out of water. He did not know how to play the game of organizational politics and did not care to learn. He became obsolete, and his daring spirit made him troublesome to the government. Modern business entrepreneurs often find themselves in the same situation when their successful enterprises reach the stage at which professional managers, corporate attorneys, accountants, and other organizational tenders become essential for continued growth.

Incremental Opportunism

Boss Tweed, leader of New York's Tammany Hall political machine, once said "I seen my opportunities and I took 'em." If one thing can be said about Cortés, it is that he had a keen sense for the opportunities that came his way, and he "took 'em" when he could. He was a remarkably decisive man. Beginning with his departure from Extremadura, a desert of opportunity for an ambitious man, he was attentive to the existence of advantageous situations, first in Hispaniola, again in Cuba, and finally in Mexico. Each of these situations represented an incremental growth in magnitude of enterprise and level of uncertainty. The journey from Spain to Hispaniola was along a path already blazed by others; the expedition to Cuba was more daring but made in the company of more experienced captains. This was his apprenticeship for the expedition to Mexico, which was on a larger order of magnitude. In Mexico Cortés was strategist, pathfinder, and commander—going where no European had gone before and pitching headlong into a situation of greater scope and immense risk. The opportunities inherent in Mexico had only been hinted at by the discoveries of Grijalva. The merest hint and most paltry evidence, however, was proof, in the mind of Cortés, of wonderous opportunities.

Hernán Cortés had a personality that we would describe today as upbeat. For him the glass was always half full, never half empty. Every roadblock and hostile encounter confirmed his confidence in what lay ahead. Through clever diplomacy he managed to reverse the fierce opposition of the Tlaxcalans from a serious negative into an important positive: a source of supplies and auxilary soldiers. The Quetzalcoatl prophesy was the ticket for the feeble Spanish force to enter the heart of Tenochtitlán without opposition. Moctezuma's gross indecisiveness, and ultimately his very person, which Cortés used as puppet and shield, was an opportunity used to advantage.

Risk Taking

George Patton admonished us to "take calculated risks; that is much different than being rash." For business people and investors, life is an ongoing series of risky ventures. By risky we mean *uncertain as to outcome* or *exposure to loss*. Starting a new product line, buying a new business or piece of capital equipment, or even hiring a new employee entails a greater or lesser degree of risk ranging from very low to very high. The rational person follows Patton's dictum, entering a risky venture only when the potential reward is commensurate with the risk. The more risky the proposition, the greater the reward should be, and vice versa. Every investor knows about this risk–reward relationship; a few know how to quantify it. If the risk of a venture exceeds its probable reward or if the risk cannot be prudently borne, that venture is passed over in favor of a more suitable one. Most of us understand this intuitively.

Since risk connotes uncertainty, it increases or decreases with the level of uncertainty. An investment in U.S. Treasury bills, for example, is considered a *riskless* investment because the range of possible outcomes is essentially nil: You receive back a predetermined amount of money on a stated date, and the U.S. government guarantees it. An investment in common stock, even of a large, comparatively stable corporation like AT&T, contains no such certainty. From a purchase price of $100 its share value might fluctuate over a period of a year between, say, $85 and $115 per share. That is not much fluctuation in today's stock market. The probability of it moving out of that narrow range of values decreases as it moves toward the extremes. Thus, because the range of probable outcomes is small, so is the risk.

The situation is much more volatile for the investor in a small, start-up company where the range of possible outcomes is immense, especially on the upside. Most of these entrepreneurial companies end in failure, and most if not all invested funds are lost. This is not always the case. Some start-ups are enormously successful, and their original investors become fabulously wealthy. Perhaps the most famous of these is Digital Equipment Corporation (DEC), a minicomputer designer and manufacturer. The venture capitalists who backed this company with $70,000 in 1957 saw the market value of their investment grow to $355 million by 1971.[17] Therefore, the set of possible outcomes for DEC investors during that time period ran from $0 to *at least* $355 million. Thus, because the range of possible outcomes was extremely broad, the risk for initial investors was considerable; and the only part of that range that could be measured with any certainty was the down side ($70,000).

Cortés and his crew faced a set of outcomes that ranged between a king's ransom and an ugly death on the Hummingbird's altar. Once he scuttled his ships at Veracruz the outcome had to be one of those two extremes: success or death. Just how he and his men calculated the risk—returns dimensions of their situation is impossible to know. On the one hand, they had seen with their own eyes the great stores of gold, silver, gems, and landed estates that would go to the victors. On the other hand, they knew very well how quickly they could be overwhelmed by their enemies. A great number of Spaniards had been killed or, worse, captured during the months of continuous combat for the capital city. On one occasion sixty-two were taken prisoner in a well-planned Aztec ambush. Over each of the next several days the Aztec priests dragged a dozen or so of these terror-stricken souls up the stone steps of their *cues* to be sacrificed in full view of their comrades, who were powerless to aid them. Even the battle-hardened Bernal Díaz confesses to the terror this inspired in him.

> I feared that one day or another they would do the same to me. Twice already they had laid hands on me to drag me off, but it pleased God that I

should escape from their clutches. . . . I came to fear death more than ever in the past. Before I went into battle, a sort of horror and gloom would seize my heart, and I would make water once or twice and commend myself to God and His blessed Mother.[18]

With the hindsight of history we must wonder if Cortés either made a poor estimate of the risks he was up against or simply threw them to the wind. His expedition did not proceed from adequate intelligence; he really had no idea what he was getting into. He simply went with what he had and handled things as they came—not exactly a plan for success. Cortés plunged boldly forward, and his success has earned him a place in history. He was brave, he was cunning, but he was also very lucky. We know from Bernal Díaz's chronicle that Cortés and his entire party were within an inch of being defeated on any number of occasions. Any single defeat could have been the end of them.

Something needs to be said here about Moctezuma because this piece of history was a contest between two leaders. It is clear from the start that Moctezuma had overwhelming resources at his command—literally at the snap of his imperial fingers. The vast forces of the Aztec nation were so in awe of their divine leader that nothing would have prevented them from smothering the feeble intruders had Moctezuma only given the word, but he never did. From the start he was too unsure of his opponent and his own position to act with courage and decisiveness. He formed an erroneous impression of Cortés based on scanty information and his own predisposition to the facts. His willingness to perceive Cortés as Quetzalcoatl, or as a demigod, disposed him to play the passive victim, and he failed to alter his assessment in the face of mounting evidence to the contrary. The battle for Mexico was lost in the mind of this one man. By the time new leadership had replaced Moctezuma, Cortés had already forged the coalition of anti-Aztec tribes that would assure him the victory.

The conquest of Mexico ended Aztec tyranny over their neighbors. It also destroyed the capital and a high culture of literature and science. In the course of bringing the native people to the True Faith, Spanish friars destroyed temples, books, artifacts, and the records of the Aztec nation. They eliminated our opportunity to learn what that unique civilization had to teach us. They banished the cruelty of human sacrifice but dealt their own draught of death and oppression in the forms of European diseases and

human enslavement. Both swept away large numbers of the indigenous people.

Last Days of the Great Conquistador

If Cortés's uncanny abilities brought him success against the Aztecs, he had little success in consolidating his own position as the
legitimate viceroy of New Spain—a title he sought from the emperor. His talent for meeting hordes of warriors head-on availed
him little against the subtle crafts of Spanish bureaucrats, lawyers,
and courtiers. In the end he accepted the less than exhalted title of
marquess of the Valley of Oaxaca.

Cortés spent years attempting to get his due from the monarch
he had served so well, futilely pursuing the honors and titles he
felt he deserved. One unconfirmed story has it that the elderly
Cortés once approached the coach of emperor Charles V as it prepared to depart. "Who is that bothersome old man," the emperor
inquired impatiently of his counselors. "Only one who has given
your majesty more provinces than he possessed towns," Cortés
replied, unheard and unrecognized as the coach's curtains were
drawn and it sped away. In his last letter to the emperor (February
1544) he wrote:

> I thought that having toiled in my youth it should profit me to find rest in
> my old age: and so for forty years I have laboured, going sleepless, eating
> poorly and at times not at all, bearing armour on my back, risking my life
> in dangers, freely spending my means and years, and all in the service of
> God, . . . spreading the fame and domains of my King, bringing under his
> royal scepter many and great realms and kingdoms of barbarous men and
> peoples, conquered at my own expense, owning no help to any man, but
> rather greatly hindered by many envious and ambitious men who like leeches
> have grown fat upon my blood. . . .
>
> I am old, poor and in debt in this realm to the tune of over twenty
> thousand ducats, not counting a hundred thousand more that I brought
> with me.[19]

The old conquistador wanted only his due so that he could
retire to his home and settle his account with God, for, as he said,
"it is a long one and I have but short time to balance it."

Hernán Cortés died near Seville in December 1547 at the age
of sixty-two, deep in debt and hounded by lawsuits. His compan-
ion in arms, Bernal Díaz, who left us the chronicle of the conquest, lived to the ripe old age of eighty-nine, and died in Guatamala as poor as he had been born.

3

Challenging the Status Quo: The Spider King Unifies France

> It must be considered that there is nothing more difficult to carry
> out, nor more doubtful of success, nor dangerous to handle, than to
> initiate a new order of things. For the reformer has enemies in all
> those who profit by the old order.
>
> Machiavelli

The birth of a male heir should have been an occasion for celebration for the court of Charles VII. But the fortunes of the French king in July 1423 were so diminished, and his realm so beleaguered, that the birth of the boy who would become Louis XI was marked by little fanfare. It was, in fact, the eighty-seventh year of the Hundred Years' War between France and England—not a good year to be born.

England's Henry V controlled much of the countryside, and already referred to himself as the king of England *and* France. His knights and deadly bowmen had annihilated French chivalry on its own soil at the battle of Agincourt just eight years earlier and continued to shred any army that took the field against them. To make matters worse, the powerful Burgundians were in the English camp, creating a grim situation for the French Crown and its heir.

Few good things can be said about warfare in any era, but in the Middle Ages, at least, campaigning was generally confined to a small area, involved few combatants, and was punctuated by frequent and lengthy truces. Armies ran out of fodder and enthusiasm, and they went home. Winter was an off-season that gave the countryside and the abused peasantry time to recover. There seemed little respite from this interminable war, however, as it came with three terrible companions.

The first of these was plague. France, with the rest of northern Europe, had caught the full force of the Black Death in 1349, and outbreaks recurred periodically. Between one-third and one-half of the total population perished from it; in some areas, entire villages were decimated, leaving no one to bury the dead.

The second scourge was the *écorcheurs* (skinners), soldiers unemployed during periods of truce or standdown. Twenty to thirty thousands of these bloodthirsty dregs roamed the countryside in disorganized bands, pillaging, raping, and burning. They descended on rural communities, leaving death and destruction in their wake. There was rarely any force to oppose them. One cleric of the era said, "They resemble wolves more than men. They leave nothing in the houses they pillage, not a hen, not a chicken, not a cock." The *écorcheurs* made commerce and the normal cycles of agriculture impossible. Many country people migrated to the relative safety of the towns, leaving rural villages deserted. In 1435 the population of Limoges fell to 5 inhabitants; the diocese of Rouen fell from 15,000 to 6,000.[1]

The third scourge, and the one that concerns us most in this chapter, was the fractured nature of power and authority that characterized France at that time. The chaos of the Hundred Years' War had reversed the gradual trend toward centralized power and authority. There was no state at this time; that is, there was no France in the modern sense. Central authority had become nonexistent. The deterioration of social order permitted the rejuvenation of the great fiefs. The country was traditionally a patchwork of feudal entities, each with its own hereditary potentate and petty interests, each jealously guarding its borders and privileges while conspiring to usurp those of its neighbor. Brittany, Lorraine, Bourbon, Orléans, Berry, Maine, and Burgundy figure among the larger "states" within the state. The king was merely one noble chieftain among many, and his standing in the pecking order was at best third behind Burgundy and Brittany.

This state of affairs quite naturally created a deadly virus of border warfare and shifting alliances. Although nominally Frenchmen, each feudal baron was capable of selling out his rivals, if not his country, for personal gain. John the Fearless of Burgundy (1371–1419) actually arranged for English troops to enter France in support of his conflict with a feudal rival. Decades after John's assassination by an axe blow to the head, someone examining the hole in his skull remarked, "This is the hole through which the English entered France." There could be no lasting peace or real progress within a body of so many princely heads.

The drive to create a viable central authority in France is a dominant theme in that nation's history from the end of the Roman era (fifth century) until the ascendancy of King Louis XIV (seventeenth century). It is a theme common to all the major nations of Europe and, for our purposes, provides an interesting laboratory in which to examine the leader who appeared on the scene to create order out of chaos—Louis XI.

Francis Bacon called him one of "the three Wise Men"—along with Ferdinand of Spain and Henry VI of England—each of whom knit together an effective national monarchy out of a patchwork of medieval fiefdoms. Parallels to Louis's accomplishment could be drawn to the feat of Washington and Madison forging a federal government out of thirteen bickering sovereign states and to John D. Rockefeller restructuring the oil industry when he built Standard Oil from the bits and pieces of many small drilling, refining, and distributing operations—replacing an era of cutthroat competition with the *Pax Rockefeller*.

Louis XI interests historians because he created a new order; he was born into the Middle Ages but moved his country to the doorstep of the modern world. He was not just carried along like a leaf in the stream of history, but he made a decided alteration in its course. He is interesting because of those aspects of his mind and character that allowed him to have such impact in the face of daunting odds.

Louis was not a man who fit the mold of the great leader. He lacked charisma, his military resources were always meager, and he liked few people and was liked by few in return. He made many miscalculations. In some ways he was the Richard Nixon of his times: often cornered, but seldom caught; counted out one day, restored the next. Had there been newspapers in those days, Louis would have provided steady employment for editorial critics and political cartoonists.

Louis did have tremendous subtlety. His modern biographer, Paul Murray Kendall, describes him as "a man of extraordinary powers wrapped in a personality so agile and various as to encompass the range of a dozen ordinary temperaments."[2] Louis was a chameleon prince who could appear to his rivals in one guise while truly being someone else. He was a man who knew his own time well, but was never a part of it; he understood peoples' fears and urges and how to manipulate them. Wile and craftiness earned him the title of the universal spider because he spun a web of diplomacy and stratagem far more intricate than anything experienced in the Europe of his day. Kendall writes that one of his great talents was to profit from his failures:

> In his life can be descried, repeatedly, variations on one of the grandest patterns of human existence: withdrawal and return. A human organism, emerging from the shelter of untested hopes and dreams, collides with a worldly reality for which it is unprepared. Cruelly wounded in spirit, an object of mockery or a victim of indifference, the organism shrinks into withdrawal. In this darkness it recharges its confidence by achieving a durable faith, a truer sense of realities outside the self, and thus rearmed comes forth to measure its strengths against the world. . . . For Louis XI it was the reiterated rhythm of his existence—failure and withdrawal and the rebound from failure.[3]

Adversity, Kendall tells us, seemed to bring out the best in him. Louis's own description of his kindred spirit, Francesco Sforza, the Duke of Milan, equally applies to him: "He was never better than when the water was up to his neck."

Remarkably, Louis's qualities can be directly juxtaposed to those of his contemporary and archrival, Duke Charles the Bold of Burgundy, whom we will meet later. Charles, we shall find, was quite the reverse of Louis.

Land of Gauls and Franks

France has never been an easy country to govern. The Romans had found the people of the land we now call France to be troublesome and untamed. Organized by regional tribal allegiances the ancient "Gauls" were either superficially subdued or in a state of rebellion against their Roman conquerors. No sooner would one tribe submit to the legions' military authority than another would go on the warpath. Only brutal military suppression and five centuries of Roman rule succeeded in Latinizing the Gauls.

In the early centuries of the Christian era the bonds of Roman authority unraveled and withered away. Barbarian tribes such as the Franks settled among the Latinized Gauls, bringing with them their own tribalisms. The ancient world with its Mediterranean culture, governance, and unity gave way to the Dark Ages of ignorance and localism; and Roman Gaul fragmented into a mosaic of barbarian kingdoms. Warlords used their ability to fight to set themselves up as local potentates. They gave their followers protection in a world of danger and violence. In return they received military service, shares of the crops, and land, and other prerequisites of power.

France, as a true political entity, floated above the Dark Ages briefly during the reign of Charlemagne (768–814), who succeeded in bringing the many threads of power together in the hands of a national sovereign. He established a royal administration, a coherent justice system, and a small standing army—all reminiscent of the efficient Roman system of centuries past. As king of the Franks, and later (beginning in 800) as the Holy Roman emperor, Charlemagne commanded something resembling a nation-state in an age of duchies, counties, baronages, and lesser entities. With Charlemagne's death and the subdivision of his estates among his descendents, however, the Kingdom of the Franks slid beneath the waves of darkness once again. The central authority he established dissipated. Power and authority again dissolved into the hands of petty feudal lords, each of whom put the expansion of his hereditary fiefdom and the increase of his own power and wealth as his primary interests.

This, of course, guaranteed continual tension—and regular warfare—between avaricious noblemen. Dutch historian Johan Huizinga has characterized the tenor of medieval life as one in which passions ran deep and often gave way to violence. The nobility, he found, were the prime instigators of violence in that they had the means.[4]

In a rural age, when wealth was based on land holding, the static availability of land collided head-on with the unsatisfied ambitions of the Frankish nobles. The idea of creating greater wealth (power) through better management of one's own productive resources was an idea whose time had not yet come. The concept of better management of agricultural estates, of promoting greater production and trade for towns and their artisans, was unfamiliar to the nobility. The size of the feudal pie was fixed; if anyone wanted a larger slice, it had to be taken from someone else's plate.

The king of France was just one of many players in this endless game. Tradition had surrounded him with an aura of sanctity: He was the "anointed of God" and his person was respected. The age of the divine right of kings to rule was still centuries in the future, and the French king had to play the same rough-and-tumble game of self-aggrandizement as everyone else. Several strong medieval French kings, like Philip Augustus, Louis IX, and Charles V had made their marks, but the fortunes of the Crown declined after their deaths. André Maurois observes that "the feudal nature of kingship eternally endangered it, for the royal domain was at the mercy of inheritances and dowries. To gather together the pieces of France was thus a labour of Sisyphus, and each generation had to accomplish anew the work of its predecessor."[5]

The malevolent influence of the English only complicated the situation. A formidable military power with hereditary claims within France since the time of the Plantagenet kings, the English continually upset the balance of power between the French Crown and its great barons.

When Louis was born in the archbishop's palace in Bourges, his royal father commanded pitifully little territory and even less wealth. Charles VII was then a twenty-one-year-old stripling without experience or kingly presence. Even his parentage was subject to speculation and public jest. The English held Paris, the Île-de-France, Normandy, Picardy, and the Bordeaux country. Their powerful ally, Burgundy, commanded Burgundy, Franche-Comté, Champagne, and the prosperous realm of Flanders. During this bleak period Charles was jokingly referred to as the king of Bourges because that was the only territory he could claim with any authority. The royal finances were so meager that he had pawned all of his family plate and jewelry and had taken to borrowing from his servants and officials. Tradespeople refused him credit.

The king, his little court, and his pathetic army were house mice among hungry cats, living hand to mouth, avoiding entrapment, and just trying to stay alive. Their fortunes would be reversed in the near future when a peasant girl named Joan of Arc rallied her country to cast out the English. Charles VII grew to be a man to be reckoned with in the thirty-eight years left to him. In the early 1420s, however, the situation was so perilous that young Louis was sent to the safety of the great castle of Loches for his upbringing.

The Apprentice Executive

Loches castle is a great pile of stone upon the high ground overlooking the valley of the Indre river. In Louis's time it was already an old structure, as its square donjon was built in the eleventh century by the count of Anjou. The young prince was raised at Loches by peasant nursemaids and the common folk of the castle and town. He had Parisian scholars to see to his education at the castle, but he also had rustic companions to teach him the joys of riding and hunting. His love of horses and hunting dogs, spawned in his youthful forays into the fields and woodlands around Loches, was to last throughout his life. We can imagine that he spent a great deal of time in the town of Loches among the merchants and tradespeople, for as an adult he showed a marked preference for the company of middle-class burghers to that of nobles. He even followed their manner of plain dress, wearing coarse brown and grey clothing and adopting a broad-brimmed fur hat to shelter his head from the sun and rain. His dress was so unnoble that years later, while riding to his own coronation at Rheims in the company of the elegant Duke John of Burgundy, the townspeople of Rheims mistook the duke for the new king and Louis for one of the duke's servants. When he traveled, he chose to lodge in the dwelling of a burgher instead of the castle of some local lord. An Italian diplomat complained that Louis took his breakfast "in the taverns like a common man." Louis's manner, behavior, and inclination were not those of his class . . . or of his age.

Business scholar Abraham Zaleznik argues that the developmental path from childhood to adulthood is critical to leadership skills. He views leaders as twice born individuals whose experiences have given them "a sense of separateness" from the world around them. Their formative experiences are less a progression of positive events than a number of stressful ones. "They turn inward," Zaleznik observes, "in order to reemerge with a created rather than an inherited sense of identity. That sense of separateness may be a necessary condition for the ability to lead."[6]

Other leadership scholars observe this characteristic of being somehow separate, detached from the times and from others. If they are correct about the source of this detachment, Louis had ample reasons for it based upon his early development. He always sensed the precarious state of the Crown and his own inheritance.

It was not until his fourteenth year that Louis took up a place in his father court. The fortunes of the Crown had improved somewhat since those dismal days at Bourges in 1423, but the English, the *écorcheurs,* and the great barons kept France in chaos.

Louis gained his first military experience (at the age of fifteen) against an English fortress, showing himself to be courageous if a little foolhardy. In this skirmish he found his thigh pinned to his horse by an English arrow. Charles VII gave him the temporary job of lieutenant-governor of Languedoc, a province that had suffered greatly from the three scourges. During his six months of duty there, Louis gained an apprenticeship in the skills of command and governance.

Life in his father's court was not a happy one for Louis. He was impatient for serious responsibilities, but was given little. He favored decisive action in his own affairs, but observed caution and dalliance in his father. Worse, he viewed the king as the captive of courtiers and mistresses, as someone weak and vacillating in whose shadow he was doomed to abide for an unknown number of years. He accepted what assignments came his way and looked to the day that he would wear the crown.

In 1447 twenty-three-year-old Louis got his first true opportunity to rule when he was given as his *apanage* the province of Dauphiné. For a century the province had been the entitlement of the heir apparent to the French throne, who ever since bore the title of dauphin; it was a pleasant but backwater land where a restive heir could be kept occupied and out of trouble until his time came to rule. The province proved to be a useful laboratory in which the young prince could learn the craft of management on a scale that matched his own limited experience.

Like an up-and-coming corporate vice president made general manager of a separate division, Louis was eager to make Dauphiné a model of the larger domain he hoped soon to rule. To that end he dedicated himself to an energetic program of reforms. Louis began by requiring that all nobles holding fiefs from him come to the capital of Grenoble to pay homage to their new overlord—something that his father could never bring himself to require of his haughty barons. High clerics—who had usurped many secular powers over the years—were forced to do the same.[7]

He set about reforming the judicial system and raising a regular army. Knowing that he must increase revenues to accomplish his ends, he looked for ways to improve the tax base of his little realm. To this end he did work on the infrastructure that enhanced commerce: repair of the roads, creation of a postal system, the establishment of market fairs, and the abolition of those taxes that inhibited trade. In this regard he showed himself to be a most unmedieval man. The practice of his time was for the nobles—who genuinely despised artisans and those who engaged in commerce—to ignore those who created wealth until they needed money, then fleece them with oppressive taxes. The idea of improving the environment that fostered commerce, wealth creation, and a healthy tax base had found an audience in Flanders and in some of the Italian states of the time, but it was an idea utterly lost upon Louis's fellow French aristocrats. Louis furthered the interests of the middle class even as he burdened those of the nobles and the clergy. In this and other ways he showed himself to be, in Kendall's words, "an alien in his age"[8] and an enemy of the prevailing order.

Louis's other reforms included steps to more equitably distribute the tax burden. Lands that tradition had exempted from taxation were brought onto the rolls, and others that had been devastated by war or disaster were given periods of relief. He created a council of advisors from among the clergy and nobility and centralized the legal system. How well these reforms worked and for how long is not clear from the chronicles of the time; however, we can be sure that Louis pursued them with energy and determination. He was not one to accept failure.

Louis spent a decade in Dauphiné: the biggest fish in a small pond. He grew more competent and comfortable in the role of decision maker, but he chaffed against the limits of the province, longing for the greater task of being king of France. He had never loved his father and respected him less. Would he grow to old age in Dauphiné awaiting his turn to command the nation?

Louis was not the first or last royal heir seduced by the thought of pushing his elder out to pasture. Business executives can at least know that mandatory retirements will make room for them at the top, and military officers can hold out for a "short war or sickly season" to cull the ranks of the senior command, but princes must await the death of kings and during that time of waiting they are subject to unnatural temptations. Two centuries earlier, Richard the Lion-Hearted had tired of waiting in his father's shadow, and France's King Philip Augustus exploited that impatience, pitting son in armed rebellion against father. Likewise, the great barons of France exploited the dauphin's restiveness by enlisting Louis in a revolt against Charles VII. The revolt collapsed, the barons quickly recanted, and Louis was left holding the bag. Charles VII dispatched royal troops into Dauphiné to bring the errant prince back to the court, but Louis escaped to the territory of his father's great rival, Duke Philip of Burgundy.

In the Enemy's Camp

Philip the Good, duke of Burgundy, maintained the most opulent court in fifteenth-century Europe. The center of tournaments, art, festivals, and lavish banquets, the court of Burgundy outshone that of the French king as the sun outshines the moon. Its emissaries were welcomed at all the great courts of Europe, where they ranked with those of kings. Its armies were among the most powerful on the continent. Burgundy had all the trappings of royalty but a crown.[9]

The dukes of Burgundy had created a formidable state between France and Germany, which included the prosperous Low Countries. Duke Philip was a man of culture. He was fond of reading, and maintained one of the best libraries and the finest collection of tapestries on the Continent. His success in war, finance, and diplomacy was said to be due as much to his choice of wise councillors as to his own abilities—a tribute to his judgment. Unlike his successor, he recognized that he was, in fact, a Frenchman, and respected the office of the king, if not the person who occupied it. When Louis the fugitive asked for sanctuary within his borders, Philip was only too glad to harbor him, enjoying the discomfort this caused his rival, Louis's father.

Philip awarded Louis a chateau at Genappe and a pension adequate to his station. For five years Louis passed the time in hunting, visiting the ducal court, and generally awaiting the "sickly season" that would open the throne to him. He also grew to know Duke Philip's son and tempestuous heir, Charles, the count of Charolais.

Charles was ten years Louis's junior. A court historian, Chastellain, observed that he was a good student with a marked interest in military subjects. He was an avid reader of histories on the life and campaigns of Alexander the Great, a popular hero during the Middle Ages. Charles grew to be tall and broad-shouldered. He was quick-tempered like his father, but he lacked the good nature to contain it. He was excessively proud, suspicious, and not open to advice. Charles inherited his father's commanding traits, but few of his human qualities. Historian Henri Pirenne tells us that Charles "never acquired even the superficial heartiness which made Phillip the Good popular. Passionate, but reserved, he held himself aloof from court life and had neither friends nor confidants."[10] During his lifetime he was known as Charles *le Témér-*

aire (the Rash), a more fitting title than the Bold used by latter-day historians.

Charles and Louis occasionally hunted together, and Louis more than once mediated between Charles and the duke when their fiery tempers got the worst of them. The young princes never developed much liking for one another, however, and there is evidence that Charles resented his father's open-handedness toward the exiled dauphin.

Charles and Louis are of interest because both were young men in the prime of life, growing older with no real responsibilities, and impatient for their chance for glory. Each had a vision and a passion: Louis to gather back to the French Crown the lands and authority that the barons had wrenched away; Charles to extend the glory of Burgundy, and possibly give it a royal crown of its own. Charles grew up aboard a smooth sailing and powerful ship of state; when his time came to rule, he would have all the material and political resources a leader could ask for. Louis was heir to uncertainty and poverty; his reign would begin under a cloud.

Louis the King

Louis's time of waiting ended in July 1461 when a fast-riding courier brought the news that Charles VII was dead. The jubilant dauphin rode with the same haste to the city of Rheims, the traditional site of French coronations, there to be crowned, at age thirty-eight, King Louis XI of France.

Louis dove into the business of ruling with the same energy that he had displayed in Dauphiné, and his unmedieval way of managing people and issues quickly rubbed many important persons the wrong way. The most aggrieved, of course, were the barons, who saw their friends at court turned out in favor of Louis's own men, mostly talented commoners. His royal officers seemed to be everywhere—disallowing their exemptions from particular taxes and disputing their rights to try certain cases in their own courts. Louis's spies intercepted compromising letters and reported their plots.[11] Worst of all, the new king could not be controlled, as had his father; he had his own ideas. The barons found themselves shut out of the corridors of power by a man who dressed like a tradesman, who sought advise from commoners, and who had little interest in chivalry or warfare. To the great lords of France,

Louis was, according to Kendall, "a changeling, a man from nowhere, a rank outsider."[12] They were not prepared to go along with his little revolution.

Moving too far too fast has been the undoing of many who have tried to change the world. Revolution gives way to reaction. Julius Caesar discovered this on the steps of the Roman senate; the Spanish Republic learned it in 1936 when a young general named Franco used his army to turn back the clock of liberal reform; Mikhail Gorbachev got a brief taste of it when the phones went dead at his *dacha* in 1991. Louis, too, learned that he had stepped over the line when his agents informed him that the great barons of France had formed themselves into the League of the Public Weal, a military alliance led by Charles of Burgundy. The league had marshaled a large army to confront the king and force him to reverse his administrative reforms. Louis met their combined forces with his own royal army near the town of Montlhéry, where the two forces fought to a standstill.

The initial skirmishes at Montlhéry were near-fatal to both the king and Charles of Burgundy. In a confused melee, Louis's horse was killed, and only the protective circle of his platoon of bodyguards saved the king from an untimely death. Charles, fighting for the opposing side on another part of the field, had advanced beyond his followers and found himself surrounded by the slashing swords of French men-at-arms. One blade battered away his armored collar, scoring his neck deeply. Only the timely intervention of his comrades saved Charles from capture or death.

Louis, who had shown tremendous personal courage in rallying his troops during the battle, drew a lesson from his experience that wars were too dangerous, too random in their outcomes for a prudent ruler to base his plans upon them. Charles, it appears, drew the opposite conclusion. He found the experience exhilarating and fell prey to the delusion that he had a great gift for generalship. Philippe de Commynes, who had ridden with Charles during the battle, wrote many years later:

> All that day the Count of Charolais [Charles] kept the field, rejoicing extremely, and imputing the whole glory of this action to himself; which has cost him dear since, for after that he was governed by no counsel but his own; and whereas before he was altogether unfit for war . . . his thought became so altered upon this point that he spent the remainder of his life in wars, in which he died, and which were the occasion, if not quite the ruin of his family, at least, of the misery and desolation of it.[13]

After several months of skirmish and standoff, Louis determined that his military position was too weak to do anything but negotiate a settlement with the league. Knowing that the barons were inclined to disunity and selfish purpose, Louis negotiated what appeared to be a humiliating set of terms that gave the barons most of what they wanted. Some received control of large provinces, others got outright payments from the royal treasury. Louis was left with little but his crown and the chance to fight another day. He could console himself only in the knowledge that once the barons dissolved the league in triumph, it would be difficult for them to put it back together again. Each would return to his estates with war stories to tell in his Great Hall, satisfied with the booty he had gotten out of the king, if not a little provoked that some had gotten more. Louis would *divide et impera:* He would withdraw when faced with overwhelming strength and attack only when the odds were clearly in his favor. "It is part of his strength," as D. B. Wyndham Lewis tells us, "that when the situation calls for it he can be utterly pliant, can submit to temporary humiliation for the sake of future gain."[14]

It is the mark of the sagacious leader to understand his own power relative to that of rivals. Sensing the distribution of power among competitors and maintaining a comfortable reserve of resources for oneself has practically developed into an art form by European statesmen since the seventeenth century. Louis was ahead of his time in developing that skill. His great rival, Charles of Burgundy, had no knack for it whatever, as we will see. Business leaders also need this capability in the formation and execution of their plans. Political scientists contend that accurately measuring the distribution of power among rivals is a tricky proposition at best, and that the frequency of warfare is a manifestation of the regular failure to do the accounting accurately. The recent war between Iraq and the U.S.-led coalition indicates that today's leaders have gotten no better at it. Witness on the one hand the foolhardiness of Saddam Hussein in taking on the most formidable powers of the world, and on the other hand the over-estimation of Iraqi capabilities by the United States. Even with its sophisticated surveillance and intelligence capacities, many in the United States credited the Iraqis with far more power than they were able to muster.

The Maturing Leader

In the fall of 1465 the League of the Public Weal disbanded and the defeated king rode back to Paris. Within a month, however, he had begun the process of undermining the individual, and now divided, members of the league, thereby eventually winning back all that he had lost.

The League of the Public Weal was but the first of four great rebellions against Louis XI during the first fourteen years of his long reign. In every one Charles the Bold, duke of Burgundy, played a dominant role. Each of the rebellions provided a healthy challenge to the king, improved his understanding of human strength and weakness, and developed his cunning. He learned that he must have trustworthy people of great ability in his service. He rewarded loyalty with loyalty and accomplishment with advancement to the highest posts of wealth and honor. He traveled incessantly to gauge the state of the realm, to hear the complaints of his subjects, and to evaluate the effectiveness of his appointees. He would record for his son later in his reign, "A prince must think about the condition of the people and go among them often, as a gardener cultivates his garden."[15] He had a collapsible bed devised to accommodate him on these far-ranging excursions. Thus the phrase, *management by riding around* was an established practice half a millennium before the phrase *management by walking around* entered the business lexicon.

As much as anything, Louis XI learned never to confront his competitors directly, unless he clearly had the upper hand. He found it better to bend than to break, to avoid dangerous encounters, and to attack only at the points of an enemy's greatest weakness. This was a highly unconventional way of behaving in an age when knightly élan and personal honor were held in higher esteem than good tactics.

These qualities were never of greater value than in the summer of 1470 when Charles the Bold launched a powerful juggernaut against Louis's northern domains. Burning everything in its path, his Burgundian army captured the small town of Nesle and massacred its garrison in a church where they had taken refuge. The fortified town of Roye was the next to fall after a siege of just two days. Panic gripped the kingdom, and Louis's advisors urged him to confront Charles with all haste. The king's dispatch to his commanders was quite typical of his cunning:

> My opinion has always been that you should not hold either Montdidier or Roye, nor put troops in any place that cannot be held . . . If you but conserve your forces and don't leave them in weak places, they will break his army. . . . As for the weak places, he gains nothing when he gains them and enfeebles himself, for he has to leave garrisons there. . . . The first place that can resist him—that will be sufficient to undo him.[16]

This is exactly what happened. After two more weeks of pillaging towns and villages, Charles's army came up against the stoutly defended city of Beauvais. He threw his forces against its walls, only to see them reel back with heavy losses. Infuriated by this resistance, he ordered repeated attacks, always with the same disastrous results. The Burgundian artillery was successful in blasting numerous holes in the defenses, but the garrison and citizens of the town invariably plugged these holes with deadly crossbow fire and, when that failed, with swords and daggers. Louis, hearing what was happening, rushed reinforcements to the town. After only three weeks of siege and failed assaults, Charles the Bold withdrew his depleted forces from Beauvais, and eventually from French territory.

Louis was a shrewd observer of men and their ambitions. Drawing confederates to his plans through persuasion and outright bribery had become part of his *modus operandi*. As Commynes tells us:

> He was . . . the most painful and indefatigable to win over any man to his side that he thought capable of doing him either mischief or service: though he was often refused, he would never give over a man that he wished to gain, but still pressed and continued his insinuations, promising him largely, and presenting him with sums and honors as he knew would gratify his ambition.[17]

In this Louis reminds us of the late President Lyndon Johnson, one of the more crafty American politicians in recent decades. In his book *Practical Intelligences,*[18] Roger Peters says that LBJ could read people like a book. Adviser Arthur Schlesinger admitted being practically hypnotized by LBJ's ability to recall the personal abilities and weaknesses of every one of the forty-eight Democratic senators. Behind his unimpressive exterior lurked a true virtuoso in the art of winning cooperation from others and building formidable coalitions.

Louis had few scruples in how he would recruit his supporters. In drawing up a peace treaty with the haughty and independent François II, duke of Brittany, Louis enlisted the duke's most important vassal, Odet d'Aydie, to his cause. Knowing d'Aydie's influence over the duke, Louis made him the recipient of cash, lucrative offices, and a member of the exclusive Order of St. Michael. Louis used the same tactic in coopting a number of leading advisers to England's King Edward IV. By far his greatest coup, however, involved Philippe de Commynes, Charles the Bold's principal advisor.

Commynes had been with the Burgundian court all his adult life. As advisor to Europe's most powerful nobleman, he knew or had dealt with most of the great leaders and statesmen of his time. Pierre Champion has described him as "one of the most intelligent men of his day." One rainy evening in August 1473, Commynes slipped away from the encampment of Charles the Bold to enter the service of the king of France. Commynes's abandonment of his prestigious position and estates without prior assurances testifies to the high regard he held for the Spider King.

Other rulers of the time used money for pleasure or dissipated it in war. Louis XI invested it for political advantage, often using money as a wedge to divide his enemies. When England's Edward IV entered France in alliance with Charles the Bold, Louis bought him off, concluding that it was cheaper to buy peace than to pay for war. He signed a peace treaty with Edward in 1475, paying 75,000 gold crowns up front and a 50,000-crown annuity for life (which in Edward's case would very shortly expire). The treaty rid the kingdom of the English army, giving Louis time to strengthen the domestic economy and concentrate all his military resources against Burgundy. The jovial French king was so pleased with this investment that he invited Edward and the English soldiers to two days of drinking and feasting, telling the English monarch that

> if he would come and divert himself with the ladies, he would assign him the Cardinal of Bourbon for his confessor, who he knew would willingly absolve him if he should commit any sin by way of love and gallantry. The King of England was extremely pleased with his raillery, and made [King Louis] several good repartees, for he knew the cardinal was a jolly companion.[19]

After forty-eight hours of nonstop carousing, the English army quite literally staggered back to its camp, from whence it departed French soil. "I have chased the English out of France more easily than my father ever did," Louis crowed; "[he] drove them out by force of arms while I have driven them out by force of meat pies and good wine." Thus, with two days of solid partying, the Hundred Years' War ended.

The Boar of the Ardennes

Unlike Louis XI, Charles the Bold learned little from the important experiences of life, and less from his encounters with the wily French king. Overfilled with his own importance, and little inclined to take advice, he fits the description made by Chastellain of the nobility in general that "princes are men, and their affairs are high and perilous, and their natures are subject to many passions, such as hatred and envy; their hearts are veritable dwelling places of these because of their pride in ruling." Failure did not instruct him, but only fed his anger; and success inflated his enormous ego.

There is nothing in the record to soften Charles's reputation for pigheadedness. Chroniclers of the time provide no glimpses of a man capable of warmth who could laugh at the world and his own foibles. All that we find is a man who was enormously wealthy, powerful, and intemperate: The Boar of the Ardennes. His volatile nature is best captured by Commynes when describing an episode in which Charles was negotiating with Louis. Sensing that he was being outfoxed by the king, Charles became so agitated that he paced his room through the entire night—Commynes in tow—occasionally throwing himself on his bed, only to spring up and resume his pacing. "On the morrow," Commynes reports, "he was in an even greater rage."

In the end, the leader who started with everything, but who failed to learn from experience and who was governed by his temper, proved no match for the leader who started with little, but who lived by his wits. By 1474 Charles had squandered the greater part of his liquid wealth on incessant warfare against the Crown, his subjects, and other neighbors. With a train of five hundred cannons and armies of feudal levies and mercenaries to support, the duke quickly ran through his inheritance and was borrowing heavily from the Medicis and other bankers.

Burgundy's undoing came at the hands of the Swiss. The Swiss cantons had allied themselves with Alsatian towns in revolt against the duke of Burgundy. In November 1474 they defeated a Burgundian armies at Héricourt, and the duke vowed to even the score. In February 1476 he sought his revenge, sending fifteen thousand men against the Swiss town of Grandson. After just a few days of resistance, the town surrendered, and Charles had five hundred of its defenders hanged and scores of others drowned in the nearby lake. Feeling supremely confident, he moved his force toward his next objective, the town of Neuchâtel. His Italian mercenaries grumbled about the miserable weather, and his commanders cautioned that the terrain near their objective would not allow them to maneuver if attacked, but the duke overruled them. On the morning of March 2, in the narrow passes near Neuchâtel, the Swiss pikemen outflanked the duke's magnificent army, sending it reeling back to Burgundy with the loss of all of its cannon, tons of field equipment, and much the duke's personal treasure.

The duke of Burgundy's defeat sent shockwaves through Europe, upsetting power relationships and alliances. The Great Man of Europe had lost most of his wealth and reputation in a single day. Political allies began distancing themselves from Burgundy; his enemies were encouraged to revolt. Instead of tending to his political problems, however, Charles chose, predictably, to revenge himself on the "bestial Swiss."

Within two weeks of the disaster of Neuchâtel, the duke had begun organizing a new military campaign. By late May 1477 he had crossed the Jura Mountains for an assault on the fortified city of Morat. His newly purchased artillery and army of Burgundians and mercenaries put the city under siege. With the duke's treatment of the defenders of Grandson a vivid memory, the two thousand defenders of Morat gave no thought to surrender and put up a stalwart defence. They held the duke at bay for over a month, giving the Swiss and their allies time to muster a force capable of raising the siege. On June 21 a Swiss army of some eighteen thousand took positions in the hills above the plateau where the duke's forces were formed up to meet them. All the next morning, the Burgundian forces stood in formation in a drenching summer rainstorm, but the Swiss would not come out to meet them. By midday, Duke Charles concluded that they had but a small force and were unwilling to confront him, so he and the bulk of his force returned to the shelter of their tents, leaving only the artillery and a small force of foot and horse to guard the plateau. When the rain stopped the Swiss debouched from the woods and ravines bordering the plateau. They quickly overran the Burgundian guard force and were upon the duke's main encampment before he could form his men into a well-ordered line of battle. The rout and slaughter that followed was a repeat of Neuchâtel, but on a larger scale. An estimated eight thousand Burgundians and mercenaries were killed at Morat, and only about half the duke's force managed to escape.

The record is silent on Charles of Burgundy's private thoughts as he galloped to safety from the disaster of Morat. Louis XI, we know, was overjoyed by the news. He sent a congratulatory letter to the Swiss, his "very special friends, by the grace of God most invincible," and he went off on a short pilgrimage in token of his good fortune.

In the months that followed, the duke of Burgundy saw his fair-weather friends distance themselves from him. He let his beard grow long and wild and was given to alternating periods of rage and senseless laughter. More ominously, he began demanding that his fiefs and towns send him the wherewithal for a new army. Meanwhile, Louis XI continued consolidating his gains. With Burgundy's star in decline, Louis's star seemed all the brighter. The duke of Milan opened negotiations with the French as did the king of Anjou; the Flemish, seeing the possibility of their independence from Burgundy improve, opened a clear channel to Louis's agents. Duke René II of Lorraine went so far as to attack and capture the Burgundian-held city of Nancy on October 6, 1477, an event that set the stage for the final act of the French–Burgundian drama.

The capture of Nancy was the ultimate affront to Duke Charles's pride. By late October, he had scrounged together two to three thousand men for a counterattack. Despite the warnings of his commanders that his force was too small and ill-equipped to conduct a winter siege of the required magnitude, Charles pushed ahead and invested the city.

Duke René had the will and the men from Alsace and the Swiss cantons to confront Charles at Nancy but lacked the money to pay them. Louis, of course, was willing to fight Burgundy to the last Swiss and gladly came up with the money! On January 5, 1478, the two armies met before Nancy. With the numbers favoring René by four-to-one, the outcome was never in doubt.

Two days after the battle, the body of Duke Charles of Burgundy was found stripped naked and face down on a frozen pond, his skull split from crown to jaw by a Swiss halbert, and his body pierced repeatedly by pikes or lances. Only scars and certain missing teeth known to his captured servants made identification of Europe's greatest personage possible.

The Twilight Years

The death of Charles the Bold, who left no male heir, spelled the end of the great Burgundian state that had for so long threatened the sovereignty of France. In the weeks and months that followed, Louis XI secured the duchy for the Crown; and other domains of the late duke began falling into line.

Louis XI would outlive his great enemy by six years, but most biographers agree that with his nemesis out of the way, Louis began to lose the fine edge of his cunning. Like a high-wire performer, the sudden presence of a safety net caused him to relax his concentration. He became impatient with the progress of events and more inclined to using force than his traditional craftiness to achieve his ends. He made more mistakes and trusted less in the counsel that his good servants provided. As his health deteriorated, he developed a paranoia about plots and assassins. He made his palace at Plessis into an impenetrable retreat, surrounded by a wall studded with iron spits. An inner iron fence lay within this outer wall, and the inner courtyard corners had watchtowers manned by crossbowmen. Four hundred archers patrolled the outer grounds; a single drawbridge offering entry. As the end approached, the king gave himself over to the influences of physicians, relics, and holy men.

Louis XI was never much loved by his people, whom he taxed heavily, but he left France in a state of peace. The English were gone, except for a toehold at Calais. The independence of the great noblemen was forever broken. Many lands were brought back to the bosom of France. The nurturing of the economy and the people who made it run had finally become a matter of state policy. The Spider King had set his nation on the path to a new era.

Challenging the Status Quo

The lesson from the life of Louis XI is that those who create change often find themselves alone, exposed, and imperiled by the power of the status quo. Fortunately, when the status quo no longer represents the fundamental interests of society (or of an organization), it tends to corruption: Its higher echelons fill up with the proud, the incompetent, and the unworthy. These are more easily defeated.

Louis had an advantage that modern change agents rarely enjoy: He was the king; and he was the king because of whom his father was. He could not be denied the levers of power. The modern change maker has no such claim to authority, but must rise to it one step at a time, avoiding fatal missteps at every turn.

The modern corporation is no lover of radicals. Most extoll

innovation, change, and creative solutions—the buzzwords of the day—but the old dogs and the old thinkers at the top will only tolerate so much of these. Change implies undoing what they have done. A good case in point was the episode of Ross Perot who, for a short time in the 1980s was a member of the board of directors of General Motors Corporation (GM). Perot had sold his very successful EDS Corporation to GM, gaining enough GM shares in the sale to have a seat on its board. He became an outspoken critic of GM attitudes and management practices and gave freely of his time to help change things for the better. The corporation's reaction was to rid itself of this nuisance—to use its scarce capital to buy back all of Perot's shares, thus ousting him from the board.

The unfortunate fact that you often get along by going along has undoubtedly ended the careers of countless potential leaders in large corporations, the military, and government. Still, some make it to the top. The case of John Reed, CEO of Citicorp, is one such interesting case. Reed came to banking via an MIT engineering background and a Wharton School MBA. In an industry whose champions rose from the ranks of corporate lending, Reed's limited lending experience and his passionate interest in the potential of back-office technology to serve customer needs made him an unlikely candidate for either survival or success. Reed had the good fortune to fall under the protective shield of Chairman Walter Wriston, who appreciated his ideas, and who gave him the freedom to try them out.

Reed backed new initiatives in retail banking—credit cards and automated teller machines (ATMs) that in their early days were such big money losers that they virtually eliminated all funds available for management bonuses within Citicorp for two years. John Reed, during those years, was the wrecker of family vacations, Florida condos, and greens fees for VPs throughout the Citicorp universe. Only the backing of Wriston saved him from certain career death. In the end, however, his new initiatives put Citicorp ahead of its money center banking competitors.

When Louis assumed the throne of France, he, too, got off to a rocky start. He first tossed out his father's advisers and top bureaucrats, only to learn later that many were highly competent and dedicated to the Crown. Years later he had the good sense to hire many of them back. His eager reforms quickly ran him afoul of the powerful barons, who responded with the League of the Public Weal, which in turn pinned his ears back and upset his timetable for change by a number of years.

Louis's life provides a lesson for people who want to change things. The hand they are dealt rarely has a set of winning cards—the people across the table inevitably start with a far larger pile of chips. The challenge, then, is the same as Louis's: to avoid situations that will get you knocked out of the game in the early hands; to be patient in building up your resources; to attack aggressively only in those situations when the odds are clearly in your favor; and when you have your opponent on the run, do not let up.

These might be valuable guides to action for anyone taking on a major business competitor. The experience of Japanese manufacturers provides, in this, an interesting parallel. At the beginning of the postwar era, the United States was clearly a ten-ton elephant. It dominated the major industrial markets: steel, automobiles, electronics, communications, finance, and so forth. It had *the* big pile of chips. To challenge it directly, Japanese industrialists would have been foolish.

The Japanese instead challenged U.S. industry indirectly, by developing products at the low end of the markets. They entered the auto business with small cars: Detroit did not care about these—poor margins! They introduced cheap little radios, small television sets and home appliances, all while avoiding America's strong suits and building up their pile of chips. Once they felt strong, they began playing boldly, introducing full-sized luxury cars, full-sized electronic appliances, and communications systems to compete head-to-head with America's best.

Today, France's Louis XI enjoys a less than lustrous reputation. Popular history has made him out to be a paranoid, a crank, and a cruel tormentor of any rival entangled in his web. In the dimly lit dungeon of the old castle of Loches, French tour guides like to show visitors the suspended iron cages, just large enough to hold a crouching prisoner, in which Louis is said to have imprisoned his enemies for months and years.

Louis XI's final resting place is in Notre Dame de Cléry, a small church he favored with regular endowments during his life. For years the church was like Louis's reputation—in disrepair. Swallows entered freely through missing windowpanes, darting across the sunlit nave and into the deep shadows along the vault. The place had a threadbare look. In the main aisle is a large, iron trapdoor, which the guidebooks indicate as the entrance to the royal crypt. The visitor can ask the sacristan to unlock this door with his huge skeleton key. Heaving back the trapdoor, the sacristan will proceed down the steps into the pitch darkness just far enough to flick on a light switch, revealing two unadorned coffins—one Louis's, the other his wife's. On a small wooden table, directly under the light, and facing the visitor is a human skull. "This," the cleric will tell you, "is the king."

4

The Power of Ideas: Two Reformers Change the World

Organized social movements cannot appear and institutions cannot function without ideas.

Carl Gustavson, *A Preface to History*

Some people lead by example, others by forceful actions; still others through their ideas. In the end, these last may be the more powerful. This is as true in business and politics as it is in science, art, and theology. Bioengineering, microelectronics, and aerospace, to name just a few, are entirely new industries based upon the ideas of a small group of innovators. Earlier in this century and in the last, the ideas of people like George Eastman (celluloid roll film), Thomas Edison (electric power and lighting, cinematography, and dozens of other innovations), General Sarnoff (radio and television), and others spawned industries that collectively employed millions and added immeasurably to the richness and variety of life. Eli Whitney had the idea of assembling goods from interchangeable parts; Henry Ford and his chief engineer, Frank Sorenson, conceived of a factory system in which work came to the workman via an assembly line; Taiichi Ohno took Ford's ideas a step farther with the "lean production" he pioneered at Toyota.

Individuals outside the realm of business whose new or synthesized ideas have changed the course of history are even more familiar: Jesus Christ had twelve very ordinary men as followers, yet his ideas about the relationship of one person to another—and to God—fundamentally altered the history of the Western world; Nicholaus Copernicus, a Polish-German monk, hypothesized a new model of the solar system that has altered perceptions of our place in the universe ever since; John Locke and other thinkers of the Enlightenment gained currency within small circles of influential people during their own lifetimes, but their writings were instrumental in igniting national revolutions that swept North America and Europe from 1775 to 1848. Mahatma Gandhi, a man whose worldly goods would not fill a gym bag, broke the back of British colonialism in India with his simple but eloquent ideas of nonviolent resistance. Of course, there was also Karl Marx, the gloomy scholar who, from the public reading room of the British Museum and his own impoverished quarters in London, systematized centuries of socialist philosophy into the doctrine of communism that changed the face of world.

People with ideas are at once the source of our discomfort and of our progress. Sociologist Lewis Coser devoted an entire book to men with ideas (obviously written before women had ideas), in which he described intellectuals from the seventeenth century onward, saying that "they tend to scrutinize the received ideas and assumption of their times and *milieu*. They are those who 'think otherwise,' the disturbers of intellectual peace."

This chapter examines the careers of two reformers—disturbers of the intellectual peace—who challenged the accepted truths of their times and offered new ideas in their place. One was a theologian, the other was a statistician. Each was a messenger of a new "religion," and each produced important, long-term change. Our attempt here is to draw insights into how and why new ideas either succeed or fail to take root.

The Wittenberg Scholar

In the fall of 1517, England's Henry VIII was an energetic young king of twenty-seven whose wife, Catherine of Aragon, was still secure enough in her marriage to complain to her husband about his bushy new beard. An ocean away in the New World, Juan de Grijalva was planning his westward voyage of exploration. In the German university town of Wittenberg, a young Augustinian Eremite and popular teacher of theology named Martin Luther rose early one morning in October, walked to the palace church, and nailed a document containing ninety-five theses—his arguments against the sale of indulgences—to the front door. If Luther's hammering disturbed his sleeping neighbors that morning, there is no record of it. In fact, the dramatic story of the theses nailed to the door may be nothing more than a story; but Luther did awaken all of Europe and his ideas disturbed it greatly for the next century.

Martin Luther's part in launching the Protestant Reformation is well known to most and will not be recounted here in detail. Suffice it to say that Luther, like many serious churchmen and fellow Germans of the time, was deeply offended by the practices of his own church and meant to do something about them. In so doing he overturned the whole apple cart of church and state and began a process that led to a new set of institutions and political arrangements. Historian Euan Cameron wrote: "No other movement of religious protest or reform since antiquity has been so widespread or lasting in effects, so deep and searching in its criticism of received wisdom, so destructive in what it abolished or so fertile in what it created."[1]

Martin Luther was hardly the first to speak out for reform of the Roman Catholic church. Earlier reformers had appeared, and most had been silenced. Religion was serious business, and the powers and practices of the church were jealously protected. It was not an age in which people could disagree agreeably on religious matters. There was the right way to God and there was heresy; the righteous got the fast lane to heaven and the heretics got fire and sword. In 1208, Pope Innocent III organized a bloody crusade, not against Islam, but against the Albigensian "heretics" of southern France, whose beliefs harkened back to Manichaean ideas about the duality of flesh and spirit, good and evil. Followers of Peter Waldo, "the poor men of Lyon," were pacifists, who also disputed the central doctrine of the Mass, and they, too, were suppressed. Followers of reformer John Wycliffe (late 1300s), called the Lollards, denied the sacramental powers of the church and were forced underground. In June 1415, a Czech preacher named Jan Hus was summoned to the Council of Constance to defend his controversial views; despite his safe passage from the emperor the council had him condemned and burned. In 1498, a friar named Girolamo Savonarola was so successful in his movement to reform both church corruption and civil tyranny in Florence that his enemies had him tried, tortured, and burned.

Luther shared much of the philosophy of these early reform-

ers, yet he not only survived, he triumphed. How did he manage
to succeed where others had failed? Why did his ideas take root
while those of the others did not? One way to find the answers is
to examine the environment in which he operated—the German
states on the eve of the Reformation.

Fertile Soil for Reform

In 1500, Germany had a population of nearly 12 million people,
mostly engaged in agriculture. Only about 1.5 million lived in
towns, of which there were perhaps 200 with more than 1,000
inhabitants. The three largest towns—Cologne, Augsburg, and
Nuremberg—each had 30,000 to 50,000 residents, and these were
controlled by the guilds and patrician families.

It was a time of economic transition; wealth had already begun its slow but steady migration from the hands of landed noblemen to the enterprises of town burghers and artisans. Commercial
families like the Fuggers accumulated capital from trade, textiles,
mining, and banking. In many respects these families were northern reflections of the greater Italian commercial dynasties that were
their contemporaries.

The profitability of landholding, the basis of Europe's medieval economy, was falling fast. In the north the great landlords felt
the pinch on their pocketbooks and responded by tightening their
grip on the peasantry, tying them more tightly to the land in classic serfdom. In the south the pace of urbanization was advancing
to the detriment of landlords: both lay and religious. As workers
migrated from farms to cities, labor on noble estates grew scarcer
(more expensive), and the landlords tried to offset this by charging the peasantry for what they once got for free—access to the
common woods, lakes and streams—and by exacting greater labor
services and taxes. Since protests against these high-handed practices had to be settled in manorial courts, no justice could be had,
and the result was a spate of rural rebellions that erupted in Germany at an increasing rate starting in the mid-1400s. These uncoordinated disturbances were put down ruthlessly by the great
landowners, but repression only kindled greater discontent.

Among the landowning class the lesser nobility, the imperial
knights *(Reichsritter),* had by this time lost most of their purpose
as warriors. Since their small estates were insufficient as economic
bases, many were forced to become mercenaries or common rob-
bers in order to maintain themselves. The provincial nobility *(Lan-*

dadel) were not much better off. Even the high nobles found themselves hard pressed as the cost of warfare and court ceremony rose and the profits on landholdings declined.

The fortunes of the Church of Rome and its ruling circle were, on the other hand, flying high. Fully one-third of German land was owned by the church. Over the centuries its great abbeys, cathedrals, and convents had amassed tremendous wealth from endowments and the sale of religious services. In an age in which true piety and primitive superstitions coexisted, the church turned a tidy profit by catering to both. Both the unlettered masses and the educated elite used charms to maintain health, enlisted liturgical rites to protect crops and animals from disease, and paid to have prayers and masses said for the benefit of souls in the afterlife. The wealthy collected relics to insure their eternal salvation. Elector Frederick of Saxony had 19,000 relics, which included such rarities as milk reputed to be from the Virgin's own breast and straw from the nativity stable. Every relic collector worth his salt had a sliver of the True Cross.

Though religion dominated everyday life and few disputed Church doctrines, the corruption and dissolute behavior of the higher clergy were universally condemned. The top jobs in the church were mostly reserved for the sons of the great families who brought little in the way of virtue or pastoral duty to their posts. Instead, they grew rich on the incomes of benefices. Many flaunted their great wealth—going about in armor and ostentatious secular garb, having a go at taverns and wenches during late night carouses, and keeping one or several mistresses. Some laypersons endorsed the idea of allowing priests to marry—so that they would stop chasing other men's wives. Albert of Brandenburg, Luther's superior, was typical of the rich clerics that Germans of all classes despised. A *doubledipper*—to use the modern term—Albert was the archbishop of Magdeburg and Mainz *and* administrator of the bishopric of Halberstadt, and he drew considerable income from each. If archbishop Albert was loathsome to the public, at least he was German. Less liked were papal clerics and bureaucrats, who were generally seen as Mediterranean leeches who drew away the wealth of Germany to the "stinkhole" of Rome. In 1520, Luther complained of the rapacious papal bureaucracy as "such a swarm of parasites in that place called Rome, all boasting that they belong to the pope, . . . lying in wait for the endowments and benefices of Germany as the wolves lie in wait for the sheep."

Nationalism was on the rise throughout sixteenth-century Europe and had led to strong, centralized monarchies in England, Spain, and France—and greater control of national churches by their kings. In Germany, however, which remained a puzzle of principalities, Rome controlled the ecclesiastical turf. If local princes wanted to set up their sons, nephews, or bastards as abbots and bishops, they first had to pay off the Roman Curia. Even outside Germany, this practice remained common, prompting Englishman Thomas Gascoigne to write that "three things make a bishop in England—the will of the King, the will of the pope or the Roman court, and money in abundance paid to the Roman court." German people of all classes grated at the idea of paying taxes and kind to a papal bureaucracy dominated by Italians, Frenchmen, and Spaniards. The Mediterranean aliens had worn out their welcome in northern Europe.

Rising German nationalism, economic change, and general disgust with Catholic church leadership and practices provided a receptive atmosphere for Luther's ideas of reform. The ninety five theses Luther nailed to the church door in Wittenberg were limited in their scope and their intentions. The theses were Luther's challenge to the practice of selling indulgences—the trading of money for the remission of sins. It is doubtful that he ever intended to raise a major ruckus. His bold action was prompted by the aforementioned Archbishop Albert of Brandenburg's commissioning of a Dominican friar named Johann Tezel to sell indulgences within his jurisdiction. Proceeds were to be split between Tezel, the archbishop, and the Pope Leo X's coffers. Within weeks, copies of Luther's theses were printed and distributed (apparently without his permission) throughout Germany, where they were enthusiastically received.

The ninety-five theses was Luther's first step down a long road that led him into deeper and deeper conflict with the papacy and with his emperor. When he and his opinions were condemned by a papal bull—*Exsurge Domine*—in 1520, the unrepentant theologian—cheered on by Germans of all classes—publicly burned the document and boldly reaffirmed his faith in a "priesthood of all believers" that relied only on the Bible, not on the ministry of the pope's agents for salvation. This brought the new emperor, Charles V, into the camp of those who wanted the preacher's hide, and only Luther's popularity with the people and the aid of his prince, Elector Frederick of Saxony, saved him from the fate that had silenced so many of his predecessors.

In the years that followed, Luther developed his framework of theological ideas, drawing generously, by his own acknowledgment, from St. Paul and St. Augustine, as well as from Bernard of Clairvaux and William of Ockham. From Saxony, his ideas and the spirit of reform spread rapidly. Aided by Luther's prolific pamphleteering and the recent invention of the printing press, the reform movement developed in other parts of Germany, then in Switzerland, France, England, and Scandinavia. In every instance, its popular acceptance was aided by a combination of nationalism, fundamental Christian piety, and economic self-interest.

Every stratum of society had one or more reasons to support Luther and his reform movement. Historian Roland Stromberg writes of the German princes, "They adopted Lutheranism in the knowledge that by so doing they might seize church lands, free themselves from papal exactions, and yet keep a relatively conservative church order which staunchly supported their authority."[2] Reformation scholar Euan Cameron cites the case of Duke Ulrich of Württemberg as a most successful plunderer of church assets: "In two years he confiscated all monastery lands, which provided twice his own original income; ultimately he seized three-quarters of *all* church property, and even had gold paint scraped off the altar paintings."[3] The all-time champ of these religiously inspired confiscators, of course, was England's Henry VIII, who between 1540 and 1547 helped himself to some £1.3 million of Church property. To these people, reformers like Luther were truly heaven-sent, not lunatics to be burned at the stake.

The reasons for Luther's popularity among the rising middle-class of the towns and among the rural peasants, is less obvious and subject to speculation. Some suggest that the urban burghers were among the first adherents of reform by virtue of the fact that they were literate and lived in cities, where preaching and pamphleteering was concentrated. The nationalistic appeal of Lutheranism had a high appeal to this group. For poor, downtrodden rural peasants, on the other hand, reform was the first cousin to revolution. The idea of tearing down the established order and destroying one set of oppressors was overwhelmingly appealing to German peasants, and many were prepared to go a step further— to rebel against their secular overlords. Luther and the secular authorities united to put down this notion in the years ahead. Revolution based upon social class was an idea whose time had definitely *not* come—at least not to fifteenth-century Germany.

Martin Luther's reformation kept Europe on a slow boil for almost a century. Conflict between Catholics and Protestants, and between warring factions of Protestants, caused tremendous loses to life and property; it also produced an atmosphere in which tremendous progress was made in political philosophy, science, the arts, and industry. Copernicus, Galileo, Francis Bacon, Kepler, Napier, Descartes, Elizabeth I, Ignatius Loyola, John Locke, and Thomas Hobbes all came of age in the tumultuous century that followed Luther's hammering on the Wittenberg church door. Even the Roman Catholic church was energized by the challenge of the new religion. The shock of Luther's rebellion gave long-silent critics within the church the opportunity to emerge and enact fundamental reforms.

In the end, the scholarly Augustinian from Wittenberg, the man with timely ideas, proved more powerful than his archbishop, his pope, and his emperor.

The Missionary of Quality

At the end of World War II, Japan's economy lay in ruins. American bombing during the late stages of the conflict had caused tremendous damage to 40 percent of the nation's urban development: Industrial complexes were flattened; major population centers were swept by firestorms, leaving tens of thousands homeless; the people of Nagasaki and Hiroshima were made victims of nuclear Armageddon. Of the 1.8 million Japanese who died during the war,[4] many were artisans, industrial managers, engineers, and trained factory workers. Like Russia and Germany, Japan lost a substantial portion of a whole generation of productive citizens. When the war ended, 6 million veterans returned from China, Southeast Asia, and the Pacific islands to a homeland that could neither feed nor employ them—at least for the moment. Only the material assistance of the United States prevented widespread epidemics and starvation.

Japanese industrialists faced tremendous problems immediately after the war. Many of their fixed assets were in ruins; some of the best workers and managers had died in battle, and the banks were as empty as peoples' stomachs—obtaining capital to rebuild homes and factories was next to impossible. In 1946, overall industrial production had sunk to one-seventh of the level Japan had enjoyed in 1941. The national output of coal, iron, textiles, electric motors, and truck chassis had all dropped to 10 percent or less of what they had been before the war against the United States.[5] Stripped of its overseas conquests, the nation was truly "a rock in the fog," barren of petroleum, iron ore, cotton, and other natural resources. Indeed, the country was (and remains) dependent upon imports for 99 percent of its oil, 95 percent of its iron ore, 100 percent of bauxite and cotton, and much of its food.

The Japanese economy sputtered along through the remainder of the 1940s, experiencing a much slower pace of recovery than did the war-torn nations of Europe. The American occupation forces of General Douglas MacArthur worked during those years to mold a new Japan based on democratic principles, with an economy stripped of its aircraft and military industries that would ultimately develop to somewhere near late 1930 levels.

The Cold War gave Japan a whole new lease on life. With the fall of China to the Communists in 1948, Japan and the Philippines suddenly took on new importance as far pavilions of the capitalistic West. With the outbreak of the Korean War in June 1950, Japan became America's principal staging and resupply center, sourcing $1.5 billion in war materials. Factory orders from the U.S. military and spending by U.S. sailors and GIs moved economic activities into high gear; with the exception of a few bumps, accelerated economic growth was to be the norm for the Japanese economy over the next forty years. The Japanese economy grew by 469 percent during the period 1952–1971 alone— more than twice that of West Germany, and five times that of the United States.[6] During the 1970s, when America's growth rate was flat to anemic, Japan's clipped along at a compounded rate of 10 percent. In the forty-eight years since its humiliating wartime surrender, Japan literally rose from the ashes to become the most vibrant and second largest economy in the world.

> For the building of a new Japan,
> Let's put our strength and mind together,
> Doing our best to promote production,
> Sending our goods to the people of the world.
> Endlessly and continuously,
> Like water gushing from a fountain,
> Grow, industry, grow, grow, grow!
> Harmony and sincerity!
>
> Matsushita Workers' Song[7]

Despite this new high-growth trajectory, the early postwar years were lean ones for the Japanese people. They were poor and they knew it—and they acted like it. Everything had to be done on a shoestring; materials, machinery, capital, and skilled hands were all in short supply. They were therefore eager to find ways to do things better with what little they had. Into this environment came an American statistician named Deming—a man who has since been described as "obsessed with precision, with performance, and with customers."[8]

Incubation Period of the Quality Movement

W. Edwards Deming was born in Sioux City, Iowa, in 1900. Six years later his father caught the bug to move west to Cody, Wyoming, and eventually to the new settlement of Powell, where he obtained homestead property. The elder Deming practiced law when he could, did some homebuilding, and ran his small farm; Mrs. Deming gave piano lessons in her home.[9] The Deming family lived a frugal existence in this frontier setting, and the habits of thrift stayed with "Ed" long after he could afford to discard them.

Deming was an able student who eventually went on to the University of Wyoming, where he earned a bachelor's degree in engineering. In 1922 he went to the University of Colorado to study mathematics and physics. His outstanding performance as a student won him a place at Yale, from which he was to earn a Ph.D in physics.[10] During the summer of 1927, while working at AT&T's famous Hawthorne plant between semesters at Yale, Deming met Walter Shewhart, a man who was to have an important influence on his career.

Shewhart was a pioneering statistician who worked at AT&T's Bell Labs in the late 1920s and early 1930s. He had successfully applied his craft to the business of quality control within Western Electric, the equipment manufacturing division of the corporation, and his ideas were later set down in a book titled *Economic Control of Quality of Manufactured Product* (1931). Shewhart recognized that all manufacturing outputs are subject to some level of variation and that excessive variation is at the heart of the quality problem. No two items passed through a milling machine or other manufacturing process turn out exactly the same. Some variation in their form or outer dimensions naturally occurs as a result of the inherent imprecision of the machinery, the material, or the skill of different machine operators. Shewhart called these "common causes" of variation, and viewed them as a natural phenomenon in a production process that was under control. Here we might use the analogy of an expert firing repeatedly at a fixed target: Even a trained person, using a rifle and ammunition manufac-

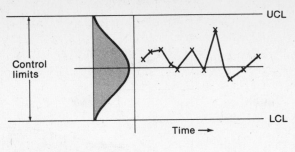

UCL = Upper control limit
LCL = Lower control limit

Figure 4.1 Control chart.

tured to high specifications, is not able to put each shot into the bull's-eye. Instead, that *expert* produces a pattern of hits clustered around the bull's-eye, the tightness of which is a measure of his or her skill and the equipment's precision.

Shewhart also noted "special" causes for variation: those originating in machine maladjustment, a worn or broken tool, an untrained operator, and so forth. In the expert shooter analogy, special causes of variation reveal themselves as periodic shots that fall far outside the normal pattern of hits or as the inability of the shooter to form *any* pattern at all: Both are evidence of a process "out of control."

Modern statistical control charts (Fig. 4.1) illustrate how the concept of variation can be used to monitor product quality over time in the manufacturing process. Measured variation is used to establish control limits that describe the natural variation of the operation. Points falling outside these limits indicate unnatural degrees of variation and must be investigated to determine the root cause. The way to assure quality, then, is to find the source of unnatural or special variation and to control it on a continuing and progressive basis. In Figure 4.1, variations form a pattern around a mean value and each variation falls within the upper and lower control limits, meaning that the process is "in control" as far as quality is concerned.

Shewhart's statistical methods for measuring variation provided managers and line workers with tools for determining whether their processes were operating smoothly or in need of attention if quality was to be upheld. He developed the mathematical underpinnings of a system that could indicate when a manufacturing

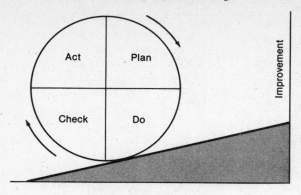

Figure 4.2 The Shewhart Cycle.

system was in or out of control. More important, he prescribed action for each case.

When special causes of variation were detected, workers and managers were to determine their locations in the manufacturing process and root them out. In the case of common causes of variation, they were to find ways of reducing them (i.e., tightening their pattern of "hits" around the bull's-eye of product specifications). This became known as the Shewhart Cycle (Fig. 4.2), and its descendent was to appear decades later in Japan under the term *kaisen* or (continual improvement).

In the Shewhart Cycle of continual improvement, managers first *Plan* a test or change in the production process, then *Do* the test, then *Check* the results, and finally *Act* to improve the process based upon what they have learned. This cycle repeats itself continually.

Shewhart's insights, which came to be called statistical process control (SPC), were implemented by AT&T, but Shewhart and his ideas were little known in the larger world of manufacturing. Deming was to extend Shewhart's concept of quality and act as its messenger. World War II provided the opportunity.

The War Years

The scope of the war required the full mobilization of the nation's resources. Academics and scientists from many disciplines were recruited by the U.S. government to help in the war effort. At places like Cal Tech and MIT, laboratory research and development proceeded at a phenomenal pace. Tremendous advances in aeronautical engineering, radar and electronics, logistics, mathematics, and—of course—nuclear physics were made by scholars-turned-civil servants. Many of the tools of operations research used by scientific management today stem from the application of statistics and mathematics to the military's problems of moving huge numbers of personnel and volumes of material, creating search patterns for submarines in the North Atlantic, and getting greater production out of the nation's factories.

During the war, Deming was asked to help train industry in the application of statistics to the workplace. He did this through a series of courses offered to managers and engineers around the country. Just as the military used crash courses to produce junior officers (ninety-day wonders), Deming and his associates set up traveling courses based upon Shewhart's ideas to train manufacturers in the methods of statistical process control. SPC, they contended, would help factories turn out high-quality materials, in much greater volume, using fewer workers. Manufacturing processes controlled through statistical methods could operate with very little error, rework, or waste. These methods would eliminate the need for the many quality inspectors who traditionally sifted through factory output, weeding out those items that did not meet specs. Some ten thousand engineers were trained in SPC during the war;[11] what they learned resulted in tremendous increases in both productivity and quality within American defense plants. Although many of their most experienced workers were away at war, American factories nevertheless produced mountains of high-quality munitions and material.

When the war ended in 1945, America's veterans came home to their old jobs. Their companies, which had prospered from government contracts, switched over to production of civilian goods, for which there was five years worth of pent up demand. With few civilian goods available during the war years, households had little choice but to stash their discretionary income in savings accounts and war bonds. These mountains of funds were just waiting to be spent on homes, appliances, automobiles, and carriages for the first wave of the baby boom.

The postwar years in the United States were a period of high demand, and industry was eager to create the supply. Strangely, however, the lessons of SPC, which Deming and others had been so successful in spreading, fell into disuse. The old managers and workers were back, consumers would buy whatever was produced, and there were virtually *no* foreign competitors. In this atmosphere, the discipline of quality was quickly lost. As Deming describes it, "Brilliant applications attracted much attention, but the flare of statistical methods by themselves, in an atmosphere in which management did not know their responsibilities burned, sputtered, fizzled, and died out."[12] Another eminent quality expert of Deming's generation, Joseph Juran, suggests that American companies were willing to use SPC as long as government contracts paid for it, but dropped it just as soon as they were required to pay for the training and analysis that went with it.[13] This seems something of a contradiction since overwhelming evidence indicates that SPC methods lead to higher quality *and* lower costs. Perhaps the mood of the times was the source of this contradiction. As Hayes, Wheelwright, and Clark relate,

> World War II now appears to be a watershed. On the production side, the very success of the war effort became the enemy of further progress. It was as if, having apparently mastered manufacturing, Americans could go on to worry about other things, safe in the assumption that production would continue as vigorous and robust as before.[14]

In any case, the methods of quality control pioneered by Shewhart and popularized by Deming generally fell from favor in American industry and were largely forgotten. Where they remained, quality often became the official province of quality control departments and teams of inspectors who examined goods as they came off the line and sent defects either to the scrap pile or to still other teams for rework—a methodology abhorrent to Deming and Shewhart. Many pieces of shoddy work were overlooked altogether and sent on to customers. Workers were encouraged to increase production by piecework incentives and numerical goals. Managers were given production quotas. More was better.

Managerial attention shifted away from the process that produced goods to the methods by which they were marketed and financed. The best and brightest of the returning young veterans and the postwar generation prepared themselves to work in the carpeted halls of corporate headquarters rather than in the engineering department or on the factory floor. Deming, and people like him, were voices in the wilderness.

Waste Not, Want Not

During the early postwar years, General MacArthur's occupation force in Japan recruited many American technical experts from both government and industry to assist in putting that war-torn nation back on its feet. Among them were three engineers—Frank Polkinghorn, Charles Protzman, and Homer Sarasohn—who were assigned to the Industrial Division of the Civil Communications Section (CCS) and given the task of advising Japanese manufacturers, particularly in the communications equipment industry. From their offices in MacArthur's headquarters building near the Imperial Palace, the three were instrumental in diagnosing Japan's postwar industrial inadequacies and prescribing cures.

By their standards, what they found was pretty dismal. Protzman wrote of Nippon Electric Company (NEC), now a world-class firm, that it lacked "understanding of production engineering fundamentals." The Japanese, he wrote in 1950, "lacked both practical engineering concepts as related to manufacturing and also fundamental management concepts and practices for effective control of the business."[15] The companies they visited were often housed in dirty, leaky sheds, and the quality of their manufactured goods was very poor. All three engineers were familiar with the statistical process control methods developed and still practiced at Western Electric. After some initial training of Japanese engineers in these methods, they decided that Deming should be invited to present them to the Japanese.

Deming had made his first trip across the Pacific in 1947 to assist Japanese statisticians with studies on housing and nutrition. In 1950 he received an invitation from the Union of Japanese Scientists and Engineers (JUSE) to present a series of lectures on statistical process control.

JUSE was the offspring of several groups of technical experts brought together by the Japanese government to help with the war effort. After the war, the group was held together under the leadership of Kenichi Koyanagi with the aim of helping reconstruct the economy. JUSE brought together twenty-one of Japan's top industrialists in July 1950 at a hotel on Mount Hakone for the first of several conferences led by Deming.[16]

Many in attendance undoubtedly had been among the thousands of leading industrial managers from Europe and Asia who had toured U.S. factories throughout the late 1940s. Since American factories were recognized as world class at that time, few passed up the invitation of the U.S government and private corporations to see for themselves how the marvelous American production system worked. It must have come as something of a shock, therefore, when the lanky, spectacled scholar told the assembled Japanese leaders that American methods were misguided and would only lead them into failure. Their own products, he told them, had a reputation as shoddy merchandise, and the adoption of American methods would do nothing to improve that negative image. Only the adoption of better methods would put Japan back on the map as an important industrial country; and that could be accomplished in less than a decade if management took the lead.

The new methods Deming proposed were based upon Shewhart's statistical process control—of sampling for process variability, identifying its causes, and rooting it out at the source. Deming, however, extended Shewhart's ideas into a far broader philosophy about the production of goods and services—one that emphasized worker involvement, management leadership, and an ultimate focus on customer satisfaction. This philosophy ultimately crystalized into his now-famous Fourteen Points that form the commandments of the quality religion. The Fourteen Points (Table 4.1) struck at the very heart of the American way of management and its techniques of evaluating individuals and business units, of segmenting activities into separate business functions, of setting quotas, and so on.

Table 4.1   Deming's Fourteen Points

---

1. Create constancy of purpose for improvement of product and service.
2. Adopt a new philosophy.
3. Cease dependence on mass inspection to achieve quality.
4. End the practice of awarding business on the basis of price tag alone.
5. Improve constantly and forever the system of production and service.
6. Institute training.
7. Adopt and institute leadership.
8. Drive out fear.
9. Break down barriers between staff areas.
10. Eliminate slogans, exhortations, and targets for the work force.
11. Eliminate numerical quotas for the work force and numerical goals for management.
12. Remove barriers that rob people of pride of workmanship. Eliminate the annual rating or merit system.
13. Encourage education and self-improvement for everyone.
14. Take action to accomplish the transformation.

Source: W. Edwards Deming, *Out of Crisis* (Cambridge: Massachusetts Institute of Technology/Center for Advanced Engineering Study, 1982), pp. 23–24.

Deming told the Japanese leaders that following this approach would result in a "chain reaction" of good things for their companies. Improved quality would result in decreased costs (less rework, fewer delays, less scrappage), which would result in improved productivity, which would lead to the capture of markets, business survival, and more jobs.

The original meeting with top Japanese industrialists was a great success and resulted in Deming giving a series of eight-day courses for over 400 engineers in Tokyo, Osaka, Nagoya, and Hakata. As he met more industrial leaders, enthusiasm for his ideas spread. JUSE was instrumental in this process, propagating Deming's methods through a series of courses taught around the country. Between 1950 and 1970, 14,700 engineers and thousands of factory supervisors were indoctrinated in SPC and the Fourteen Points. Quality became something of a religion in Japan, and Deming was its high priest. In 1951, JUSE established the Deming Prize awards that today honor both the man who brought the idea of quality to Japan and those corporations that most fully adopt his principles.

Positive results began to appear not long after Deming's initial consultation. In 1951, Furukawa Electric Company, an adherent of Deming's methods, reported a 10 percent reduction in the level of rework needed in the production of insulated wire and cables. Tanabe Pharmaceutical Company reported producing three times the level of one of its chemicals with the same level of personnel, equipment, and materials. Fuji Steel lowered its energy requirement for a ton of steel by 29 percent.[17] Although the full effects of the quality movement would not be seen until the mid-1970s, Japan was successfully employing Deming's ideas about quality and taking the first step toward its winning the competitive battle to produce higher quality goods at lower cost.

Other Americans developed useful ideas that Japan eagerly embraced. One of these was Phillip Crosby, another quality expert, who helped Martin Marietta Corporation to develop a technique called zero defects in the mid-1960s. Martin Marietta was a substantial defense contractor and missiles were one of its products. The U.S. Department of Defense (DoD) had been obtaining missiles from the firm on a two month cycle from order to required delivery, but it asked for delivery in just two weeks due to military requirements at the time. The firm had to find a way to produce a highly technical product that was error free at each stage of its production and that would not require the normal tests and readjustments that accounted for its normal two-month cycle. Martin Marietta developed the ability to "do it right, every time, the first time" at each stage of missile production, and it was successful in meeting the DoD's demanding schedule with an error-free product. This method found its way to Japan in 1965 through the Nippon Electric Company.[18]

The success of these methods in Japan raises some interesting questions. Why did the ideas of Shewhart, Deming, and other Americans take root halfway around the world in an alien culture while they died on the vine at home? Were the ideas themselves more suited to Japanese industry than they were to American industry? Was there something related to culture or to prevailing circumstances in Japan that made the adoption of these ideas more likely? Or both?

The fact that quality ideas based on statistical process control originated in the United States and were applied successfully at AT&T during the 1920s and 1930s, and in American industry more generally during the war years, suggests that this approach to management was well-suited to the culture of American industry. There was nothing alien in the nature of SPC, based as it was upon applied mathematics, one of Western society's great achievements. The Shewhart Cycle, the basis for continual improvement, is another concept that resonates with traditions of Yankee inventiveness and the uniquely American belief in constant progress.

The acceptance and rapid dissemination of Deming's management principles in Japan between 1950 and 1980, and their failure to take hold in the United States, was surely related to the competitive situation and relative availability of resources that prevailed in those two nations during that period. As noted earlier, Japan was seriously constrained in material, human, and capital resources. If it hoped to get back into the game as an industrial nation, then all of its scarce resources would have to be put to their highest uses. The Japanese would have to become *optimizers,* leaving no room for waste. The philosophy and method of quality management served this end extremely well. SPC helped to identify and eliminate the sources of variance within productive systems, and the tangible results were immediately visible as reduced scrappage, reduced rework, reduced numbers of quality inspectors, lower production costs, and higher quality goods that could capture markets abroad. For the Japanese, it was an idea whose time had come.

This same attitude about limited resources is reflected in the successful development of the JIT (just-in-time), or Toyota, system of production, which is credited to Shigeo Shingo and Taiichi Ohno. "The fundamental doctrine of the Toyota production system," Ohno wrote, "is the total elimination of waste."[19] In his antipathy to waste, Ohno was simply following the tradition of Kiichiro Toyoda, who built the firm's first automobile plant in 1935 using General Motors (GM) and Ford as his models. "We will learn American-style mass production methods," he told his colleagues at the time, "but we will not imitate them blindly . . . We will conceive a production system in keeping with the resources of our country."[20] In developing his JIT system, Ohno viewed the U.S. approach to mass production as productive of waste at every step in the manufacturing process: overproduction, time-on-hand for workers, too much transporting of parts from place to place, unnecessary stock inventories, wasted motion, and too many defects ending up in the scrap pile. Management consultant Kiyoski Suzaki said that Ohno's Toyota system views anything but the minimum amount of equipment, materials, parts, space, and worker's time not essential to adding value to it products as wasteful.[21]

America Rediscovers Quality

In adopting the ideas of Deming and Ohno, Japanese industrialists were in fact creating a production system that—in Toyoda's words—was in keeping with the resources of their country. This helps to explain why those ideas found a home in Japan, but not about why it did not in the United States. On this, perhaps, the words of Robert Hayes are enlightening. While the Americans chose to shift their attention from manufacturing to marketing and finance, "The Japanese have never considered the production problem solved, never underestimated the challenge of building and improving the 'factory of the present.' There are no magic formulas—just steady progress in small steps and focusing attention on manufacturing fundamentals."[22]

U.S. manufacturers eventually began to recognize that marketing and finance never had and never would produce a first-class product. By 1980, the world had discovered the Japanese quality movement through its outstanding industrial and consumer products that were now ubiquitous in North America and parts of Europe. These products were well-designed and attractively priced, and they grabbed top ratings in objective assessments of quality. Within a relatively short time, the little nation once known for cheap merchandise had become the world quality king.

The larger world now also discovered—or rediscovered—Dr.

Deming. In the late 1970s, American corporations that were getting a shellacking from Deming's Asian disciples began lining up to see the venerable doctor for their own dose of his medicine. As he approached his eightieth birthday, a stage in life when 99 percent of people have finished their productive careers, Deming became something of an industrial celebrity—this time in his own country—and his private consulting practice exploded in North America. Among his new clients was Ford Motor Company. Many credit Deming's consulting work at Ford with the success of its Taurus automobile, which earned top honors in many quality assessments, and helped the company to surpass—for the first time in a generation—the profitability of rival GM.

As Americans fretted about their declining position among industrial nations, Deming and the quality movement gained greater visibility. Corporations enlisted quality consultants and sent their top people to workshops, conferences, and traveling seminars that preached the new gospel of quality. *Quality* became the business buzzword of the 1990s and virtually every leading business magazine devoted a cover story to it. Books by (and about) Deming sold well, as did those of Juran, Crosby, and lesser-known experts. Phillip Crosby opened the Crosby Quality College in Florida. IBM and other large firms established internal quality consultancies to serve their many subunits, suppliers, and customers.

As in Japan in the 1950s, the positive results of American quality initiatives in the 1980s were soon forthcoming for those firms that had gotten aboard the quality bandwagon in a serious way. Motorola, where quality had became an obsession, experienced dramatic improvements. From a nadir of six thousand defects per million components in 1987, Motorola whittled its defect rate down to forty per million in 1992. The firm estimated that this progress saved it $700 million in manufacturing costs alone during that period.[23] American firms in electronics, autos, steel, machine tools, and other industries followed suit, and the result was a dramatic narrowing of the quality gap between their products and those of their Japanese competitors. Unfortunately, the number of American firms that adopted the quality approach to management was relatively small. Consultant V. Daniel Hunt estimates that by 1990, only 16 percent of American business had adopted what he calls quality first principles; furthermore, he estimates that only 50 percent will have done so by the year 2000.[24]

Ideas and Change

We can learn from the histories of these two very different reform movements—Lutheranism and the industrial quality movement—that ideas have the power to create change, particularly when environmental conditions are favorable. As we have seen, Luther was not the first ecclesiastical "protester"; rather, he was the first to have real and long-lasting impact. Precursors like the Albigensian heretics, the Lollards, and the Hussites were impeded by the mismatch of their ideas and their times. The medieval world in which these early religious reformers operated was not prepared to receive their ideas to the extent needed for germination and diffusion. The authority of the Catholic church was too strong and universal, the force of nationalism too weak, and the means of communication before the general availability of printing presses too limited for these voices to gather adherents. In sixteenth-century Germany, on the other hand—and throughout northern Europe—the moral authority of the church had already been undermined by its own corruption, and its political authority eclipsed by the rise of nationalism. The mood of the public was receptive to the new ideas of a reformer like Luther, who, in his condemnation of the established church, was simply articulating the deeply felt beliefs of the larger society. And society roared back its approval.

In postwar Japan, Deming struck a responsive chord because his methods were in tune with the necessities of the moment: to eliminate waste wherever it appeared. The failure of earlier efforts to institutionalize SPC-based quality management within American industry was related to the lack of perceived need for these programs.

Among scholars, sociologists seem to have had the greatest interest in the phenomenon of new ideas (innovations) and the part they play in change, and that interest is reflected in a literature of research, most of it written within the past thirty years. The focus of sociologists has been on the diffusion of new ideas, viewed as a process, and their work undoubtedly stems from initiatives made by governments and international development agencies to diffuse modern ideas for social and economic change throughout the Third World (i.e., getting Peruvians to boil their drinking water, spreading modern agricultural practices in India, encouraging family planning in high birthrate countries of the sub-Sahara, etc.). Sociologists have theorized for decades on just how new ideas enter a social system and how they affect change. A landmark book on this subject is Everett Rogers's *Diffusion of Innovation*. To Rogers, "diffusion is the process by which an innovation is communicated through certain channels, over time, among members of a social system."[25] Certain characteristics of an innovation in the minds of the public explain its rate of adoption—or its failure:

- the advantage of the new idea relative to accepted ideas;
- compatability—its consistency with existing values, past experience, and needs;
- complexity—the difficulty of understanding and using the innovation;
- "triability"—the degree to which one can experiment with the innovation;
- observability of results from adopting or experimenting with the new idea.[26]

Thinking back on earlier parts of this chapter, most of these factors favored the diffusion of Martin Luther's innovation in religious beliefs, but even more so the doctrine of W. Edwards Deming. In the case of Deming's gospel of quality in the workplace, it was an idea with obvious advantages, it was compatible with the values of postwar Japan (and chastened America), it was not too complex for even the line supervisor to understand, it could be tried as an experiment, and its results could be observed.

Perhaps the level of public support for *old* ideas should be added to Rogers's list of factors influencing the adoption rate of new ideas. Are the old ideas still potent, or are people already chafing against them? As we have seen, in sixteenth-century Germany, in postwar Japan, and even in America beginning in the early 1980s, the old value systems were losing their hold on peoples' minds. Political and economic change, and dissatisfaction with church bureaucracy had weakened the hold of orthodoxy over of the German people. Likewise, the disasters of war had broken the old Japanese establishment and its practices, paving the way for the diffusion of new ways of thinking. By 1980, America could feel the loss of world economic leadership in its bones; it smarted under the too-obvious fact that many of its products were considered second-class, and it was open to new ways of doing things.

Becoming a Change Agent

Men and women who hope to lead and manage in turbulent times must see themselves as agents of change, not as conservators of traditions, however successful. It should be their mission to continually adapt the form and function of their organizations to the changing world rather than to operate under the assumptions of the past. This does not come naturally. Change creates high levels of tension and ambiguity for an organization and its members. Change is always painful, but it remains the sine qua non of human progress. Ideas must play a large part in this process. As Carl Gustavson wrote; "Organized social movements cannot appear and institutions cannot function without ideas. They are the threads which bind the minds of men together sufficiently for joint action to occur."[27]

Rogers describes change agents as figures with one foot in the old world and one in the new—creators of a bridge across which others can travel. In this way, they are conduits for the diffusion of new ideas. In his analysis, successful change agents fulfill seven critical roles:

- They develop the need for change. Change agents show others what the problems are, and convince them that they can and must grapple with those problems if they hope to improve.
- They make themselves accepted by others as trustworthy and competent. People must accept the messenger before they accept the message.
- They diagnose problems from the perspective of their audience. "The change agent must psychologically zip him or herself into the clients' skins, and see their situation through their eyes."
- They create the intent to change through motivation.
- They work through others in translating that intent into action.
- They stabilize the adoption of innovation.
- They foster self-renewing behavior within others so that they can "go out of business" as change agents.[28]

Where should change agents target their efforts? Should they be missionaries to the leadership or to the rank and file? Which is most likely to offer support or resistance? According to Rogers, it depends on the circumstances and on the innovation being advanced. In his article "Social Structure and Social Change," he proposed that "power elites act as gatekeepers to prevent restructuring innovations from entering a social system, while favoring functioning innovations that do not immediately threaten to change the system's structure."[29] This very effectively describes the relationship between the established church and reformers throughout the Middle Ages until Luther's time. New doctrines would be considered as long as they did not threaten the authority, power, or bureaucracy of the church. Those that did were banned as heretical.

Two other proposals by Rogers are worth mentioning here.

The first is, "bottom-up change is more likely to be successful at times of perceived crisis," especially "when headed by a charismatic leader"—this fits the case of Luther and sixteenth-century religious reform very well. The second proposition is, "Top-down change in a system, which is initiated by the power elites, is more likely to succeed than is bottom-up change," which explains the very successful adoption of Deming's ideas in Japan—where commitment to quality methodologies was initially made by top industrialists—and its failure in early postwar America—where top management was largely uninvolved.

In a society like Japan's, tradition has favored change from the top. Perhaps no greater or more far-reaching example of top-down change can be found than in the late nineteenth-century reforms of that nation. A small cadre of progressives took on the task of mastering the technologies and military–industrial practices of the West and developed a modern constitution for their medieval nation. They were successful in creating fundamental changes in a very short time. In 1871 the traditional Chinese calendar was dropped in favor of the Western calendar. The Bank of Belgium became the model for the Bank of Japan created in 1872. In 1882 Hirobumi Itō and a large staff went to Europe to study constitutional systems, and their work bore fruit just seven years later when Japan adopted a constitution based upon the Bavarian model. Other Western institutions and methods were studied and adopted almost entirely (e.g., the British navy became the model for a new Japanese navy). Some 5,000 foreign technical experts *(yatoi)* were brought to Japan to transfer their skills to their Japanese counterparts.

Within just one generation, a small group at the top of Japanese society successfully changed an insular and feudal nation into a growing industrial nation with modern armed forces. This process was undoubtedly abetted by a culture that looked for direction from established authority. In the United States, that sort of top-directed change is unlikely at a public level because power is diffused to localities and individuals, but it is very possible within its institutions. Here, notable examples are to be found in corporations that have fundamentally altered their strategies and operations because of strong, directed leadership at or near the top. Under Donald Petersen's direction, the Ford Motor Company restructured itself in the early 1980s and reformed its methods of design, manufacturing, and utilization of human resources in the very successful Project Taurus, a five-year effort that produces

America's most successful new automobile and saved the company from financial decay. Likewise, Xerox Corporation, beginning in the late 1970s, saved itself from a slow slide into industrial obscurity through strong leadership at the top.[30] While the impetus for change in these instances came from the top, success was only possible because of the ability of top management to win the adherence of lower- and middle-level personnel to their goals.

Studying the careers of people with new ideas is extremely satisfying. Luther, Galileo, Christopher Columbus, Karl Marx, Charles Darwin, Henry Ford, Thomas Edison, and people like them, fascinate us not only with their achievements, but also with their determination to create change. Almost all were outsiders; all were violators of the conventional wisdom. How they eventually overcame the opposition of the narrow-minded and the powerful of their day makes for edifying reading. We should remember, however, that people with ideas are not curiosities from the past. They are always among us—in our universities, our churches, and our places of work—though we often fail to recognize them at the time. They are the people who make us angry and uncomfortable with their methods, and our instinct is to ignore or to get rid of them.

5

Strategy and Fate: Yamamoto Overplans at Midway

As individuals we move into the future on the mingled accident and design of our lives.

Robert L. Heilbroner, *The Future as History*

The empire of the Rising Sun seemed unstoppable in early 1942. Success followed success on land and at sea. With much of the U.S. Pacific Fleet underwater after the attack on Pearl Harbor, Japanese forces chalked up a string of land and naval victories in the Philippines, Malaya, and the Dutch East Indies, routing the British, Dutch, and Americans from their colonial citadels. These conquests were all part of the strategic plan worked out by Japan's leaders as early as 1938.

Japanese military adventurism had begun in Manchuria in 1931 and had spilled onto the Chinese mainland by 1937. The armed forces, which came to dominate Japan's national government, were bent upon establishing dominance over Southeast Asia and extending their power throughout the western Pacific. The Western powers, the United States in particular, seriously menaced that ambition. American bases in the Philippines threatened Japanese lines of supply and communications; their very presence in that part of the world was an affront to Japan's new sense of itself as a power of the first order.

Diplomatic relationships between the two Pacific powers were strained by Japan's aggression in China, and they deteriorated rapidly when Japan signed the Tripartite Agreement with Hitler and Mussolini in 1940. Military thinkers on both sides viewed armed conflict as inevitable and planned accordingly.

Japan's strategic planning rested in the hands of the Imperial government and the naval general staff, which was dominated during the years prior to Pearl Harbor by Admiral Isoroku Yamamoto. The general staff was fixated by America's potential to overwhelm them with superior naval resources. In 1940 they estimated that the naval power balance between the two nations was in a 10:7 ratio unfavorable to Japan. Even so, they viewed this imbalance as acceptable. The thinking among Tokyo's war planners was that for every thousand miles a fleet operated from its home base, 10 percent efficiency was lost. With that formula, the Imperial Navy could hold its own in its home waters against the Americans, even in a 10:5 situation. While both navies were expanding their tonnage during the prewar period, however, America's greater resources were fast changing the equation. By 1941 the United States was producing capital ships at a rate *three times* that of Japan.[1] As time went by, the relative strengths of the two navies would grow increasingly unfavorable to Japan. For an island people whose very lifeblood and national ambitions depended upon controllable sea-lanes, an inferior navy was shorthand for second-class nationhood.

Few in the Japanese leadership appreciated the power and resources of America better than did Yamamoto. As a graduate student at Harvard in the early 1930s, and later as a naval attaché in Washington, D.C., he had come to know his future adversary and its culture well. He had traveled widely in the United States and had developed a respect for its industrial prowess. Though not a Christian, it is said that he read the Bible regularly as a source of inspiration and wisdom. From his Harvard classmates he learned poker and bridge, which suited his knack for detail and bluff, and these became lifelong addictions.

Yamamoto was too well-traveled, too scientific in his thinking, to be bitten by the epidemic of jingoism that consumed his fellow Japanese in the 1930s. He viewed war against the United States as suicidal for his homeland, and said so publicly and repeatedly. Extreme nationalists denounced him as a pro-American traitor, and friends feared that he would be assassinated for his unpopular views. When war became inevitable, however, Yamamoto closed ranks with his compatriots and fellow officers. Even after the die was cast, he remained sanguine about Japan's ability to achieve lasting victory: "I can raise havoc with [Britain and the United States] for a year or eighteen months. After that I can give no one any guarantees."[2]

For Yamamoto and the rest of the general staff, time was the great enemy. Every week, every month allowed the Americans to grow stronger. Once the United States embargoed oil and other strategic materials, Japan's capacity for action progressively dwindled. Japan had to make a move quickly, or not at all. The solution was to strike a devastating blow that would bring the scales into favorable balance—if only for a time. Toward that end Yamamoto and the navy built a fleet based on six carriers with state-of-the-art aircraft and well-trained crews. Naval air power, in Yamamoto's view, was the way of the future. "The battleship," he told his staff, "will be as useful to Japan in modern warfare as a samurai sword." He practiced attacks on shipping—a revolutionary tactic for naval aircraft of the time—in a series of war games, and studied how the British had successfully used carrier-based aircraft against the Italian fleet at Taranto in November 1940. His forces developed the capacity to strike hard and fast.

The instrument for the blow against the Americans was to be the surprise attack, a tactic that had brought Japan overwhelming success in the 1905 war against the Russians—and again in China. Shogun Hideyoshi had been the first Japanese to use the surprise attack in a naval engagement when he struck a decisive blow against the Koreans in 1596, even as he engaged them in peace negotiations.

Yamamoto and his staff spent eighteen months planning the attack on the American fleet at Pearl Harbor, developing and rehearsing it in detail, cajoling the doubters to accept it as the way to rebalance the power discrepancy between the two navies. The plan succeeded beyond everyone's expectations. Only the fact that the U.S. carriers were at sea at the time of the attack made the strike on Pearl Harbor less than a total debacle for the Americans and a complete victory for the Japanese navy.

Japan's Strategy in the Pacific

Pearl Harbor was the opening move in a strategic plan to accomplish three further objectives: (1) clear the western Pacific of American forces, (2) build a line of outer defenses for the home islands running from the western Aleutians through the mid-Pacific, and (3) win a "decisive battle" against the American navy, one so damaging that the United States would have to recognize Japan's sphere of influence in the Pacific.

By late May 1942 successful completion of the plan was ahead of schedule and had been achieved with remarkably minor losses. Ship losses at the Battle of the Coral Sea (May 1, 1942) had been the only sour note thus far. Only two tasks remained: (1) to set up forward outposts in the Aleutians and at tiny Midway Island and (2) to draw out what was left of the U.S. Pacific Fleet for the decisive battle.

For these remaining tasks a powerful fleet was assembled under the overall command of Yamamoto. It was a force of five separate elements, each slated to play a unique role. Two elements would provide the muscle to wrest Midway Island from its garrison of U.S. Marines. These were the Midway invasion force, made up of troop transports and support ships, and the carrier strike force under the command of Vice Admiral Chuichi Nagumo. Another force with two light carriers would proceed to an attack on small American forces dimly known to be stationed in the frigid Aleutians. A separate force of submarines would position itself between Oahu and Midway to detect and report the advance of the U.S. fleet. Yamamoto himself would command the fifth force, the main body of battleships and cruisers; these would remain in the background, ready to steam forward into any American force foolish enough to rush to the defense of Midway Island.[3] To preserve secrecy, the various forces sallied from different home island ports under radio silence, each striking its own course toward the objective. But the main actor was to be Nagumo, however, whose aviators had performed so brilliantly at Pearl Harbor.

At the heart of Nagumo's force were four fast carriers, all veterans of the Pearl Harbor attack: *Kaga, Hiryu, Soryu,* and his own flagship, *Akagi*. Collectively, they carried 325 aircraft and the world's most experienced naval aviators. Their first task would be to destroy U.S. planes based at Midway, and to provide tactical air support to the landing force of 5,000 troops scheduled to storm the beaches on June 5. Their second task was to find and destroy the U.S. fleet that would surely venture out from Hawaii to challenge them.

The Midway invasion was a baited trap. Once the Americans rose to the bait, Nagumo's skillful pilots and Yamamoto's fast battleships would deliver the one–two knockout blows upon which the empire's entire strategy rested. The American public, it was thought, would have no stomach for a long and costly war over trackless miles of empty ocean just to win back a few insignificant coral islands. They would negotiate a grudging understanding with Tokyo that recognized its legitimate sphere of influence; and over the years relations between the two Pacific powers might return to normal. So went the thinking behind the plan. As for the U.S. Navy, Japan's commanders and crews had so far tasted easy victories and fully looked forward to another. "Japan was awash in a sea of self-adulation."[4] They did not think of their adversary as either skillful or eager to fight. They believed that their plans and positions were a well-kept secret. Unknown to them, however, another fleet was steaming out of Pearl Harbor to meet them.

The Notion of Strategy in Business

Strategic planning has long been embraced by military leaders. Its adoption by business organizations—at least in a formal manner— is something fairly new. Peter Drucker first addressed strategy in his 1954 book *The Practice of Management*. It was not until the 1960s, however, that management scholars like Kenneth Andrews and C. Roland Christenson of Harvard articulated the notion of strategy as a tool that could link together the separate functions of the organization.[5] In *The Concept of the Corporation,* Andrews showed business managers how they needed to look outward to the external environment for potential opportunities and risks as well as inward in assessing their own distinctive competencies and resources. These outer and inner worlds then had to be considered together in developing a competitive strategy for the organization.[6] By the late 1970s, strategic planning was all the rage in graduate business schools, consulting firms, and corporate headquarters. Many surely thought that if they could just develop the right strategy, success would be assured.

"There is many a slip 'twixt the cup and the lip," and many of the brave new strategies that emerged from corporate war rooms failed miserably in the mean streets of everyday competition. Important financial institutions like Continental Illinois and Shearson Lehman charged forward with great new strategies designed to make them much bigger players, only to be tripped up by poor execution and human venality. Retail giant Sears Roebuck concocted a bold strategy to remake itself into the merchandising powerhouse of decades past, but only slipped farther behind its rivals. The introduction of "new" Coke took lots of planning but fizzled when it came to market. The great synergies assumed by corporate strategists during the last two merger booms have likewise failed to materialize as planned. Some survey data indicate that 75 percent of mergers and acquisitions are considered to have been mistakes within just a few years of their consummation.

It would be easy to say that pointing to these highly visible failures is to be pointing to companies that had *bad* strategies. Perhaps. There have been so many, however, and most were developed by supposedly bright people who apparently believed strongly in them. Many followed the advice of the best strategy merchants from top-tier consulting firms and business schools.

Failures could be dictated by the complexity of the world in which strategic plans must be both developed and executed. Most of the things we need to understand about ourselves and our competitors to be successful will always remain hidden from us. Assumptions that seem so reasonable in foresight often appear foolish in hindsight. Many things just happen by chance, and these things can make enormous differences.

The Radio Intercept

In a windowless basement on the U.S. military compound at Oahu, 120 men and women of the Combat Intelligence Unit (CIU) had been working night and day to intercept and decipher coded Japanese messages. They had had a great deal of success during the preceding several months in breaking Japanese codes, and on May 20, 1942, they intercepted a message from Yamamoto that indicated a large invasion at a location designated only as AF. What AF stood for was anyone's guess. On Oahu, Pacific Fleet Commander Chester Nimitz and his people believed it to be Midway Island, while the naval brass in Washington took it to be Oahu itself. To determine the truth, Nimitz had a radio operator stationed on Midway send a message in the clear that the island's water distillation plant had broken down. Two days later the CIU intercepted another Japanese message saying that AF was low on drinking water. Was Midway the target for the invasion, or were the Japanese merely feeding false information? No one could be sure.

Acting on deciphered messages is a dangerous business. Deliberately planted signals, like Nimitz's phony message about the distillation plant, were nothing new in the game of intelligence and counterintelligence, and accepting them as genuine poised considerable risks. Yamamoto had once before deceived American intelligence with false transmissions. Before the attack on Pearl Harbor he had radio traffic near the Japanese home islands stepped up, creating the appearance that the entire Japanese fleet was safely tucked away even as his carriers crept silently toward Oahu.

Naval officialdom was reluctant to accept the theory of a Midway attack. Nimitz decided to override Washington's objections and accept his codebreakers' intelligence as genuine, and dispatched two carrier task forces to ambush the Japanese.

Task Force 17, commanded by Rear Admiral Frank Fletcher, was composed of the carrier *Yorktown,* two cruisers, and a screen of six destroyers. *Yorktown* had suffered heavy bomb damage during the Battle of the Coral Sea and had seemed a doubtful starter. (Japanese intelligence believed that the carrier had been sunk at that battle.) Repairs estimated to take ninety days in dry dock, however, were miraculously completed, at least enough to get her battle worthy, in just forty-eight hours by a crew of fifteen hundred working around the clock. The repair crews continued their work even as *Yorktown* was being piloted out of Pearl Harbor on its way to battle.

Task Force 16 formed around the carriers *Enterprise* and *Hornet,* with a larger force of cruisers and destroyers. Rear Admiral Raymond Spruance had been assigned to command this task force as a last minute replacement for William Halsey, who had been hospitalized with a severe case of dermatitis. A steady and reliable man in his mid-fifties, Spruance was known for his cool, cerebral approach to tactics, much different than the brash and aggressive Halsey. He had made his mark in naval gunnery, but was clearly untested as a commander of a carrier force. Still, Nimitz trusted Spruance and Fletcher to carry out his directive to "be governed by the principle of calculated risk, which you shall interpret to mean the avoidance of exposure of your force to superior enemy forces without good prospects of inflicting . . . greater damage on the enemy."[7]

With less than eleven hundred miles of empty sea between Midway and Hawaii, Nimitz was cautious about putting in peril the last large piece of U.S. naval power in the Pacific after Pearl Harbor. His concerns were well-grounded: The force Fletcher and Spruance were steaming toward had four times as many surface ships and much more suitable aircraft.

The Pacific Ocean is a very large place. In the days before

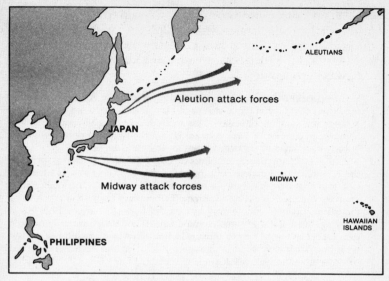

Figure 5.1   Fleet movements toward Midway.

recon satellites, large fleets occupying fifty to sixty square miles could, by observing radio silence, cruise undetected amid its vastness. Even when the peering eyes of enemy submarines and long-range scout planes were present, fleet commanders knew how to conceal themselves in darkness, storms, and fog.

On June 3, the Midway invasion force approached its target from five hundred miles to the southwest. Nagumo's carrier strike force was about the same distance from the island, but to the northwest. A weather front stood between these forces and Midway. The U.S. task forces were then some three hundred miles northeast of the atoll (Fig. 5.1); at this point, they inferred that a large enemy force was out there, but they could only speculate as to its location and order of battle. Both sides were like sparring opponents in a blackened room; however, the Japanese had the great disadvantage of thinking that there was no one else in the room.

Yamamoto and his commanders had not planned on any U.S. warships being in the area until *after* the Midway landing on June 5; they had no knowledge of the lurking presence of the two U.S. carrier task forces, and had only planned on them as a remote possibility. Five weeks prior to the scheduled invasion, Yamamoto and his staff had conducted lengthy tabletop rehearsals of the Midway plan and subsequent operations. Captain Mitsuo Fuchida, a carrier aviation commander who was present at these rehearsals, expressed his amazement at how flawlessly the complex operations played out in the simulation, even when an uncomforting contingency was introduced.

> Every operation from the invasion of Midway and the Aleutians down to the assault of Johnston [coral atoll] and Hawaii was carried out in the games without the slightest difficulty. This was due in no small measure to the highhanded conduct of Rear Admiral Ugaki, the presiding officer, who frequently intervened to set aside rulings made by the umpires.
>
> In the tabletop maneuvers, for example, a situation developed in which the Nagumo Force underwent a bombing attack by enemy land-based aircraft while its own planes were off attacking Midway. In accordance with the rules [dice were cast] to determine the bombing results and it was ruled that there had been nine enemy hits on the Japanese carriers. Both *Akagi* and *Kaga* were listed as sunk. Admiral Ugaki, however, arbitrarily reduced the number of enemy hits to three, which resulted in *Kaga* still being ruled sunk but *Akagi* only slightly damaged. . . . even this revised ruling was subsequently cancelled, and *Kaga* reappeared.[8]

Even before the Japanese force had set out, the forewarned U.S. Marine garrison on Midway Island had been working night and day to entrench its positions, mine the beaches, and bring in supplies and aircraft. The island's small airfield was crowded with a mix of offensive and defensive planes, including a squadron of B-17 bombers. A flotilla of Catalinas—long-range reconnaissance seaplanes—was moored in the lagoon. The Catalinas and B-17s flew out in broad arcs to the west-southwest and west-northwest in search of the enemy fleet; these flights extended as much as seven hundred miles from the island.

First Contact

At 0900 on June 3 a Catalina piloted by Ensign Jack Reid was at the far end of its tether. Reid's plane could stay aloft for thirteen to fourteen hours, and he was already near the halfway point and preparing to head back when he spotted eleven ships on the horizon west of Midway heading east. This was part of the Midway invasion force. From this first sighting, other players in this drama would eventually reveal themselves to each other, and ultimately lock horns. Later that day, B-17s were sent out to attack the intruders, but their high-level bombing attacks produced no hits.

Aboard the *Akagi*, Nagumo had, by the first hours of June 4, used the weather front of low clouds to maneuver to within 220

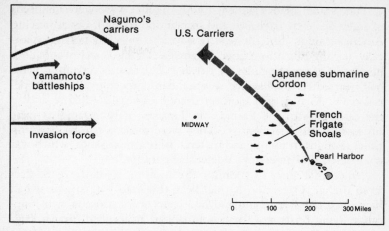

Figure 5.2 Midway–Hawaii area, June 4, A.M. Nagumo launches first wave against Midway Island.

miles west of his target without being discovered. He would soon be in position to strike. At 0230 he had the pilots awakened for their breakfast and briefings. The air that day was clear with high-level clouds, and the sea was calm: perfect conditions for launch and attack. They would bomb Midway shortly after daybreak, destroying its aircraft, fuel and ammo dumps, and defensive positions before the invasion force arrived (Fig. 5.2). At 0430, the Japanese carriers turned into the wind, deck lights came on, and amid cheers and high hopes 108 planes roared off to the attack. Among them were several planes designated for reconnaissance, including two seaplanes of the cruisers *Tone* and *Chikuma*. The plane from the latter was slow in getting off because of engine trouble; and that trouble forced it to turn back shortly thereafter. The *Tone*'s plane was delayed for forty-five minutes by a faulty catapult, which in the end proved to be quite costly.

The possibility of an enemy air attack while their own planes were off attacking Midway was a bothersome possibility to the Japanese commanders. Planes of the first attack wave would be away from their nests for some four hours. That opened a window of opportunity to the enemy, whose location and strength was unknown. To hedge his position, Nagumo held back ninety-three planes of his most experienced units. These would be a second attack wave against Midway Island, or, if an enemy carrier stumbled upon him, a force to destroy it.

The search planes launched with the first wave were hundreds of miles away by daybreak and in position to spot any advancing American ships. But the searches were conducted nonsystematically, leaving much to chance. In any case, a few search planes over hundreds of square miles of ocean could assure very little. This half-hearted reconnaissance was standard procedure in the Imperial navy. As historian Gordon Prange observed, "Before and in the early days of the Pacific war, Japanese naval strategists were obsessed with the offensive. They were most averse to devoting time, thought, training, and material to reconnaissance, which was considered fundamentally a defensive concept."[9]

An earlier plan to monitor the movement of the U.S. fleet from the air, Operation K, had been thwarted by a stroke of bad luck. Japanese fleet command had proposed stationing two long-range flying boats at a small uninhabited atoll called French Frigate Shoals. From this outpost, located between Midway and Oahu, the seaplanes could undertake long-range reconnaissance all the way to Pearl Harbor, thereby detecting any fleet activity by the U.S. navy. Three submarines would stand by the shoals to refuel the planes. On May 30 one of these submarines arrived at the shoals and found that it had unexpected company: Two U.S. seaplane tenders were anchored within one of its coves. The Americans had already staked the place out and were using it as a base for their own seaplanes. With nowhere else to conduct refueling operations, Operation K was scratched.

The Japanese submarines sent out to form an early warning line between Pearl Harbor and Midway also had problems. A typo in their orders sent them in the wrong direction. By the time the mistake was discovered and the submarines had moved to their correct coordinates, the American ships had already slipped by their cordon undetected.

The U.S. Catalinas also left Midway in the early morning darkness on June 4, flying out on assigned bearings to initiate search patterns. After weeks of boring and fruitless reconnaissance, cramped in their planes for over twelve hours at a stretch, this would prove to be an eventful day for the crews. Beginning at 0520, radios at Midway crackled with reports from the Catalina pilots; first with a sighting of enemy search planes; then with the first waves of attack planes; and finally the most important revelation, the position of Nagumo's carriers.

The Midway defenders scrambled their ragtag force of vintage fighter planes to take on an overwhelming force of Japanese bombers and Zeros. It was an unequal contest in both numbers and the quality of the opposing forces. Fourteen of the twenty-six U.S. planes that rose to the island's defense that morning never returned to base, and most that did return were too badly shot up to return to the fray. The attackers pounded the island's fuel tank farm, power station, hangers, and antiaircraft positions, but inflicted only minor damage on the airfield. It was left unscathed, and it was clear to everyone why: The Japanese intended to use the runway themselves in a matter of days.

Flight leader Joichi Tomonaga, limping back with a damaged aircraft, radioed *Akagi* at 0700 that "there is need for a second wave."[10] Even as his message was being received, other Midway planes began an attack on the now-revealed carriers. These strikes were ineffective and driven off, but they confirmed in Nagumo's mind the need to hit Midway again. Neither his carriers nor the landing force would be safe until Midway's aircraft were eliminated.

"Planes in second attack wave stand by to carry out attack today. Re-equip yourself with bombs." This was the order sent to Japanese carriers at 0715. Planes parked topside with torpedoes for use against possible U.S. carriers now had to be brought below decks and rearmed with bombs for the second Midway strike. This was a one-hour job and was begun as ordered.

Where Are the American Ships?

For Task Forces 16 and 17 approaching Midway from the northeast, the early morning hours were clear and serene. The sun rose at 0457 into a blue sky. There was little wind, and the temperatures were in the sixties.

Fletcher was confident that this would be the day that he and Spruance would tangle with the enemy carriers. When Midway's Catalinas reported Nagumo's location, the transmissions were picked up by the U.S. fleet, and the contents were no big surprise to some. (A week earlier, Captain E. T. Layton had predicted the time and place of Nagumo's first discovery to within five minutes and five miles.[11])

For Spruance, the location of Nagumo's carriers was all he required to take action. His plan was to hit them with everything he had just as soon as he could while he still held the advantage of surprise. He knew that it would only be a matter of time before his own position was discovered. Launching now, he reasoned, would permit his planes to strike the enemy carriers just as they were recovering and refueling their Midway attack aircraft. All the wasps would be in the nest.

The problem for Spruance was that the enemy flattops were 200 miles away. Many of his aircraft—particularly the Devastator torpedo planes—would be unable to cover the distance out and back with any appreciable time over the target. Many would have to splash on the return trip, and many fliers would surely be lost. His problem was whether to move in closer and risk discovery or launch immediately and lose many of the fliers whose names and faces he had come to know. Spruance briefly pondered his dilemma and then gave the order to launch. By 0708 *Enterprise* and *Hornet* were hurling planes from their decks. Fletcher soon did the same from the *Yorktown*. Some 116 American planes took the air that morning: F4F Wildcat fighters, Dauntless dive-bombers, and the lumbering Devastators.

Twenty minutes after the Americans had begun launching, the scout plane from the Japanese cruiser *Tone* radioed the sighting of what appeared to be ten ships. This report might have come an hour earlier had *Tone* not had trouble with its catapult. The message was brought to Nagumo at 0728 and, according to his staff, the admiral was visibly shaken. This was an unsettling piece of information, and it could not have come at a worse time. He had already committed his force to one course of action—rearming for land targets; however, there were now these ships. But what kind of ships were they? The scout pilot had failed to provide this one important detail. If no carriers were among them there would be no immediate threat to Nagumo's operations. A carrier, however, would require another course of action—and right away! Nagumo needed more information to make a decision, but he did not have it.

At 0745 the scout plane was asked to identify the enemy ships by type. At the same time, Nagumo reversed his earlier directive, ordering that bomb loading be canceled and that torpedoes be reinstalled on the second wave of planes. These would be essential if the scout identified any of the enemy ships as aircraft carriers. It was not until 0820 that the scout confirmed Nagumo's worst fear: One of the unidentified vessels appeared to be a carrier.

The first U.S. carrier aircraft to reach Nagumo were torpedo planes. U.S. tactics called for torpedo planes and dive bombers to attack simultaneously—one group from ship-deck level, and the other dropping from high above—but the different units had become separated and the torpedo squadrons had to go in alone. Most of their pilots must have known that they would never make it back, at least not in their planes—the range was just too great. The sluggish Devastators, which could only muster 175 miles per hour, encountered withering fire from the destroyers and cruisers that screened the carriers some 8 miles out. Those that broke through that ring of fire ran up against swarms of faster and more nimble Zeros. Each Devastator squadron that came in was successively destroyed by the defenders. Of the forty-one Devastators that attacked the carrier strike force, only six returned. In one squadron all fifteen planes were lost and only one of the thirty crew members survived. A sense of what these pilots experienced is captured in the testimony of that sole survivor, Ensign George Gay:

> Zeros were coming in from all angles and from both sides at once. . . . The planes of T8 [squadron] were falling at irregular intervals. Some were on fire, and some did a half-roll and crashed on their backs, completely out of control. Machine gun bullets ripped my armor plate a number of times. As they rose above it, the bullets would go over my shoulder into the instrument panel.[12]

For all their sacrifice, the Americans had not yet managed to even chip the paint on Nagumo's ships.

From Nagumo's perspective, things had not gone badly. From the first attack by Midway-based planes at 0728, his carriers had been under intermittent siege for over three hours. The American planes had come in uncoordinated waves, and every one had been either shot down or driven off without scoring a single hit. His crewmen were wildly enthusiastic over their ability to knock down whatever the enemy threw at them.

Nagumo's first Midway attack wave returned to the carriers during the last of this commotion, and the business of refueling and switching over to torpedoes was nearly finished. Bombs were stacked in the servicing areas and gasoline lines stretched across the decks. Planes loaded with fuel and explosives revved their engines in preparation for imminent launch against the newly discovered American carrier. The air overhead churned with the fury of Zeros pursuing the last of the ill-fated Devastators.

At 1020 the sun smiled warmly on the empire's skillful sea warriors and their great mission. It was now time to begin the final phase of the plan. The enemy fleet had been located, and the time to destroy it had come. The Japanese carriers began turning into the wind.

Six Fateful Minutes

Just an hour earlier, at 0921, Lieutenant Commander Wade McClusky found himself and his two squadrons of Dauntless dive bombers over an empty expanse of blue water where the Japanese carriers were supposed to be. His was not the only group to draw a blank. Almost forty planes from the *Hornet* had done the same, going into a fruitless search pattern. Some of these eventually made it to the airfield at Midway and the rest splashed nearby.

With his fuel indicator dropping rapidly, McClusky decided to play a hunch as to where the carriers had gone. He turned onto a new bearing and signaled the others to follow. If his hunch was wrong, the two squadrons would end up in the drink; if he guessed right, they would have a crack at the enemy carriers. Later, Nimitz would credit McClusky's decision to follow his intuition as the most important of the entire battle. After some time on this new course, the trailing elements of the carrier strike force loomed on the horizon. McClusky noted their course and charged ahead with his squadrons. Before long, the outlines of three Japanese carriers appeared in the distance.

Within minutes, and almost unnoticed, McClusky's planes were over *Akagi* and *Kaga*. Quite by chance, another squadron from the *Yorktown* appeared over *Soryu*. From an altitude of fourteen thousand feet, they dove at a gut-wrenching seventy-degree angle onto the carriers, sighting on the huge red sun symbols painted on the yellow flight decks. Most released their bombs at 2,000 feet, then strained to pull out of their dives. Standing on the deck of *Akagi*, Mitsuo Fuchida saw them coming:

> A lookout screamed "Hell Divers!" I looked up to see three black enemy planes plummeting toward our ship. Some of our machine guns managed to fire a few frantic bursts at them but it was too late. The plump silhouettes of American Dauntless dive bombers quickly grew larger, and then a number of black objects suddenly floated eerily from their wings. Bombs! Down they came straight toward me! . . . The terrifying scream of the dive bombers reached me first, followed by the crashing explosion of a direct hit.[13]

Two bombs tore through *Akagi's* flight deck, their blasts throwing deck crews and parked planes into the sea, and setting off secondary explosions among the gasoline lines and heavily armed planes. Within minutes *Kaga* and *Soryu* were also hit. All three carriers were mortally damaged and destined to sink, taking with them all their aircraft and many of the Imperial Navy's best sailors and fliers.

Separated from the other carriers by five miles, *Hiryu* remained unnoticed and unscathed. From that distance the crew of *Hiryu* could see flames and black smoke belching from their sister ships and knew that they alone remained to avenge their loss. Within minutes, *Hiryu* launched twenty-four aircraft toward the reported position of the American carrier (they still knew of only one). The correct course would not be difficult to find in any case, as all they needed to do was trail the returning American planes.

Radar on the *Yorktown* picked up the attackers some forty miles out, and a number of returning U.S. planes were waved off to the *Enterprise* so that *Yorktown's* fighters could be scrambled to intercept them. Half of the Japanese planes never got past the American fighters, but of those that did, three scored hits on the *Yorktown*. A second wave from *Hiryu* put two torpedoes into her. She was too damaged to be saved and sank the next day.

At 1530, *Hiryu* was located and its position radioed back to the *Enterprise,* whose planes dealt her a fatal blow. With the last of their carriers drifting out of control and burning like a torch, and having nowhere left to land, dozens of Japanese pilots circled the area until their fuel ran out and their planes dropped into the sea.

The Battle of Midway cost Yamamoto all four of his Strike Force carriers, over three hundred aircraft, and an estimated twenty-five hundred men. Along with them Japan's opportunity to score the decisive blow upon which their strategy relied was lost forever. On June 5, Yamamoto signaled the fleet: "Midway Operations Canceled." He had been the victim of the very trap he had set for his opponent.

Smelling the opportunity for even greater victory, and still unaware of the enemy battleship group that lay in wait, Spruance's staff (mostly Halsey people) urged him to pursue the "retreating" enemy and finish them off. Most speculate that the aggressive Halsey would have done just that. Spruance, however, opted for caution, and his prudence saved the Americans from blindly sailing into the guns of Yamamoto's battleships.

Good and Bad Fortune

The causes of Yamamoto's defeat and America's victory at Midway have been debated ever since the two adversaries disengaged. Some Japanese participants point to the lack of adequate aerial reconnaissance as the primary cause of their defeat; had they been more systematic in their search patterns and discovered the U.S. fleet sooner, they would not have been caught in so vulnerable a position. Others suggest that Yamamoto's faulty assumption of secrecy was the cause of the debacle. Still others see overconfidence and contempt for the abilities of the enemy as the fundamental flaws from which other errors emerged.

Whatever the criticisms of Yamamoto, it remains clear that but for a number of fortuitous events the battle would have had an opposite outcome, underscoring Ecclesiastes's suggestion that "the race is not to the swift, nor the battle to the strong . . .; but time and chance happeneth to them all." Nimitz's decision to gamble on the deciphered messages, the incorrectly transcribed orders to the surveillance submarines, the catapult malfunction that delayed launching of the *Tone* search plane, the botched plan to station boat-planes at French Frigate Shoals, McClusky's fateful hunch as to the location of the carriers, and his fortuitous arrival when all the enemy planes were either occupied in low-altitude defense or sitting on the flight decks full of fuel and explosives—even the fact that Spruance got command because Halsey was in sickbay—were all circumstances that suggest a malevolence of nature toward the empire. Gordon Prange, who has probably researched the battle more than anyone (on either side of the Pacific), concludes that "The final debacle was due to a stroke of luck on the U.S. side— the uncoordinated coordination of the dive bombers hitting three carriers at once while the torpedo strikes were still in progress. Except for those six short minutes, Nagumo would have been the victor." [14]

In his foreword to Fuchida's chronicle of events, Admiral Raymond Spruance remarks, "In reading [Fuchida's] account of what happened on 4 June, I am more than ever impressed with the part that good and bad fortune sometimes play in tactical engagements." [15]

Keeping It Simple . . . and Robust

The Battle of Midway has been required reading for students of naval science for half a century now, and it suggests useful lessons for leaders and strategists in other fields. The Japanese operational plan was one of enormous scope and required the coordinated efforts of many units operating independently over broad expanses of ocean. This was typical of Japanese naval planning at the time. As John Winton has observed:

> Whenever possible, the Japanese liked to overelaborate, split their forces into separate groups with separate objectives, inviting defeat in detail. They laid elaborate traps, with complicated diversions, sacrificial decoys, and optimistic pincer movements. Japanese plans demanded a degree of co-operation between their own ships and commanders which no navy in history has ever achieved. They made few allowances for the contingencies of war. Most dangerous of all, they often relied upon the enemy doing what was expected of him.[16]

We know from experience with complex plans, with mechanical devices of many parts, and from working in large organizations that complexity opens windows to failure. Product designers have learned this and, particularly in the past decade, have sought to eliminate failures by reducing their opportunities (i.e., by simplifying designs and reducing the number of component parts). The IBM Selectric typewriter provides an excellent example. Originally a device of over 2,300 components, the current model now has less than 200, and its reliability is said to have increased by a factor of 10.[17] With fewer parts to break down, failures are reduced. When failures do occur they are more quickly identified and remedied. Writing in the *Harvard Business Review,* former IBM executive Ralph Gomory relates the success of another of the firm's office products, the Proprinter dot-matrix printer, which had been developed for use with the IBM PC in the early 1980s. PC printers then on the market were observed to have about 150 parts. "This was too many parts, and it was an invitation to wasted motion: the more parts you had, the more you had to design, purchase, account for, and store." By the time IBM's development team finished its work, they were able to introduce a printer of only sixty-two parts that outperformed its competitors. In addition to the usual benefits of simpler manufacturability, fewer parts meant that "The Proprinter proved unusually reliable in the field. Fewer parts meant fewer assembly errors, fewer adjustments, and fewer opportunities for things to go wrong later. No screws will loosen in the customer's office if there are no screws in the product."[18]

Like manufactured products, organizations are likewise afflicted when they become too complex, and for the same reasons. As anyone who has worked in a large company can tell you, once you get too many people working under one roof, snafus multiply. In particular, the narrow span of control, with its many layers of management so characteristic of modern corporations until just recently, created multiple opportunities for miscommunications and poor execution down the long chain of command.

These are *internal* problems (i.e., things that can go wrong within the machine, the organization, or the plan). Yamamoto certainly created the potential for many internal problems when he and his staff developed the Midway plan. His force was divided into five elements—some of which were, in turn, subdivided—and all were broadly dispersed and operating under radio silence. Misinterpretation of orders, equipment failures, missed signals, and poor execution were offered numerous opportunities to do their mischief. Like all grand schemes, this one had little time bombs built into it, each waiting to go off at random times.

There were *external* problems as well; both natural and artificial. Surface naval operations have been at the mercy of the weather since warriors first went to sea. The Japanese had been the great beneficiaries of cruel weather when in 1281 a fierce ocean storm—a *kamikaze* (divine wind)—destroyed the invading fleet of the Mongol emperor, Kublai Khan. Yamamoto's forces did not suffer from nature's caprice, but an unforeseen typhoon could certainly have thrown a monkey wrench into his operations.

The external force that mattered most at Midway, of course, was the U.S. Navy, which refused to play the role of the mindless, obliging victim that the Japanese planners had written into the script. The Americans, in this case, were not the sleeping prey of Pearl Harbor; rather, they were an enemy that came out of the darkness as a confident predator, poised to attack. Yamamoto's tabletop rehearsal of the battle worked just fine as long as the Americans behaved as they were supposed to. As in war, business planners who assume the passive compliance of competitors are equally imperiled. Like chess players, they must always examine their plans through the eyes of their competitors, being alert to the range of possible countermoves. Effective contingencies must be developed for each of these countermoves. They should heed the warning of Disraeli, "What we anticipate seldom occurs; what we least expect generally happens."

Life has a random quality to it. Things happen that defy the ability of even experts to predict or forecasts prove faulty. The complexity of the real world frustrates planners by its perverse ten-

Figure 5.3 Linear causal relationship.

dency to undercut their bedrock assumptions. Like stock prices, events do not follow patterns traced out in the past.

Our scientific tradition encourages us to think in linear, cause-and-effect patterns. Some change in *A* results in *B,* and that leads to *C,* and so forth (Fig. 5.3). A securities analyst might look at Ford Motor Company and conclude that its fortune will improve next year because interest rates have dropped, which makes financing costs lower for both Ford and its customers, which makes Ford cars more affordable, which increases sales, and so on. Life, however, unfolds in ways that confound this tidy string of causal relationships.

Consider the fiasco of the U.S. electric utilities industry between the first Arab oil embargo in 1973 and the collapse of the oil cartel a decade later. Most of the nation's electric utilities had bought into the assumption that energy use and gross national product were tightly correlated. After all, economic progress and energy consumption had always marched to the same drumbeat. American economic activity had been growing at a high rate of growth for three decades, and energy use had grown with it. At the same time, the oil cartel had managed to jack up oil prices from $5 per barrel in 1970 to $47 per barrel in 1982 (in 1991 dollars). Oil experts spoke about $100 per barrel without blushing. With economists forecasting continued economic growth and oil sages projecting continued price increases, the electric utilities committed billions of dollars of capital to nuclear power plants and to "take or pay" contracts to purchase natural gas at high fixed prices over many years.

Unfortunately, these plans almost universally went sour. First, the price of oil did not grow to the sky. Consumers did not behave as they were supposed to; rather, they either conserved energy or found substitutes for oil. With demand slumping, the oil cartel broke down and the price of oil dropped like a stone, falling to $18 per barrel in 1991. Second, the growth of the American economy slowed down dramatically (in part because of high fuel prices). Demand for electricity slowed even faster, disproving the assumed linkage between the two. In the end, many electric utilities found themselves stuck with unneeded and unwanted nuclear plants, mountains of debt, commitments to buy fuel at high prices,

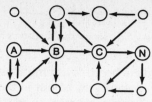

Figure 5.4   Nonlinear causal relationship.

and a chastened view of the reliability of forecasts. Writing on the value of strategic business planning in that same period (1978), Paul, Donovan, and Taylor warned:

> In the past five years, a period no longer than most strategic planners deal with, several major changes have affected almost all U.S. corporations, including the most severe recession in modern times, severe shortages in raw materials in many basic industries, sharply rising costs for energy, a doubling of interest rates, depressed and inflated stock prices without any apparent relation to EPS, record levels of inflation and high unemployment (an impossible condition in most economic theory), and abrupt shifts in consumer income attitudes and purchasing behavior.[19]

They point out that while these developments are explicable in hindsight, there is little evidence that any of them were forecast in the plans of business strategists of the time.

The reality that planners and strategists must deal with more closely resembles what we see in Figure 5.4. In this case, dozens of chaotic forces impinge upon events in ways that are unequal, difficult to measure, and often unseen. This representation of unfolding events does not lend itself to the kind of planning and analysis that most of us can handle. In this reactor of colliding influences, outcomes are less certain and result from interactions we have little ability to understand and even less to predict. Nobel laureate Herbert Simon tells us that "The capacity of the human mind for formulating and solving complex problems is very small compared with the size of the problems whose solutions are required."[20]

The chaotic view of external forces in Figure 5.4 defies the linear thinking on which most large-scale planning relies. It calls for the *configural* thinking that seems to be the gift of a few chess masters, superb quarterbacks, and consistently successful military commanders. Even these people make their share of mistakes, especially when they are pitted against each other.

What seems important for us to understand is just how much is beyond our ability to anticipate and control. This is not to say that leaders and managers should not plan or develop strategies. It merely underscores the importance of developing strategies that are *robust*—strategies that are able to stand up to unforeseen contingencies. In fact, good strategies are those that pursue a single goal with the flexibility to accommodate constantly changing circumstances. The flaw in Yamamoto's strategy was twofold: (1) it failed to include an information system capable of determining where and how circumstances were changing *in real time,* and (2) it made no contingencies for those changing circumstances. His staff developed and rehearsed an overengineered plan that was based upon a static set of assumptions. An anecdote told by Ben Ball, Jr., former vice president for Gulf Oil, seems useful here. According to Ball, a senior manager of the firm once said, "You tell me what the future will be, and I'll prepare the strategy." Ball's reply was, "If I know what the future will be, *anyone* could prepare the strategy."

The Battle of Midway was perhaps an uneven contest from the very beginning. Yamamoto, being the "leader" in the Pacific, had sufficient resources to entertain a variety of options. As a result he succumbed to the temptation of taking on a broad set of objectives (capture Midway; attack the Aleutians; destroy the U.S. fleet). As underdogs with limited resources, the Americans were constrained to pursue a simpler, more straightforward mission: defend Midway Island. As a result, their strategic responsibilities were much different: To be alert to whatever opportunities might arise within the context of their single mission and to be sufficiently flexible to act on them.

We might speculate that the general failure of corporate diversification and conglomeration, popular business strategies in the 1970s and 1980s among giant firms with substantial planning departments, is further evidence of the tendency of organizations to overextend their strategic responsibilities and to be oblivious to the contingencies of competitive warfare.

The Emperor's Sword

The Battle of Midway was the beginning of a gradual downhill slide for the Japanese navy and its strategic plan for hegemony in the western Pacific. The ability of the Americans to decipher intercepted coded messages had undermined one of the fundamental assumptions of that plan. That ability remained unknown to Tokyo throughout the war and was used by the Americans with the utmost discretion, for fear of tipping the enemy. Yamamoto's fleet had run afoul of the American codebreakers at Midway, and he would be one of its personal victims less than a year later.

On April 17, 1943, Yamamoto was inspecting military personnel and facilities at Rabaul on the island of New Britain. Morale had been poor, and he was aware that his presence had a way of boosting everyone's spirits. He decided, therefore, to spend the night at Rabaul and fly to Truk the next morning with a number of his staff. A communications officer at Rabaul radioed this itinerary ahead in coded form. When one of the admiral's aides objected to using a radio message to announce Yamamoto's movements, the communications officer assured him that a new code had just been introduced and that the enemy could not possibly decipher it.

At 0600 on the following morning, two Mitsubishi "Betty" bombers took off from Rabaul with an escort of six Zeros. Three and one-half hours later, flying over the jungles of Bouganville, sixteen American P-38 Lightnings appeared as if from nowhere. The Americans had, in fact, intercepted and deciphered the Japanese code and put together a hasty plan to intercept the leader of the enemy navy.

The Zeros did their best to defend the bombers against the faster, more heavily armed U.S. fighters, but they were quickly overwhelmed. Yamamoto's "Betty" dove from about two thousand feet to the level of the jungle canopy with one P-38 in pursuit. The American pilot raked the bomber with machine gun and cannon fire and observed black smoke and then flames erupt from the starboard engine. The wing was soon afire. As the P-38 continued firing, the bomber careened into the tree tops and exploded.

Yamamoto had said that he could raise havoc with the enemy for twelve to eighteen months. Fifteen months had passed since the Pearl Harbor attack and the admiral had kept his part of the bargain.

> *I am still the sword of my Emperor.*
> *I will not be sheathed until I die.*[21]
> Admiral Isoroku Yamamoto

6

Global Management: Hadrian Consolidates the Roman Empire

Old men who have followed the Eagles since boyhood say nothing is more wonderful than the first sight of the Wall.

Rudyard Kipling, *Puck of Pook's Hill*

August, A.D. 117. Marcus Ulpius Trajanus was 250 miles from Antioch on his homeward journey when death overtook him. Rome's greatest military emperor succumbed to a paralytic stroke in the Cilician coastal town of Selinus at the age of sixty-four. The empire had reached its greatest geographic limits under his leadership. When Trajan came to power, Roman control already extended eastward into the lands of Syria, Judea, and Arabia, northward to the dark German forests, and still further to wild and misty Britain. The lands that are now Spain and France had been effectively Latinized for generations. To the south, Egypt and the Mediterranean coast of Africa were in the Roman orbit. Each of these added to the luster and wealth of the Eternal City. Spain contributed foodstuffs as well as silver and lead from its fabulous mines. Egypt's grain and exotic animals brought from below the Sahara gave Romans their bread and circuses. The Greeks and the culture they had disseminated throughout the Near East and northern Africa set the standards for learning, science, and *haute culture* in the ancient world. Slaves, gathered from many battles,

Figure 6.1 The Roman World—114 A.D.

provided the empire with human resources for everything from brute labor to the arts, medicine, and education.

Like a 1970s-style CEO, Trajan expanded the Roman conglomerate still further, annexing Dacia as a new province in A.D. 106 and conquering Armenia in 114. That same year he led his legions into Mesopotamia and to the capture of the capital of the Parthians—Rome's most resourceful enemy. When he died on the road from Antioch, however, Trajan was rushing back to Rome to take charge of a gathering imperial crisis, not to accept his hero's laurels. The empire was coming loose at its edges. "The people whom Trajan had subdued were in revolt. Moors were provocative, Sarmatians were attacking, and the Britons were defiant. Egypt was prey to sedition, and Libya and Palestine had risen in rebellion."[1] To make matters worse, imperial finances were a mess.

At the time of Trajan's death, Rome's empire was an entity of forty-three provinces peopled by tribes and nationalities that had little in common: the barbarous Belgicas and the cultured Greeks; followers of the Persian cult of Zoroaster and the adherents of Judaism; urban merchants in Alexandria and backward rural Gauls; and Christians of many nationalities who had forsaken the polity of this world for the City of God. Languages and civic customs varied dramatically. The empire contained over 2 million square miles, and its many strategic cities were connected to Rome and to each other by 50,000 miles of roads, Roman justice, and a system of decentralized governance.

The distances between Rome and its furthest outposts were daunting, particularly by the transportation standards of antiquity. Between Rome and the legionnaire town of Cologne were 67 days of hard marching. Travel from the Italian port of Puteoli to the strategic city of Alexandria on the coast of North Africa required 9 days of sailing in the best of seas; forty-one under normal conditions. Antioch could be reached only after 124 days on the road and 2 at sea.[2] Governing the mosaic of peoples within these vast spaces, and defending their borders was a challenge more monumental than anything faced by modern international business organizations. How the Romans succeeded in this challenge commands our attention.

The Modern Global Organization

Every decade, the business community gets wrapped up in a new set of buzzwords. *Global* is the business buzzword of the 1990s. Hardly an issue of a major business magazine fails to include an article about some company's "new global strategy."

This is something new to many in the United States. Until recently, attention to commerce beyond American borders received scant attention in business education, the media, or, apparently, most corporations. Having the world's largest markets for autos, steel, petroleum, pharmaceuticals, frozen foods, flea collars, and just about everything else has that effect. By the 1960s, the United States had only 6 percent of the world's population, but about half of its total wealth. America was the biggest and best market in the world, and every producer wanted to be part of it. Still, a number of U.S. firms cultivated international business and enjoyed good trade overseas: GM and Ford had major foreign operations for decades; grain traders like Cargill had always been global players; and IBM maintained foreign subsidiaries around the world. Aircraft, electronics, and machine tool firms did very well overseas in the post–World War II era. Until recently, however, most Americans rarely thought to pursue markets beyond their borders. Indeed, business schools in the United States offered courses in international business as specialized electives, something out of the mainstream of commercial education.

Others have taken a broader view. As major industrial producers, the British, the Germans, the Dutch, and the Japanese have had relatively small domestic markets, especially in the early postwar period—and for consumer products in particular. Exports have always been a national imperative. The British and the Dutch were not only active as exporters, but as purchasers of income-producing assets in foreign countries. The cash-rich Japanese followed their example in the 1980s, but exporting one's output and buying control of foreign corporations is not the essence of global business. It is the next step—setting up shop on foreign soil and inviting foreign nationals into the executive suites—that makes a company a truly global player.

The global view has enjoyed an awakening among American producers. Companies like Johnson & Johnson, Gillette, Corning, Coca Cola, Caterpiller, Colgate, Xerox, and Dow Chemical now generate more than half of their revenues outside U.S. borders.[3] American firms in computers, software, and even services are doing more and more business abroad. In all cases this represents more than just good salesmanship; it indicates the extent to which these entities have embedded themselves into the fabric of the countries that support those sales in terms of joint ventures, subsidiary operations, and local distributors.

The extent to which firms have become global as opposed to national enterprises provoked Robert Reich to pose his now-famous question: Who is us?[4] Reich observed that while U.S. politicians busy themselves with ways to protect or enhance the competitive capabilities of domestic corporations, many of those same corporations may not be very domestic at all; rather, they are floating free of national identification and allegiance altogether. In the United States, companies like IBM, Hewlett-Packard, and Texas Instruments, Reich argued, are no longer purely American firms operating globally, but global firms operating in America and elsewhere. The same phenomenon is observed in Europe. Whirlpool, for instance, employs more workers abroad than within its domestic borders, as do Holland's N. V. Phillips (79 percent) and Britain's Imperial Chemical (58 percent). Both Ford Motor Company and Matsushita Electronics employ over 40 percent of their workers outside of their respective borders.[5] S. G. Warburg & Company, London's premier investment banker, locates more than 40 percent of its 5,000 staff in the financial centers of North America, Europe, Australia, and Japan. These companies, according to Reich, draw their inventive and managerial talent from many sources around the world, and they locate design, manufacturing, and assembly wherever capabilities and costs dictate. The clear national identity of these firms has begun to fade. Shareholders are scattered broadly; product designers and engineers are on one continent, assembly workers are on another, and the customers are everywhere. The case of Otis Elevator and its development of the Elevonic 411 is representative. Six research centers in five countries contributed to its design; special motor drives came from Otis's facilities in Japan; its German subsidiary handled the electronics; Otis in Spain contributed gear components.[6] The auto industry provides similar examples. As Reich explained it, Mazda's popular sports car, the Miata:

> was designed in California, financed from Tokyo and Chicago, its prototype was created in Worthing, England, and it was assembled in Michigan and Mexico using advanced electronic components invented in New Jersey and fabricated in Japan.[7]

As revolutionary as these cross-border projects and sales may be, perhaps more profound is the extent to which the nationality of key personnel has diversified. Ciba Geigy may be a Swiss corporation based in Basel, but its executives and scientists carry many passports. Arthur D. Little, Inc., calls Cambridge, Massachusetts, home, but its offices are in most of the world's leading business centers and its consultants hail from Belgium, the Middle East, the United States, Germany, India, and wherever else managerial and scientific talent is to be found. Coca Cola, a name that has traditionally meant USA, is headed by a Cuban émigre, Roberto Guisueta, and its managerial ranks are broadly multinational.

Perhaps the firm that has gone the furthest in globalizing its operations is Asea Brown Boveri (ABB). Its corporate headquarters is in Zurich; its CEO is Swedish. Its quarter-of-a-million employees are broadly scattered around the globe. ABB states its financial reports in U.S. dollars and uses English as its official language. ABB's executive committee includes Swedes, Swiss, Germans, and Americans. CEO Percy Barnevik described it as a "multidomestic organization."[8]

The globalization of business is testing the skills of managers everywhere. The idea of suddenly having colleagues and subordinates who do not share the same first language, political traditions, and customs of business practice is truly disturbing and mystifying to many. Creating a sense of coherence, identity, and mutual purpose for the far-flung members of truly globalized enterprises is a new managerial challenge.

Business Week of May 14, 1990, heralded the coming of the "stateless" corporation—an economic entity that is a state unto itself, whose true domicile is unclear. Perhaps the term *suprana-*

tional is more appropriate, but history tells us that others have traveled this road. In this chapter we explore the Roman Empire and the organization it created and successfully managed for many centuries.

The New Spanish Emperor

Trajan's successor was a cousin, Publius Aelius Hadrianus, a man in his early forties whom the late emperor had adopted as son and heir. Adopting an adult male heir was the Roman convention for choosing a successor. Hadrian, like the late emperor, was a Spanish provincial, coming from the town of Italica, where he was born in A.D. 76. Italica had been settled by retired legionnaires some two centuries earlier. Its citizens remained largely of Italian stock, and most could still trace their lineage back to some soldier who had followed the Eagles for enough years to earn his pension and a parcel of land. Like most boys of good family, Hadrian received an education in letters and sports, and then spent two years as a minor bureaucratic official. At age nineteen he was commissioned as a junior officer and stationed with the Second Legion (Adjutrix) at Aquincum (modern Budapest).

When Trajan became emperor in A.D. 98 he called Hadrian to Rome, where he gave him a series of increasingly more demanding administrative responsibilities. Hadrian became the emperor's quaestor, the curator of senatorial records, and tribune to the plebs. During the Second Dacian War (105) he commanded a legion. In 114 he followed his emperor into Parthia. Three years later, Trajan made him governor of Syria, Rome's military linchpin in the Middle East. With the death of his kinsman and patron, Hadrian inherited the imperial cloth that Trajan had been rushing home to mend.

Rome's expansion from a small Italian city-state to an imperial power had taken place over a period of many centuries. It had taken from the Bronze Age until 270 B.C. for it to become master of the Italian peninsula. From that time until the death of Augustus in A.D. 14, Rome managed to triumph over its only Mediterranean rival—Carthage—and extended its power over Spain, North Africa, the Middle East, Greece and Macedonia, and Gaul. From that time until Hadrian's Principate, Rome expanded to Britain, the Caspian Sea, what is now modern Iraq, and beyond the Rhine and the Danube.

The glory of conquest and the desire for land, tribute, and

slaves surely played a part in Roman expansionism, but not all of its acquisitions can be condemned as purely imperialistic. The ancient world in the West and Middle East was an untidy and unpeaceful place filled with marauding tribes and subject to longstanding regional feuds. Rome's interest was in maintaining peace within its own borders, stability along them, and security against incursions by the quarrelsome and often barbaric people who lived outside. Rome solved its security problems through expansion (i.e., by casting the net of Roman peace and order farther and farther from its homeland). It was often drawn into neighboring kingdoms at the invitation of one of several warring parties to put down intertribal disorders. Its general policy in these cases was to pacify the area and set up a client king to keep a lid on things, usually with a Roman garrison stationed nearby to assure order. The first of the client kings was Hiero of Syracuse, who, at the time of the First Punic War, apparently saw that Rome's star was brighter than that of Carthage, and wanted his kingdom to bask in its light.

Rome generally resisted the temptation to annex neighboring states. It did not want to be in the expensive business of managing and defending any more territory than absolutely necessary, nor of embroiling itself in the internal problems of adjacent states. The notion of having a client relationship with the rulers of these states was much preferred.

Perhaps the best-known of these client kings to most readers was King Herod of Judea, who received his royal status from the hand of Mark Anthony in 40 B.C. Herod presided over an opulent court and maintained his own army of German and Thracian mercenaries commanded by Roman officers. He was despised by his Jewish subjects as an alien and a public sinner, but he and his offspring nevertheless ruled Judea on behalf of the Romans for forty-eight years.

The client kingdom bore some resemblance to the foreign-owned business subsidiary of today. One of the natives was left in charge and saw to it that the cogs kept turning and that satisfactory revenues were funneled back to the foreign owner. This local top manager journeyed periodically to the parent headquarters to report results. Local practices and personnel decisions were generally respected as long as results were acceptable. The foreign parent company kept clear of unwanted entanglements through this arrangement, and the subsidiary enjoyed the security of having a powerful ally.

The client kingdoms of the Roman world were allowed to be self-governing as long as taxes were collected and the peace maintained. Their leaders traveled to Rome periodically, and disputes were resolved in counsel with the Roman Senate. If these kings faced internal or external armed threats, they knew that the long arm of the legions was there to assist them.

Time and circumstances undermined the client kingdom system. By Hadrian's Principate all of these territories had been absorbed into the empire as provinces. In the case of Cyrene, its king, Ptolemy Apion, bequeathed his state to Rome upon his death in 96 B.C. King Amyntas of Galatia died in battle in 25 B.C., and his kingdom passed to Roman rule. In the case of Cappadocia, Emperor Tiberius coveted the kingdom and annexed it when its king was forced to commit suicide on a trumped-up charge of treason.

With rare exceptions, the acquired provinces accepted Roman authority, which brought tranquility, status, and a rational framework of justice. Historian Edward Gibbon regarded life under Rome during this period as perhaps the happiest in human history. Others agree. Speaking of the early first century of the Christian era, M. P. Charlesworth stated:

> Our own war-torn generations can appreciate what this solid Augustan peace meant. Occasional local outbreaks there might be—a rising in Britain or Gaul—a vendetta in Spain or a chieftain giving trouble in Africa—but they were mere ripples on a placid surface. War had vanished from the experience of men.[9]

The taxes imposed by Rome were often lighter than were those of previous indigenous rulers, and they were more equitably levied. Governors were instructed in Tiberius's maxim that "the good shepherd shears his sheep; he does not skin them."[10] Still, as would be expected, not everyone was thrilled about having Roman overlords. The Britons, according to Tacitus, complained that "the legate tyrannizes over our lives and the procurator tyrannizes over our property." The Jews, seething first under the rule of Herod and his family and then under a string of unpopular Roman procurators, plotted the day of national liberation. To them, *Pax Romana* was just another spelling for imperialism. Still the Romans made an effort to do two important things that true imperialists rarely do: respect the culture and practices of their subjects and give native people real authority.

Unlike other conquerors, Romans did not hold themselves out

as missionaries of some superior culture. They were not interested in forcing compliance to their own standards in matters of religion, language, or political ideology. Only in rare cases were native religions suppressed. Here the causes for suppression were either a strong tie between the religion and anti-Roman nationalism or the association of the religion with practices deemed inhumane or repugnant.

The suppression of Judaism is an example of the first case. Strong Jewish nationalism in Judea resulted in civil disturbances, attacks on Roman auxiliaries, and, in A.D. 66, open warfare. Legions commanded by Vespasian put down the Jewish revolt after three years of fighting and destroyed their Temple and its precincts. Restrictions on the practice of the Jewish religion followed. Another Jewish revolt in A.D. 132 led to the forcible dispersion of the Jews from their capital city and native land—a situation that persisted until this century.

The suppression of rites of human sacrifice, as practiced by tribes in North Africa—and possibly among the Druids—were undertaken in the name of humanity. Christians were periodically persecuted because they would have nothing to do with the deities of the state—an attitude that made them unpopular with their neighbors. Except for these instances, life in the new provinces went on much as when they were independent of Rome. Rome did not become systematically abusive of nontraditional religious practices until the totalitarian edicts of Emperor Diocletian in the early third century.

The allies of Rome (as the provincials were called) were little interfered with: They continued to lead the life to which they were accustomed and to manage their own affairs. The system of administration was adapted to the conditions of each province and the Roman government respected the liberty of its subjects.[11]

Nor did Rome block its subjects from participation in government or the military, even at the highest levels. This may have been Rome's greatest innovation. Emperors Trajan and Hadrian were both of provincial birth, yet they rose to the highest office of the state, as did others who followed. The army had come to be staffed and commanded by non-Romans. By Hadrian's time, only about 2 percent of the army were of direct Italian stock. In A.D. 70 a Roman general addressed an audience in Gaul with the observation that "you yourselves often rule over Roman provinces or command Roman legions; nothing is excluded or shut off from you." In A.D. 47 Emperor Claudius pushed the Senate to open its ranks to Gauls, thinking that this was an important way to assimilate their leadership into the Roman family. By the second century Greeks and Middle Easterners were also being admitted to that exclusive club.[12]

By the second century, the importance of non-Romans to the functioning of the empire had become fundamental. They acted as magistrates, military commanders, teachers to Roman youths, artists, and as common soldiers. In part to cure the illogic of having aliens in positions of power and in part to reward service and achievement, Roman citizenship was often given. The grant of citizenship had been made in the first century B.C. by Julius Caesar and Pompey to native nobles who joined forces with them. In the first and second centuries, communities were often declared *municipia*, thus investing their magistrates, and eventually their entire populations, with citizenship. The status and rights that accompanied this grant were no small matter. Roman citizenship guaranteed the right to justice and appeal, to travel, to making a will, and to marry; these rights were not guaranteed to others. It was an enviable status. In A.D. 212, Emperor Caracalla granted Roman citizenship to virtually everyone within the borders.

Decrees do not change the hearts of men and women, but one cannot help but think that the granting of citizenship helped to unite the diverse peoples of the empire, giving them a greater sense of ownership in it and winning their allegiance to the goals of the state. Almost two millennia later, the United States would invite a flood of aliens to its shores, invest them with the full benefits of citizenship, and see many of them rise to the highest levels of government, business, and the arts. Within two generations, most of these former aliens would become indistinguishable in manner, politics, and outlook from the native-born population. The same spirit seemed to have infected many newly minted Romans. Roman ways, language, deities, and institutions were widely adopted from Britain to North Africa. The empire's borders came to be defended by German barbarians, Spaniards, and Gauls. Service in the army resulted in citizenship status. The regular movement of legions from province to province along the frontier broke down the soldiers' sense of national origin, replacing it with a Roman identity.

If Americans are correct that mass enfranchisement has enriched their nation, then we must assume that the Romans could make an equal claim. The big difference, of course, is that America made citizens of those who traveled to its shores; Rome created citizens where it found them.

In contrast to the Roman model, Great Britain in the heyday of its empire produced a truly imperial relationship with its colonies. In Africa, Asia, and the Middle East, Britain set up colonial governments in which all important posts were filled by British civil servants and appointees. Unlike the Romans, the British viewed themselves as agents of a superior society and were not reluctant to hold out their own religion, art, education, and sports as superior to native forms of the same. As we will see later, Japanese economic *imperialism* (to stretch the term) has much in common with the British model, while contemporary American global business shares the spirit of the Romans.

The Roman Commonwealth

Hadrian was a capable leader and just the right person to head the global enterprise his predecessors had pieced together over the centuries. He had a keen sense of limits and a manager's sense for the smooth functioning of political administration and defense. He was the right person to deal with the simmering problems that Trajan had left unresolved.

His first observation was that the empire was overextended relative to its resources. There were not enough legions to defend its far-flung borders, not enough capable civil servants to administer its many provinces, and too few funds in the treasury to pay all the bills. Bold thinking and action were called for.

Armenia and Mesopotamia, recently annexed by Trajan, were Hadrian's first order of business. They hung by thin threads to the body of the empire. The client kings set up to hold these areas were losing control in the face of insurrection. Heavy campaigning would be required to bring these areas to heel. Holding them would mean living with constant disturbance along the broad eastern frontier and, to Hadrian's thinking, a drain on Roman resources far exceeding any offsetting contribution of wealth or greater security. He was interested in consolidating the Roman world within borders that could be economically maintained. Therefore, Hadrian divested the empire of Armenia and Mesopotamia and withdrew all Roman forces back to early frontiers.

Hadrian's bold step in reverse was unpopular with many conservatives in the Senate and with a number of high-ranking military men. Walking away from hard-won conquests was not the Roman way. But the emperor was unfazed by these complaints, and he moved quickly to other business.

Managing by Walking Around

"He loved not only to govern," wrote a contemporary, "but also to perambulate the world." Hadrian ruled the empire for almost twenty-one years, and he spent half of those away from Rome. "He went round all the provinces on foot, outpacing his companions," we are told. Inclement weather did not dissuade him from his journeys, "He wore no covering on his head either amid Celtic snows or in Egyptian heat."[13] In an age when travel was difficult, dangerous, and frustratingly slow, Hadrian nevertheless made it his business to see and be seen throughout the empire. No other emperor before or since was so widely traveled, so intimately knowledgeable about local conditions and problems. Augustus had established an efficient messenger system to link the center of leadership with provincial governors and magistrates; eventually, he upgraded this system with relays of chariots so that face-to-face communication would be possible. Hadrian, however, needed to see and hear for himself.

Some ascribe Hadrian's journeys to his natural curiosity and love of travel. There is ample evidence of this. It is likely that he wanted to assure himself of the allegiance of his armies. The role of the army in making and breaking emperors and causing civil war had been endemic since the time of Julius Caesar, and Hadrian wanted to know his troops and them to know him. In that end he was remarkably successful. "No emperor," says historian Michael Grant, "was ever closer to his soldiers than Hadrian. . . . His constant presence with the armies, sharing their tasks and knowing their habits, ensured him great popularity with the soldiery."[14]

Hadrian knew that the success of his plan to consolidate and effectively manage the empire was dependent upon peace. Warfare, as now, added incrementally to the cost of defense; it interrupted the collection of the universal land and property taxes as well as tributes upon which the imperial treasury depended. Peace would solve the empire's chronic fiscal problems. It would also assure that the least Latinized of the provinces—places like Britain, Judea, and Dacia—would have an opportunity to be integrated into the commonwealth of Roman nations. Peace would also have a better chance if two things prevailed: if the frontier armies were thoroughly prepared and professional and if those armies were positioned on logical and defendable borders. As a longtime military man, Hadrian understood how aggressive tribes along the borders were tempted to raid Roman territory whenever they perceived weakness. He knew that the lack of clear and defensible borders created preconditions for turmoil. He would have neither. His insistence that the legions be kept in a state of continual training and utmost readiness prompted one barbarian leader to remark, "The Romans prepare for peace by acting as if they are at war."

To reduce the preconditions for armed conflict Hadrian manipulated borders. His withdrawal from Armenia and Mesopotamia was previously noted. He also ordered the construction of elaborate border defenses at possible flash points.

Hadrian's initial journey began in A.D. 121 and kept him away from the capital for almost five years. His first destinations were the legion camps along the Rhine. Twenty years of peace along this frontier and the garrisoning of troops in fortified positions had made their discipline and field effectiveness highly questionable. Modern leaders know that lack of regular testing against effective opponents dulls the edge of organizational competence, and Hadrian recognized the same in these northern forces. He meant to remedy the situation through intensive drill and field maneuvers. He ordered an intense regime of training, and shared its hardships with the men, including regular twenty-mile marches in full armor.

From the Rhine he traveled to Britain, where, after a two-month tour of inspection, he ordered the building of a wall clear across the country to separate Roman Britain from the warlike Brigantes to the north. He then went on to Gaul, Spain, North Africa, and the sophisticated cities of the east: Ephesus, Athens, and Rhodes. During his three years in the east, he commissioned the building of bridges, fortifications, and temples. A number of towns were founded or renamed in his honor—Hadrianopolis (there were three with this exact name), Hadrianotherae, Hadrianoi, and Adrianople—all of which must have caused confusion for mapmakers and travelers for centuries.

The emperor returned to Rome in the fall of A.D. 126, where he stayed for two years before setting out again for North Africa, again to Greece, to Cappadocia, Syria, Judea, and Egypt. As far as we can tell, he returned to Rome in A.D. 131, but insurrection of the Jews in Judea took him to Antioch, from whence he directed military operations during the first stages of a three-and-a-half-year war. These hostilities, it seems clear, were sparked by Hadrian's own ill-considered ideas of founding a Roman colony called Aelia Capitolina on the ruins of the city of Jerusalem and of building a temple to Jupiter upon the foundations of the Hebrew Temple destroyed by Roman soldiers six decades before.

It is likely that Hadrian returned to Rome, for the last time, sometime in A.D. 133 or 134. Julius Severus, a general highly regarded by the emperor, had been brought in from Britain to put down the Jewish rebellion.

In the few years remaining to him, Hadrian strengthened the civil service on whose daily work imperial policy was dependent. Like all successful managers, Hadrian learned that he needed competent and reliable people to whom he could delegate the regular business of the state. Augustus had done much to establish and professionalize the civil service, and others, notably Vespasian, had built upon that foundation. In earlier times, higher civil and military positions went to members of senatorial families—Rome's unofficial nobility—and, by tradition, they served without pay. By the second century, however, an increasing number of the top-tier jobs went to members of the equestrian class. Like the senatorial class, the equestrians were propertied and educated, but they were men of trade. They represented the upper-middle managerial class, and they collected the taxes, ran the courts, and saw to the smooth running of the machinery of imperial and provincial administration. The emperors came to depend upon these "new men" just as the kings of medieval Europe would come to depend upon Jews and clerics. In neither case would this dependence endear either set of rulers or servants to the nobility. Hadrian's development of the civil service and his promotion of equestrians within its ranks seems to indicate that he meant to be served by a superior class of administrators.

The effectiveness of the civil service over long periods of time—despite periodic rot at the top—was a primary factor in the longevity of the Roman imperial system. Between Augustus and Hadrian more than a few emperors abandoned their responsibilities to the machinery of government to pursue their own pleasures and perversities. Tiberius in his twilight years allowed the reins of power to slip into the hands of one of his guards, the ambitious and murderous Sejanus. Tiberius was followed by the psychopathic Caligula. His life was brought to a well-deserved end by the Praetorian Guard, but Romans had to muddle through another fourteen years of inept leadership—this time in the person of Gaius Nero, another deranged character. After his assassination, four men assumed the purple in the span of two years. The fact that the Roman world held together through those years of incompetence and corruption attests to the strength of Roman institutions—in particular, the army on the frontiers and the civil service.

Large numbers of provincials were recruited into the civil service. This was an important means of Romanizing the diversity of tribes and nations within the empire in that it produced a core of Latin-speaking citizens whose loyalties were to Rome, not to Lusitania, Lower Moesia, Mauritania, or to any other province. Over time these people rose to positions of leadership.

Hadrian played an important role in converting an empire of subject states into a manageable commonwealth of people and places with shared institutions and goals. As historian Richard Haywood has said:

> The movement of the second century toward a commonwealth was an attempt to do with all the varied people of the empire what the earlier Romans had done with the peoples of Italy. To unite the peoples of Italy instead of merely subjecting and exploiting them had been a brilliant idea. To unite the men of the whole empire from Britain to Mesopotamia, and from the Atlas mountains to Hungary under the rule of law and with ideas and ideals which they could all accept, was one of the great ideas of all time.[15]

By the middle of the second century A.D. the term *Roman* could be broadly applied. Its institutions—the military, civil service, and commerce—could draw freely from a large and diverse pool of human talent whose individual members shared a core set of values and traditions. Those institutions were strong enough to take in large numbers of aliens and not become alien themselves—at least not for some time. The army could recruit undisciplined barbarians from along the Rhine and produce from them soldiers who would march in formation, live up to the traditions of Roman fighters, and respond to orders given in Latin. It was the development of this core set of values, disciplines, and traditions that transformed the empire of many states into a supranational organization.

Hadrian died in 138, leaving Antoninus Pius as his designated heir. He was buried in a magnificent tomb on the banks of the Tiber, an edifice that today bears the name of the Castel Sant' Angelo. The ancient world would enjoy another four decades of order and peace. During his successful reign he provided a number of examples that the modern student of leadership and the managerial arts should emulate:

- He divested the empire of those parts that his predecessor had acquired thoughtlessly. He made the Roman world smaller, but more coherent and manageable.
- He shored up strategic weak points and brought his soldiers back up to the high stardards of Roman arms.
- Instead of remaining glued to his headquarters, where decisions would be made on the basis of reports and hearsay, he went to see the problems that affected the empire first-hand. His presence among the frontier legions and the provincials served as a visible symbol of Roman authority and the concern of its top leadership.
- He advanced competent and reliable people into key managerial positions.
- Most important, Hadrian supported the Roman tradition of unifying the diverse peoples of the empire with a universal language, a common culture, and a set of civic values.

The Roman Model

The Roman state survived Hadrian in the West by some three-and-a-half centuries, depending upon how you count, and persisted for yet another thousand years in the East.[16] Few other institutions can boast so long a run. Almost two thousand years after its heyday, the relics of Rome's achievement dot the landscape of Western Europe, North Africa, and the Middle East. In Britain, Hadrian's Wall remains as a visible reminder of Rome's engineering prowess; water still courses into the city of Segovia along the graceful arches of its Roman aqueduct. Roman bridges and roads still serve travelers in Tuscany, France, and Spain. Less visible, but more important to the way we live today, are Roman military forms, which shape the organization of all modern armies, Roman law and language, and Rome's legacy of civil governance.

The Roman Catholic church is undoubtedly the most dynamic of the surviving offshoots of the old empire. Some fifteen hundred years after the Visigoths sacked the Imperial City, the church remains the dominant religious institution of the Western world, and its pontiff represents the longest lasting monarchy in human history.

Having grown up in the shadow of the old empire, the church quite naturally patterned itself on the Roman model of administration, and that pattern persists. Its global headquarters in the

Vatican employs a professional staff (curia) of bureaucrats, theologians, diplomats, and advisors. In the field, church governance is in the hands of appointed cardinals and bishops whose seats are in the old provincial capitals of the empire. Like provincial governors of antiquity, the cardinals report to Rome regularly. Papal legates represent the views of the central leadership in far-flung corners of the world.

Like ancient Rome, the modern church has a core set of beliefs, yet tolerates local extensions and traditions. Catholic liturgy in France is very different from that found in sub-Saharan Africa; religious celebrations in Mexico borrow freely from pre-Columbian paganism and are a world apart from the celebrations observed by Catholics in Milwaukee, yet all are Roman Catholic. Its adherents speak many tongues, but the church and its professionals share the Latin language. The different orders of the secular clergy and monastics follow their own rule. The top ecclesiastical ranks throughout the world are not reserved for Italians, but go to indigenous leaders. Even in the Vatican, the church's willingness to recruit from its far-flung constituency is apparent. The top job, at this writing, is filled by a Pole.

The Roman Catholic church, perhaps better than any other large contemporary organization, provides an instructive model for the supranational corporation. Its philosophy, leadership, and bureaucracy are drawn freely from the thousands of locales it serves; yet, except for a small parcel of land in the midst of Rome, it has no national homeland. It is a service firm with employees and clients on every continent. If today's business thinkers need a living model from which to draw lessons for global effectiveness, then the Church of Rome is worthy of serious study. As corporations attempt to carve out global turfs in competition with others, they will need to adopt some of the organizational values that led to the success of Rome and to that of the Roman Catholic church.

The Contemporary Challenge

The wunderkinds of global competition over the past fifteen years have been the Japanese. First, they beat everyone by the price and quality of manufactured goods produced in Japanese factories. From that foundation they have carried their flag right into the heart of their competitors' territories, building manufacturing facilities outside Japan and hiring and training locals to work in them. In the United States, Japanese auto firms have built new plants, staffed them with American workers, and produced products that have matched—and sometimes surpassed in cost and quality—those previously imported. They have demonstrated the universality of their style of management and organization; they have also shown that non-Japanese workers, if managed by Japanese methods and employed in well-designed facilities, can achieve much higher levels of efficiency and quality output.

Despite these successes in spreading their operations beyond Japan, it may be that the Americans are better prepared to make the transition from national firms operating internationally to global firms operating in many nations. As a country of many cultures, the United States is accustomed to diversity in races, religions, foods, surnames, and, in some localities, languages. Over the past quarter century, the American workplace has been forced by law to deal with the thorny issues arising from differences in race, ethnicity, and gender, with the result that the concept of managing diversity has taken on the aura of a positive ideal within leading firms. American business has sought to accommodate itself to human diversity and get the best of what it can offer, both at home and abroad. Its domestic R&D laboratories, engineering staffs and those in the ranks of management are today liberally staffed with skilled and talented people from Europe and Asia. Overseas, American subsidiaries traditionally have been fairly independent operations—and usually run by native managers.

The extent to which local talent and customs direct America's overseas subsidiaries is seen in the case of Motorola's Asia-Pacific semiconductors division. Its president in 1992, Tam Chung Din, felt obliged to check the spirits (*fengshi*) of the company's new $400 million Hong Kong plant by calling in a respected soothsayer.[17] Motorola leans heavily on the talents of managers like Din, not just within their subsidiary units, but within the entire organization.

By contrast, Japanese firms rely almost exclusively on homegrown talent, and they will need to make some fundamental adjustments if they hope to become truly global. It is a great irony that firms of the nation most feared and respected for their ability to capture foreign markets and to shift production to foreign locations are so poorly equipped to take the important next step—to supranational status.

Japan is a homogeneous, male-dominated society that views itself as unique, separate, special, and otherwise distinct from other societies—which by most accounts it is. These characteristics and the dedication of its people to group consensus, discipline, and hard work have served it well. These same characteristics and attitudes, however, now put it at a serious disadvantage in terms of the changing picture of supranational enterprise.

Since the early 1980s, Japanese firms have been aggressive in transplanting their operations abroad. Financial service behemoths like Nomura, Nikko Securities, the Industrial Bank of Japan, and Mitsuo Manufacturers Bank have opened branch offices in the United States. Industrial firms like Mitsubishi Motors, Toyota, Honda, NEC, Toshiba Electronics, and Seiko have built and staffed new facilities, often from the ground up. By 1992, nearly four hundred thousand Americans (including some fifty thousand managers) were working for almost two thousand Japanese firms in offices and factories scattered around the United States.[18] While the majority of the personnel employed in these operations are Americans, real decision-making power invariably rests in the hands of Japanese. More often than not, big decisions are made in the home office in Japan. Many blue-collar and clerical workers have been generous in their praise of the Japanese management style as practiced in the United States. But American managers at many of these same firms complained that their employers maintain two unequal societies—one of native managers handling day-to-day affairs and a Japanese preserve that holds most decision-making authority.

An American ex-employee of a Japanese trading company once described to the author how important decisions were made at his firm. A meeting would be called, but only Japanese employees would be asked to attend on the premise that the native managers "wouldn't be interested" or, when pressed, that "they couldn't speak Japanese." Evidence indicates that this is typical. While some firms have stated their intent to gradually Americanize the higher management of their U.S. operations, having Japanese nationals in key positions with direction from Asia is the rule. As Jeremiah Sullivan writes:

> This kind of firm keeps Japanese management in all key posts. When an American of necessity is put in a high position, a Japanese advisor often is appointed to keep him in check. Instructions flow in a constant fax stream from Tokyo or Osaka, and information useful for strategic decision-making flows back the other way.[19]

Sullivan's research points to virtually the same practices in Japanese operations sited in Europe.

Interviews conducted by Dennis Laurie on 250 American white-collar workers employed at thirty-two different Japanese-owned companies corroborate Sullivan's statement. But these go on to reveal one very important, if somewhat misdirected, strength of Japanese firms: their ability to inculcate employees with the culture, values, and mission of the firm. Laurie cites the extensive training, job rotations through different departments, and general grooming that goes into the development of broadly experienced, loyal, and mature executives of Japanese firms.[20] Like the civil servants, commanders, and diplomats of the Roman Empire, these managers are nurtured to command and carry on the best traditions of their firms.

That these efforts are slightly misguided is evidenced by the fact that this sort of career development is reserved for Japanese nationals. Native managers and workers are hired for their particular expertise and are seldom rotated or molded for promotions to key positions. A recent article in *Across the Board* cites a rising level of lawsuits (an occupation in which Americans have a clearly competitive advantage) against Japanese employers involving issues of promotion practices.[21] Laurie attributes the penchant of U.S. managers to jump ship to competing firms as a partial explanation for this disparity of treatment. Tribalism surely explains the rest.

Some American firms see this tradition of running foreign operations out of Tokyo as the Achilles heel of their Japanese competitors. According to a recent story in the *Economist,*[22] executives at United Technologies believe that Japan's strength has been its ability to deliver products of extraordinary quality, first by exportation and then by building foreign factories on greenfield sites run from Japan. United Technologies believes that once it is able to match Japanese product quality standards, its decentralized system of global operations will give it a competitive leg up in providing for local adaptability and choice.

Nationalism and Corporations

Will the supranational corporation become a dominant form of future enterprise? There is no telling at this time. Nationalism has been such a potent force in the world for so long that the ability of economic entities (or their employees) to shed their allegiance to one nation-state or another is open to serious question. Still, we might speculate on some consequences if this were to happen.

Nationalism has probably outdone religion as a source of conflict in the modern world. When people have national destinies to fulfill and national pride to assuage, they must inevitably find themselves in conflict with neighbors out to do the same. The separation of peoples and their economies along national lines has led to hostility and warfare on an almost continual basis for the past two centuries. What, though, might world affairs be like if households across the globe depended for their incomes on dozens or hundreds of supranational business firms that maintained vital stakes in traditionally antagonistic nations? For example, suppose that half of the working adults in Germany, France, Russia, Japan, India, the United States, Great Britain, Korea, and Brazil were engaged as employees, shareholders, or suppliers to one of a dozen major supranationals that supported operations in these and other locations. Millions of households around the world would look to those firms for paychecks, medical insurance, and pensions; their governments would look to them as continuing sources of tax revenues. How likely is it, in this situation, that a dispute between governments would be allowed to escalate into open warfare, undermining those sources of income and benefits?

Imagine that you worked for XYZ Computer Corporation in its software development center in Cambridge, Massachusetts. XYZ equipment uses chips designed and made in its Tokyo plant. Color monitors come from Seoul under a joint venture agreement with a Korean company. R&D takes place in Cambridge, Brussels, and London. Disk drives are made by a single German supplier, and assembly takes place in a new state-of-the-art plant near Moscow. Customers for XYZ products are broadly distributed throughout Europe, North America, and the Pacific Rim. Your paychecks, bonuses, and pension depend on the collaboration of all these parties. What, then, would you say to a political representative who supported trade embargoes or military initiatives that would threaten this web of commerce? What would your fellow employees in those other locations say to their leaders?

When commerce is not allowed to cross borders, armies will. International trade and the linking of nations through global business operations may be the best chance for a peaceful world—for the decades of prosperous tranquility that characterized the Roman world under Hadrian and the string of "good" emperors who followed him.

7

Managing in Turbulent Times: Hutchinson Misreads the Revolution

To lead the people, walk behind them.

Lao-tzu

Sometime around 10:00 P.M. the sergeants were sent to rouse their men. The troops had slept in their uniforms that night, so it took only a short time to turn them out into ranks on the common meadow. A nearly full moon broke out from scattered clouds on that cool and windy night as the officers formed up companies of light infantry and grenadiers for the short march through the north end of town to the river, where boats waited to ferry them across to Charlestown. From there a six- or seven-hour march through the outlying farming villages of Medford, Manomet, and Lexington would bring them to Concord, their objective, shortly after sun-up.

The clash between British soldiers and Massachusetts colonists at the end of that night's long march is a story known to every American schoolchild. The new day would clatter with the first shots of the American Revolution, and Britannia's sons would engage their American cousins in an armed conflict destined to last six years and end in permanent separation.

How could it come to pass that people who spoke the same language; who shared the same traditions, values, and laws; and who until so recently had seen themselves as loyal subjects of the same king, would find themselves desperately sighting down musket barrels at each other on a fine April morning in 1775? Could no one have prevented it? These question were as puzzling to contemporaries as they are for many today. In searching for the answers we find lessons about how people deal with fundamental change—how some ride in its wake while others are swept away.

Two men whose lives are instructive in this episode were far from the fighting that April morning, yet each played a major role in its inevitability. The first was a shrewd Boston political organizer named Samuel Adams, who had slept in Lexington the night before and who fled at the first alarm of the approaching redcoats. The second was Thomas Hutchinson, the last civilian governor of Massachusetts Bay Colony, who would be blamed by many—on both sides of the Atlantic—for the great catastrophe. Hutchinson, in favor of military rule, had already retired to England where news of the armed clash arrived several weeks later.

Hutchinson had spent his entire adult life in political service to the Bay Colony and to the Crown, climbing up through the ranks of the colonial system in a series of elective and appointed positions. Learned, genteel, and experienced in the ways of colonial administration, Hutchinson was nevertheless hounded from office by developments for which his previous experience rendered him ill-prepared. Indeed, his great misfortune was to have been born twenty years too late.

Over the past few years, a growing number of major corporate leaders have likewise been sacked or convinced to step down. In October 1992, Robert Stempel, chairman of General Motors, was shown the door by a frustrated board of directors. A thirty-four-year veteran of the firm, Stempel had climbed the ladder to increasingly responsible positions, becoming the first engineer to make it to the top of the giant of U.S. automakers. Outside board members, however, grew impatient with his inability to make rapid progress in the company's plan to adapt itself to the automotive environment of the 1990s.

A few months earlier, Kenneth Olsen, the computer pioneer who conceived and built Digital Equipment Company (DEC) over a period of thirty-five years, decided to step down. DEC was experiencing massive losses, and had changed from a profitable company with a perfect record of no forced layoffs to one drowning in red ink, from which thousands of managers, engineers, and other workers were being furloughed. Even at IBM, where layoffs of forty thousand were announced in the summer of 1992, John Akers stepped down after not keeping his company apace with advancing computer technology. In 1991, the leadership of Sears Roebuck found itself on the defensive as Robert A. G. Monks and a coalition of rebellious shareholders waged a campaign to get Monks elected as a reforming outsider on the firm's board.

These headline events are merely symptomatic of growing efforts to shift leadership from the hands of executives comfortable with the traditional values of their institutions to others thought to be more suited to the times. Stempel's departure prompted management professor Warren Bennis to say, "It's really a wake-up call. With the galloping changes that are taking place—demographic, geopolitical, global—if you think you can run the business in the next 10 years the way you did in the last 10 years, you are crazy."[1]

Change comes so quickly today that technology-based firms have trouble keeping up without a continuous infusion of newly minted research scientists and engineers. The core competencies that assured their commerical success in one product generation are sometimes of little value when a new product generation appears in the market. For example, the competencies that supported the great success of NCR and its management during the era of electromechanical cash registers did not serve it well when computer-based cash registers invaded its market in the early 1970s. The company lost 80 percent of the new cash register business in a period of just four years. Catastrophic losses led the NCR board to remove its longtime chairperson and the core of top executives, replacing them with managers who seem more likely to lead the firm into the new computer age.[2]

In business, as in politics, each generation of leaders seems to develop visions and competencies that address the competitive challenges that confront them during their formative years; in fact, they form themselves to these challenges. Once formed, they seem less able to adapt to the next set of challenges, and other leaders are called for. There is tragedy in this, of course, as often sincere and otherwise competent individuals who have served their organizations well over many years suddenly find themselves unable to cope with contemporary challenges. The transition between generations of leadership is usually painful for all concerned, as demonstrated in this episode from American history, in which the failure of an otherwise able and well-meaning man to deal with revolutionary change cost him both career and country.

The Colonial Condition

A decade before the outbreak of the Revolution, life for the average British citizen in the American colonies was about as good as anyone then living anywhere on the planet could find. The 2.5 million colonists scattered up and down the Atlantic coastline enjoyed a bountiful if rustic existence. Food was cheap and plentiful; land was obtainable for those who would work it; the sea, the rivers, and the forests provided occupation and abundance. British-American cities like Williamsburg, Philadephia, New York, and Boston were repositories of arts and sciences transported directly across the Atlantic.

As an important part of the British mercantile system, the American colonies were expected to serve the interests of the mother country: exporting raw materials to the factories and mills of England and Scotland and importing finished goods in return. In America, Britain had a ready source of agricultural commodities, fish, rum, and the forest products upon which her navy depended for lumber and tall, straight masts. America was also an important market for the manufactured goods that poured out of its dark, satanic mills. By 1760 the colonies absorbed almost 13 percent of all British production.

Exports from America, even to other nations, always had to be first shipped through Britain, on British ships, with British crews. This restriction was less an imposition than it would first appear. As British citizens themselves, colonists could own and man these same vessels; in fact, they controlled half of the tonnage that moved the transatlantic trade in the decade before the revolution.[3]

Their commerce, cities, and settlements prospered under the shield of His Majesty's Army and Navy, which protected them without charge from Indian incursions, pirates, and Britain's European rivals. As for restrictions on trading outside the British system, American merchants made an art form of smuggling and bribing royal customs officers. The coastline of British North America was a vast sieve through which illegal shipping penetrated almost without challenge, theories of mercantilism notwithstanding. Yankee traders like John Hancock amassed fortunes from shipping, little of which passed through the king's custom houses.

The American colonies had the good luck of having been established during a period in British history when the powers of the monarchy were being systematically reduced in favor of the people, as represented in Parliament. The Puritans who came to

New England in great numbers throughout the 1630s and 1640s were, in fact, contemporaries of the great revolution that pitted Royalists against the forces of representative government. They carried the tradition of that struggle to America, where the king appointed a governor, judges, and, typically, an advisory council in each colony; however, a lower chamber, an assembly, was selected by popular election. The Crown provided no funding for the business of government or the salaries of its governors, judges, or councils, so each colonial government had to raise its own revenues. Over the decades of the colonial period, the assemblies gathered the purse strings of taxing and spending into their own hands, and through these powers they came to dominate the day-to-day affairs of government. Although royal governors had veto power over them, and although they existed solely at the pleasure of the Crown, freely elected colonial assemblies were the de facto parliaments of British North America.

The mother country held her colonies in a very loose grip. The elected assemblies carried on much of the government business within the colonies, passing statutes, maintaining local militias, and imposing and collecting internal taxes. Britain exercised the right of setting and collecting customs duties on *external* trade. Parliament maintained authority over the colonial assemblies in theory, but it found no compelling reason to exercise it. It was a system of salutary neglect, and it worked very well for the colonies and for the mother country for a very long time.

This comfortable arrangement changed abruptly after Britain's victory in the French and Indian War (1754–1760). The outcome of the war stripped France of its vast Canadian domain and added Spanish Florida, a few Caribbean islands, and all of France's North American possessions east of the the Mississippi to Britain's colonial orbit. It changed Britain's place in the world fundamentally, elevating it to the position of an imperial maritime power for the first time.

As Americans have learned time and again since their own great victory in World War II, being a world power is an expensive proposition. Britain's victory over France left the Exchequer with a staggering debt of £130 million. The cost of holding, protecting, and providing administration over its expanded North American domain was estimated to cost another £300,000 per year. This burden was viewed as insupportable in London, and the king's ministers began casting about for new revenue sources; the American colonies seemed a good place to find them.

A Very Good Gentleman

By all accounts the Massachusetts Bay Colony was a thriving little estate. In 1760 it had 210,000 white inhabitants, 95 percent of British ancestry. The city of Boston enjoyed a vibrant economy of sailors, shipbuilders, fishers, mechanics, rum distillers, and merchants. Some five hundred ships left its harbor each year bound for the West Indies and Great Britain.[4]

The Hutchinson family was among the oldest in New England and prominent within Boston's merchant class. When Thomas Hutchinson was born in 1711, he was already a fifth-generation American. The family had produced no poets, teachers, or preachers, but it had demonstrated a knack for business. Young Thomas had all the genes of the merchant. His father gave him a small emolument when he entered Harvard at the age of twelve, and he turned that into a sizable sum and was the owner of several income-producing enterprises in fishing and shipping by the time he finished school. (After the Revolution his properties were auctioned off for £98,000——a princely sum at the time). It would be difficult to find a person—or a family—in New England whose well-being was more intimately connected with the colony and its growing prosperity.

An Edward Truman portrait of Hutchinson at age thirty reveals a slightly built man of delicate features with an air of serene self-assuredness. He was intelligent, a good scholar, a capable merchant, and a sober and totally respectable fellow. James Otis described him as tall, slender, and fair-complexioned, and "a very good gentleman." Those who knew him remarked that he was always composed and revealed little of his inner feelings. There were no high jinks in Thomas Hutchinson. An heir to the Puritan traditions of sobriety and self-denial, his passions were cerebral and expressed in logical, carefully worded, and pedantic discourse. Harvard historian Bernard Bailyn tells us, "Hutchinson did not respond deeply to the physical qualities of life; his sensuous apprehensions were never keen. . . . He spoke fearfully to others, especially to the young, of the temptations of dissolute living and of its disastrous consequences."[5] John Galvin describes him as "a man ridden hard by inhibition." "My temper," Hutchinson wrote, "does not incline to enthusiasm," but this did not imply disinterest.

As an educated and sophisticated man, he could appreciate opposing points of view, and when he pushed back against those with whom he disagreed, he did so with carefully formed arguments. There was no fiery oratory in Thomas Hutchinson. Today we would call him a stuffed shirt or an egghead. We have evidence of his feelings only in letters to his closest friends and to his family members. Indeed, Hutchinson withdrew from society to his close circle of friends and relatives at every opportunity, and by all accounts he was a very happy man and entirely dedicated to those he loved.

Above all else, Hutchinson was a political conservative who saw the world as one in which, according to historian John Galvin, "the most highly skilled and worthy men of the land pitted themselves in constant battle against the forces of decay, decline, sloth, corruption, and self interest."[6] The barbarians were always at the gates of the prosperous and well-ordered world that Hutchinson and people like him hoped to maintain.

Thomas Hutchinson entered politics at the age of twenty-six, first as a Boston representative to the Massachusetts House, and later as a member of the governor's council. He advanced his political career as he advanced his business, through hard work and well-made alliances. His marriage to Margaret Sanford, daughter of an important Boston family, was followed by the marriage of Margaret's sister to Andrew Oliver, Hutchinson's closest political ally. Years later, when Hutchinson had become governor and Oliver his lieutenant governor, Hutchinson's eldest son would marry Oliver's daughter. The Hutchinson-Oliver-Sanford alliance became a powerful force in the business and government of the colony. They succeeded in monopolizing most of the top political offices of the colony, prompting John Adams' impassioned complaint that Hutchinson and kin had created an "amazing ascendency of one family, foundation sufficient on which to erect a tyranny."

Hutchinson's public career spanned four decades and elevated him to the lofty posts of lieutenant governor, chief justice, and eventually governor (1770–1774). During those years he established himself as the most knowledgeable and experienced politico in the colony: learned at dealing with London, the subtleties of the assembly, and the interests of the colony's many factions. He even found time to write the most authoritative book to that time on the history of the colony.

Hutchinson emerged as the leader of the loyalist faction in Massachusetts. He represented its view that the best interests of Massachusetts lay in its connection to Great Britain, and that both its economy and safety were bound to it. "Is there anything which we have more reason to dread," he confided to a friend, "than independence?" Without its ties to Britain, he reasoned, Massachusetts shipping would be easy prey for French and Spanish marauders, the economy would founder, and demagogues would inflame the baser passions of the public, jeopardizing both personal liberties and property rights.

Hutchinson's thinking about the proper relationship between the mother country and the colony emerged from the Enlightenment philosophy of the eighteenth century—the same philosophical roots tapped by the Adamses, Otis, and other revolutionaries, who drew from them quite different conclusions. In Hutchinson's view, the British political system was the best practical guarantor of individual liberties in the world. In this he represented the core of loyalist ideology throughout the colonies. Historian Janice Potter simply described that ideology as, "The British tie was a positive historical and contemporary force which was associated with prosperity, liberty, and unity."[7]

In Hutchinson's view, Parliament was the logical sovereign of colonial governments; still, he felt that a place had to be maintained for the colonial legislatures, the rights of colonists as English citizens, and some representation of their views on matters of law and taxes. As Robert McCluer Calhoon described him: "He believed to the core of his being that the only way to defend colonial liberties was to submit prudently to British authority and, without denying the subordinate status of the colonies, to expand quietly the scope of colonial autonomy."[8] Hutchinson spent a good deal of time trying to develop a philosophical framework for that viewpoint—one that steered a middle course between the conservatives of his own social order and the colonial radicals.

His were not the views of a tyrant, a usurper, or a villain who conspires to rob his neighbors of their rights and property, as his enemies described them. Indeed, it is remarkable how much of a philosophical base Hutchinson shared with his most venomous detractors. Far more informed and liberal in his views than the interests he represented, Hutchinson was no political dinosaur, however, his thinking was not evolving at the same pace as the great body of other colonial leaders and thinkers. This fact put Hutchinson on a collision course with the popular party of James Otis, John Adams, Joseph Warren, and Ben Franklin. He would become a favorite target for rabble-rousers like Samuel Adams and the street thugs who made Boston practically ungovernable for a decade. Josiah Quincy, Jr., complained that "all the measures against

America were planned and pushed by [Governor] Bernard and Hutchinson." John Dickinson counted Hutchinson among the "villains and idiots" who turned the people against the mother country. Mercy Otis Warren called him a "dark, intriguing, insinuating, haughty, and ambitious man." John Adams, whose obsessive dislike for Hutchinson spanned the decades before and after the Revolution, described him as a manipulator of "the passions and prejudices, the follies and vices of great men in order to obtain their smiles, esteem, and patronage and consequently their favors and preferments." Most of all they despised him because he was one of them—a native-born American—who had cast his lot with those whom they perceived as their oppressors.

Hutchinson had not always been held in such low esteem. As early as 1742 he had made a name for himself in fighting the practice of impressment. British naval commanders had regularly filled out their crews by grabbing able-bodied men off wharfs and civilian ships at sea. This became a hot issue in New England during the War of Jenkin's Ear (1739), when British captains began impressing colonials to fill holes created by desertion and casualties. Riots ensued in Boston, and the issue remained a touchy one for decades. In 1742 a housewright named William Pratt, a man with a business and family, was impressed by HMS *Astraea,* and Thomas Hutchinson succeeded in negotiating his release. Another case involve a Marblehead sailor named Michael Corbet, who killed two members of a British press gang that had attempted to kidnap him for HMS *Pitt Packet*. Corbet was hauled into the Admiralty Court on murder charges. His lawyer was a young and inexperienced John Adams, who was interested in using the case to test the entire principle of impressment. Hutchinson was a judge on the court and, being a practical man (and not a lawyer), was more interested in the fate of the defendant than the fate of impressment. Before final pleas could be entered, Hutchinson recessed the court and later issued a not-guilty verdict by virtue of self-defense. This infuriated Adams, who saw his chance to use Corbet's impressment as a test case disappear. Years later, when he was appointed chief justice of the Massachusetts General Court, Hutchinson earned a reputation for fair-mindedness and good judgment.

The Road to "Absolute Dementation"

Had British policy toward the American colonies not changed at the end of the French and Indian War, Hutchinson would have lived the orderly, comfortable life that so suited him. The inhabitants of Massachusetts were loyal to the mother country; local governance kept business and society on an even course. It was the ideal world in which to be a public official, but it was not to last.

The end of this period of "salutary neglect" marked the beginning of a new era of British innovations in colonial policy, intended to either extract greater revenues or impose more direct political control. There was little sympathy in Parliament and the British government for the American colonists, who were accounted to be a pack of ingrates who had made fortunes off government contracts and from illegal trading with Britain's enemies during the late war, even as the mother country had defended them at great cost in blood and treasure.

The first evidence of the new attitude in London appeared in the person of Francis Bernard, sent to Boston in 1760 to become the Bay Colony's new royal governor, with the charge of enforcing customs laws and tariffs already on the books. Bernard was nearing retirement and looked to his new assignment as easy duty and a way to feather his nest a bit after a long career of service. He had a large family to provide for, and Boston seemed the kind of place where good appointments could be found for his sons and suitable matches for his daughters. "I am assured," he wrote, "that I may depend upon a quiet and easy administration. . . . The people are well disposed to live upon good terms with the governor and with one another . . ." Bernard was accounted to be a no-nonsense fellow, not particularly sharp, but sharp enough to know that he would receive one-third of all contraband seized by customs officials under his authority. It was in his interest, therefore, to haul as many smugglers into court as possible and to have judges who would be sharp with the law. To that end he appointed Hutchinson, his lieutenant governor, to the post of chief justice. Every seizure and conviction improved the retirement prospects of the new governor.

The new British policy got its first set of real teeth with passage of the Sugar Act of 1764. New England was a center of rum distilling, which was based upon the importation of molasses from the Caribbean islands—an important source of the region's prosperity. The Sugar Act both revised the tariff on imported sugar and its derivative—molasses—and changed the way violators would be prosecuted. By tradition, customs transgressions were tried in common-law courts with local juries. It would seem from the record of these that colonial juries could neither see nor hear any evil, as convictions were scarce. Under the Sugar Act, however, smugglers were tried in vice admiralty courts before judges appointed by the Crown. These innovations were designed in London with neither the counsel nor consent of the colonists.

The Sugar Act and its enforcement made the Americans howl, particularly in New England, where the availability and price of molasses was critical to the rum distilling business. Massachusetts alone had sixty operating rum distilleries, and the British West Indies—the only source of *legal* molasses under the Sugar Act—could only supply about 25 percent of their requirements.[9] The more abundant and cheaper molasses of the French and Dutch islands was officially off limits. Politicians like Thomas Cushing, speaker of the Massachusetts House, opposed the act from a constitutional viewpoint, declaring that such parliamentary acts, contrived without colonial consent, "have a tendency to deprive the colonies of some of their most essential rights as British subjects." Leaders of the budding popular party—the lawyers—ranted and raved about the principle involved, and many ordinary citizens wondered about the growing numbers of British customs officials in their midst. The Sugar Act did not bring people into the streets. Britain had always taxed sugar imports, and most people were not involved with the rum business. Smuggling continued, and life went on.

Few realized that Hutchinson had opposed the Sugar Act from the very start. In a letter sent to Richard Jackson, the Bay Colony's London agent, Hutchinson was as critical as anyone of the legislation, and impressed on Jackson the damage it would do to the economy and how it should be opposed in London. Unfortunately, the lieutenant governor thought it best to make his view unofficial, lest his opposition to Crown policy be thought disloyal. This reluctance to personally oppose the official line was typical Hutchinson. Deference to authority, adherence to the chain of command, and reliance on logical discourse—speaking to the head and not the heart—were so part of his nature that it would not occur to him to personally and publicly oppose the British policy that so offended both him and his fellow colonists. This weakness, and his lack of leadership in publicly opposing the Sugar Act, were to cost him dearly; he would be seen as one of its supporters in the mind of the public.

The great mass of people are not easily provoked. They seldom make waves as long as they are fed and clothed and feel secure in their persons and occupations. This fact would explain the longevity of so many of the inept and banal regimes around the world, past and present, that have made life so unpleasant for so many for so long. Considering the oppressions and human miseries that prevailed elsewhere, the colonists of British America were among the least abused people on earth in the late eighteenth century. The ruckus over the Sugar Act was insufficient to move them to desperate measures. Hardly good candidates for riot, let alone revolution, they already held the reins to most of the government affairs that directly affected their lives and businesses; and royal control was generally benign. The issues that put them at odds with the mother country were more theoretical than tangible. By 1768, however, disorder within Boston would reach the point where royal customs agents had to seek refuge behind the walls of Castle William, and Governor Bernard sought a transfer, declaring that "the people seem to me in a state of absolute dementation."

Not content with the Sugar Act, Prime Minister George Grenville concocted yet another money-making scheme to pay off his government's debts: a tax on court documents, land titles, newspapers, legal contracts, and other printed materials. The idea of a stamp tax was not new. Indeed, it had been first levied in England in 1694, where it brought in the handsome sum of £290,000 each year. Extending this to the American colonies, it was reasoned, would raise enough to pay for the maintenance of the ten thousand redcoats stationed in North America.

Colonial leaders and their London agents voiced their opposition to the Grenville plan in the strongest terms. Parliament had never before laid a direct tax on the colonies—that had always been the prerogative of local assemblies. This Stamp Act would be a dangerous innovation, an alteration in the traditional relationship between the mother country and its colonial subjects. Benjamin Franklin told Grenville, "If you choose to tax us, then give us members in your Legislature, and let us be one People." That proposal went nowhere. Hutchinson counseled privately against the stamp tax; it would be stupid and dangerous and bound to cause outright defiance. He knew the public mood, and it would not accept an imposed tax.

In wrestling with the philosophical principals that underlaid the relationship between Parliament and colonies, Hutchinson reached the conclusion that the will of the King-in-Parliament was theoretically superior to that of the colonial legislatures. The colonists, he reasoned, had surrendered some of their rights as Englishmen when they left British shores. In return, they had received colonial charters and the protection of the Crown from the dangers that were all around them. To Hutchinson, Parliament had every right to pass such an act, but he was no theoretical purist. He could imagine what would be the result of a spitting contest between Parliament and the colonies over theoretical rights. It would only lead to big trouble. In a long letter sent to Richard Jackson, Hutchinson listed a number of practical reasons for not imposing a stamp tax, none of which challenged the authority of Parliament. His opposition to the Stamp Act was contained within this and other private communiques. Hutchinson's approach to dealing with the burning issues of the day was always with reason and logic, believing that one's opponents could be won over with carefully constructed arguments, generally delivered through personal letters. It was not his way to deal from the heart or harangue in public. Passion eluded him, but passion was what the times required. When the emotions have been inflamed, appeals to logic neither influence nor lead.

Prime Minister Grenville had plenty of warning that the Americans would never accept his new tax. Eager to put this constitutional issue to the test, he asked the House of Commons if anyone doubted the power and sovereignty of Parliament over its colonial dominions. If there were doubters they did not speak up.

The Stamp Act was passed in March 1765 with an overwhelming majority. Beginning November 1, 1765, a British stamp would have to be purchased and affixed to every manner of legal and printed documents. Violators would be tried in the vice admiralty courts. For good measure, Parliament passed the Quartering Act, requiring that the colonies provide housing and supplies for soldiers sent to their shores.

In May 1765 a ship arrived in Boston harbor with the details of the new tax act. It unleashed furies beyond anyone's imagination. It was a red-hot ember tossed heedlessly into a parched field. Unlike the Sugar Act, the stamps did not just affect importers, distillers, or New Englanders, it touched almost everyone in every colony. It was the one point of grievance that every disaffected colonist could get behind. In no time at all, disciplined street mobs were making the life of stamp agents impossible. Many resigned their commissions out of fear for their lives and property; many who did not were chased out of town. In August 1765 Boston's Sons of Liberty carried an effigy of the colony's stamp tax collector, Andrew Oliver—Hutchinson's in-law—through the city's narrow streets. After burning the effigy they proceeded to a new building owned by Oliver and gleefully destroyed it.

In most cities of British North America, patriot mobs maintained a not-so-subtle campaign of intimidation against anyone suspected of lacking the proper zeal in defiance of the Stamp Act. Anyone whose business or personal interests were linked with those of the British government was automatically targeted. Boston was a hotbed of these extralegal activities. On the night of August 26, 1765, while Lieutenant Governor Hutchinson and his family were having supper, a mob began bashing in the front door of his brick home—reported to be one of the finest in the city. He hustled his family and servants out the back door, instructing them to seek safety with a neighbor. Hutchinson was not a physical man, but he had a great deal of personal courage. He intended to stay behind and confront the invaders, but his daughter said that she would not leave without him. So together they exited through the back entry as the mob burst through the front.

The Hutchinson house was considered a "mansion": well appointed and filled with rich furnishings, books, and the lieutenant governor's unique collection of archives relating to the history of the Massachusetts Bay Colony. According to Hutchinson biographer, Bernard Bailyn,

> the rioters smashed in the doors with axes, swarmed through the rooms, ripped off wainscotting and hangings, splintered the furniture, beat down the inner walls, tore up the garden, and carried off into the night besides £900 sterling in cash, all the plate, decorations, and clothes that had survived, and destroyed or scattered in the mud all of Hutchinson's books and papers, including the manuscript of volume I of his History and the collection of historical papers that he had been gathering for years as the basis of a public archive.[10]

According to Governor Bernard, the mob worked through the night at dismantling the house. "The next day," he wrote, "the streets were found scattered with money, plate, gold rings, etc., which had been dropped in carrying off."

A day later, Thomas Hutchinson appeared in his courtroom without judicial robes, which had been lost to the mob, wearing a mismatch of clothing borrowed here and there. He recounted to the court the misfortune that had befallen him and his family. "I call my Maker to witness," he pleaded, that

> I never, in New England or Old, in Great Britain or America, neither directly nor indirectly, was aiding, assisting, or supporting, or in the least

promoting or encouraging what is commonly called the Stamp Act, but on the contrary did all in my power, and strove as much as in me lay, to prevent it. . . . I hope the eyes of the people would be opened, that they will see how easy it is for some designing, wicked men to spread false reports, raise suspicions and jealousies in the minds of the populace and enrage them against the innocent.

Although the vandals of Hutchinson's "mansion" were never officially identified or charged, the "designing, wicked men" who inflamed them were known in and about the city of Boston. The foremost of these incendiaries was Samuel Adams.

The Provocateur

To men and women of the loyalist party, Sam Adams was a "pimp" for James Otis—the opposition's most thoughtful and eloquent advocate—and a "journeyman scribbler" of provocative and baseless broadsides against the government. Peter Oliver described him as "all serpentine cunning. . . . He understood human Nature, in low life, so well, that he could turn the Minds of the great Vulgar as well as the small into any Course that he might chuse." Sam Adams was, indeed, the friend and provocateur of the working classes of Boston.

Adams's father had owned a malting business in the city from which he made enough to support his family in good style and send Sam to Harvard, where he studied history and law. The elder Adams was an enterprising man; he had started a land bank in the 1740s, in which he and hundreds of other merchants invested heavily. The bank issued paper currency backed by its own assets and the assets of its investors. The Parliament and many in the colony, however, feared the inflationary effects of paper money. Thomas Hutchinson was one of the most outspoken colonial critics of the land bank. Together, they succeeded in closing down the bank to the ruination of elder Adams and his fellow investors. Young Sam, then at Harvard, had been used to having his meals prepared and served to him in his private quarters, but after the bank closure he was forced to take his meals in the Commons, and even had to wait on tables to make ends meet. It was a humiliating experience for him, and he held a grudge against Hutchinson and British government for the rest of his life.

After Harvard, Sam Adams joined what was left of the family business, a brewery, if only for lack of anything else to do, but he seemed to have no knack for the trade. Within just a few years of the elder Adams's death, the brewery failed. In 1758, in need of steady income, Sam Adams became one of several tax collectors for Boston, having responsibility for three of the city's wards.

Adams may well be the only tax collector ever to have won the affections of his collectees. He achieved this through sheer dereliction of duty. He had an annual collection quota and was paid nine pence on every pound he collected; however, the records show that he never once met that quota.[11] By 1767 he was several thousand pounds in arrears and made it his practice to use the first payments of the new year to pay off his shortages from the old.

A creature of the wharfs and workshops, Adams haunted the city's labyrinth of narrow streets and crowded docksides. He knew the sailors and shopkeepers, the stevedores and fishmongers. He was most comfortable among the working class in their places of labor and entertainment. A natural politician, he made a point of being known to just about everyone in Boston—which in those days was not that hard to do. Aiding in this objective was his ability to move comfortably between the world of the working class and the more cultivated realm of the merchants and lawyers. That made him a unique character because it was the lawyers who would eventually develop the language and philosophy of separation from Britain, while the merchants would give it respectability. The masses would provide the muscle. Adams became an important link between these different elements of Boston society, and, in a sense, an eighteenth-century equivalent of the urban political boss. This unique position was not achieved overnight. Sam Adams spent nearly a decade pressing the flesh and developing a reputation as the man-in-the-street's defender against the elitists of the loyalist party and the presumptions of royal authority.

The image of Samuel Adams that comes down to us from nineteenth- and early-twentieth century historians is one of a troubled, neurotic man whose interests in politics had less to do with the rights of man than an escape "from his tiresome mental problems."[12] Others called him a professional agitator—a man who taught his dog, Queue, to bite Redcoats. During and after the Revolution, many claimed that Sam Adams had been bent upon the notion of American independence from the very beginning of his public career and that he used any real or imagined infringement of the colonists' rights as a pretext for whipping up resentment and rebellion. This was certainly the impression held by loyalists in London and New England. A closer look at the record, however, and at Adams's writing and correspondence, reveals a less demonical, more principled character, but still one dedicated to putting it to the British and their American friends at every opportunity.

To those who approved of the rebellion, Adams's reputation at home and abroad during the 1770s was immense, so much so that John Adams, in France during the war as the representative of the Continental Congress, always had to disappoint his French hosts that he was not in fact the "famous Adams," but merely his cousin.

Like most of America's revolutionary leaders, Sam Adams had not been bent on separation from Great Britain, but had only come to that course over time. Britain had held the colonies with such a loose leash for so long that every attempt to rein them in, to discipline them, or to impose taxes and penalties was viewed as a tyrannical infringement of longstanding rights. This was a slow process of progressive disaffection. The Sugar Act (1764), the Stamp Act (1765), the Townsend Act (1767) that took the governor and judges off the payroll of the assembly and into the direct pay of the Crown, the stationing of troops in Boston (1768), and so forth, all moved the process along. Whenever pushed, the colonists pushed back. By degrees, the shoving match moved closer and closer to a brawl, and Sam Adams was always there to cheer on his team. More than anyone in Massachusetts, Sam Adams understood the temper of the people and how to channel it. He saw his task as a popular leader to "keep the attention of his fellow citizens awake to their grievances; and not suffer them to be at rest, till the causes of their just complaints are removed."

Writing on the challenge of socialism to capitalism in the 1940s, economist Joseph Schumpeter said:

> Neither the opportunity of attack nor real or fancied grievances are in themselves sufficient to produce, however strongly they may favor, the emergence of active hostility against a social order. For such an atmosphere to develop it is necessary that there be groups to whose interest it is to work up and organize resentment, to nurse it, to voice it and to lead it.[13]

Samuel Adams played that role on the eve of the American Revolution—encouraging and organizing active hostility against Hutchinson and his masters. In keeping Bostonians "awake to their grievances," Adams was something of a master. He kept up a continual barrage of criticism and biting invective against Hutchinson and his supporters both in the Massachusetts House, of which he was a leading member and clerk, and in the popular press. He had, as John Galvin describes it,

> The eagle's eye for the slightest weakness or the phrase that can be turned around and used with sarcasm against the originator; the polite insolence couched in words of submission; the feigned righteous surprise at assertions made; the surface appearance of objectivity and calm while the fire shows through only too plainly; the lipservice to respect for authority is actually the target of attack.[14]

Bungling British ministers gave Adams plenty of opportunities to practice his craft. In fact, their inept handling of colonial affairs made it possible for Sam Adams to become a popular figure. Were it not for the Stamp Act, Adams would have remained a marginal local politician, an annoying crank, and his place in history confined to minor footnotes. The times were ripe for Adams's brand of political theatrics, however, and he rushed to grab the reigns of power over the Boston radicals and held them throughout the period of the Revolution. It is as if he anticipated Otto von Bismarck's remark that "we can only wait until we hear the footsteps of God in history and then leap forward and try to catch on to His coat-tails."

Adams's chosen instrument of attack was the printed word. Under a number of pen names—*Candidus* being a favorite—he used every opportunity to assail British policy, taxes, the behavior of its troops in New England—and most of all the suspected ill intents of Hutchinson and his party. His writings were enormously popular in Boston.

From the day the Stamp Act officially went into effect in November 1765, Boston became practically ungovernable. Unruly gangs of workers and street toughs destroyed the property of stamp agents and known sympathizers with the Crown, and intimidated anyone suspected of using stamps. Governor Bernard could do little but look forward to repeal of the Stamp Act and his own retirement from this madhouse of mobs and radicals. It was Hutchinson's bad luck to be in line for the governorship when Bernard did retire in 1770, and the next few years were, for him, a living nightmare. Tormented by the deteriorating situation and the furies around him, he pleaded to London to be allowed to turn his post over to someone else. His request was eventually granted, and Hutchinson and his daughter left Boston in June 1773 aboard the British ship *Minerva*. Governorship of the colony passed into the hands of military authorities, who stationed troops in the city, inviting still greater disorder and—eventually—armed rebellion. Ultimately, the incendiaries against whom Hutchinson had labored carried the day.

The Right Person at the Right Time

Tempestuous times call forth new leaders and usually retire old ones to the scrapheap. New leadership is not necessarily *better* or more humane, but more suited to the time.

Thomas Hutchinson was one of those leaders who would have done quite nicely by his constituents in a quieter time, but he was incapable of adapting to the post-1760 colonial world. Worse still, he was temperamentally disposed to identify change with social decline. In the end, his reserve, and his inability to evolve his thinking as rapidly as the pace of changing events, made him ill-equipped to survive the revolutionary times in which he lived. As Bailyn tells us, "He needed a stable world within which to work, a hierarchy to ascend, and a formal, external calibration by which to measure where he was."[15] The times demanded a different type of leader: not necessarily "a very good gentleman," but one with fire in his belly and in his heart. Hutchinson was the wrong man for the times, and he could not make himself to be otherwise.

We have all observed men and women in business life who have become victims of changing times: good *managers* who failed because good *leaders* were needed; dynamic leaders shoved out the back door because caretaker managerial skills had become more important. The same applies in politics: British voters brought in Winston Churchill in 1939 and followed his leadership to victory in World War II. When the war was over, so was the British love affair with Churchill, whose party went down in defeat. In late 1992, with forty years of Cold War over and done with, the American electorate cast aside President George Bush, a man whose views had been formed in an age of hot and cold war. Bush was a product of the years in which he matured. His views and his nature had naturally crystallized around his personal experience of war in the Pacific, the Soviet menace, nuclear standoff, and American dominance in the world economy. It was in the context of those events that Bush formed his opinions and values. But in a world without a nuclear arms race, in which American economic supremacy had faded, Bush was no longer a man for the times. Try as he did to project a keen personal interest in the concerns of frustrated working people in factories and urban centers, George Bush was too much a product of Phillips Andover, Yale, World War II, and the Cold War to convince the electorate to stick with him.

The problem for many corporations today is that so many of them are in transition from a long period of stability to a new period of instability—the same problem that confronted the Massachusetts Bay Colony in the 1760s and 1770s. Their top managers, like Thomas Hutchinson, have spent decades rising through positions that rewarded a set of skills that are no longer appropriate. Some management experts suggest that the process for grooming and selecting top managers should focus less on specific skills—like finance, marketing, or engineering—and less on years spent with the firm as well, but more on the individual's ability to cope with change.[16]

Farewell Forever

On March 17, 1776, almost a year after the first armed conflicts at Lexington and Concord, 170 vessels sailed out of Boston Harbor. Three British men-of-war hovered protectively nearby. The Continental Army under George Washington had effectively surrounded the city of Boston with cannon, making evacuation imperative. Some one thousand American loyalists, few of whom would ever see the land of their birth again, were aboard the ships with the soldiers.

As the ships cleared the harbor and the green islands that lay around it, they turned onto a northeasterly bearing for the British base at Halifax, Nova Scotia. Many on board must have speculated on the course of events that had so altered their lives and driven them to exile and on how intelligent and well-meaning leaders might have averted such a catastrophe.

8

Revitalizing Enterprise Through Innovation: English Arrows Defeat the Iron Men

Steed threatens steed, in high and boastful neighs
Piercing the night's dull ear; and from the tents
The armourers, accomplishing the knights,
With busy hammers closing rivets up,
Give dreadful note of preparation.

Shakespeare, *Henry V*

In August 1346, England's King Edward III was concluding a successful campaign against the French right in their own backyard. He had entered France with a small army to stake his claim to certain lands, and had proceeded with great success, and little opposition, through Normandy and almost to the walls of Paris. From there he headed north to link up with his Flemish allies. Along the way, at the rural village of Crécy, Edward was overtaken by a much larger French force. Estimates of this force range wildly, from Froissart's 120,000 to the more conservative figure of Edward himself of "more than 12,000 armed men of which 8,000 were gentlemen, knights and squires." His own force was probably about 8,000, of whom 5,000 were archers. The English were far from home, outnumbered, and without lines of support.

Forced to give battle, Edward had his supply carts drawn into a circle with all the horses placed inside. In defiance of medieval traditions, his entire force would fight on its feet, and its front line would be the yeomen archers.

Long hours of practice had made English and Welsh bowmen extremely effective. Edward's edicts made archery a compulsory hobby, and public competitions raised it to a respected art. Good archers could hit a human target at one-hundred meters; they could hit a formation target at three-hundred meters; and they could nock and deliver between ten and fifteen arrows per minute.[1] It is said that an English arrow could penetrate two to three inches of oak, which meant that it was capable of piercing chain mail and, if struck directly, some of the armor plate worn by knights and men-at-arms.

In the front line with the English archers at Crécy were pikemen, and behind them heavily equipped knights and men-at-arms, who wore chain mail and plate armor. To the rear on a hilltop, King Edward observed his formations and the empty field that lay before them. He watched as runners carried bundles of yard-long arrows from the circled supply carts to the lines of archers. With his rear protected by high ground and dense woodlands, he knew that the enemy force would attempt a frontal assault, and the bowmen would have to hold their ground.

When the French took the field late in the afternoon, they did so as a disorganized crowd. The great *fervetus* (ironclads), France's mounted knights, pushed with their horses toward the front. They were the nation's glory, and each man wanted to shine that day. The footmen who supported them were feudal levies, mostly conscripted within the past few days under the terms of traditional obligations. These crowded in behind the knights. Thousands more were congested upon the narrow road that led toward the battlefield. Unable to move forward, many despaired of ever getting into the fray.

Up to the very front of the French line marched a contingent of Genoese mercenary crossbowmen. The crossbow had been introduced in the twelfth century, and these men of Genoa had become masters in its deadly use. A skilled operator could get off two well-aimed bolts each minute, and these traveled at such high velocity that even heavy armor could be pierced. The nobility complained bitterly about the crossbow because its great penetrating power made it possible for a lowly poltroon to bring down the bravest knight, a possibility that did not square with the then current concept of valor and comparative worth. The Catholic Church forbade the use of this weapon by Christians fighting other Christians, but this restriction was largely ignored. Despite its fearsome reputation, the crossbow's slow rate of fire and the failure of commanders to utilize it with tactical imagination condemned the device to a marginal role on the battlefield.

The Genoese usually placed large wooden shields in front of their positions as shelter against incoming missiles. On this day, however, the shields were on carts still tied up in the traffic far to the rear, so the crossbowmen took up their forward positions without them.

Upon a signal from the French commander, the Genoese cranked up their crossbows and let their bolts fly at the English, but this first volley fell short. Before they could reload and advance into range, the English archers unleashed a barrage that must have appeared like a dark swarm of hornets lofting into the sky, hanging there briefly before raining down with a thousand hissing voices. Another volley followed within seconds—and another, and another.

The Genoese tumbled by the hundreds. Without armor or shelter they were totally defenseless against the murderous rain of English arrows. The few unscathed among them fled in terror toward the French lines, and the wounded crawled off where they could.

Impatient for glory, the pride of France, spurred their chargers forward, stampeded through the remnants of their Genoese hirelings, and rumbled in a wave of horses and men and iron toward the English front. Their plan was simple and conventional: smash through the English line in a powerful frontal assault. The shock power of armored men on heavy warhorses moving at speed would break their formations and force them to scatter, at which point they could be cut down like wheat with broadswords and axes.

As the first line of horsemen approached the middle of the field, however, it was struck by the same deadly storm of missiles that had devastated the Genoese. The rounded surfaces of armor successfully deflected most English arrows, but chain mail, flat metal surfaces, and open helmets did not. The horses were the most vulnerable. They were hit repeatedly and fell with their riders, or they bellowed and ran off in panic. Once downed, the knights were practically helpless against the English footmen who ran out to slaughter them with daggers and axes.

Over the course of nearly two hours the French sent fifteen

separate mounted assaults against the English line, but each was beaten back with terrible loses. Only the gathering darkness and a mist that settled over the battlefield halted the slaughter.

The next day a count was made of the victims of Crécy, and it was reported to Edward that some 16,000 Frenchmen had perished, and that he had lost about 300. Even discounting for exaggeration, this made the battle one of the most lopsided military outcomes in Western history. The defeat was so enormous for France that almost every noble family was directly touched by the disaster.

Edward's victory was based upon innovative tactics developed over years of border warfare with the Scots and Welsh, during which the use of the longbow was introduced and perfected. Military archers had been employed in the Western world for over two thousand years, but the English made a major technological improvement in both the equipment and its tactical use in the field.

The English longbow was of Welsh origin. Usually made from yew or elm, it has been described as being the height of a man (scarcely over five feet at the time). This length gave the projectile greater range (twice that of the shorter bow employed on the Continent), improved accuracy, higher velocity, and greater penetrating power. More important, English commanders learned from their own painful experiences with the rebellious Welsh just how effective longbows could be against the prevailing military technology of the day: the armored horseman.

The knight on horseback was the M1A tank of the Middle Ages. His heavy armor, field mobility, and powerful weapons made him largely invulnerable to lightly armed yeomen conscripts. He could tear great holes through their formations, creating panic and flight. The rise of the mounted warrior was itself the result of a technical innovation. According to medievalist Lynn White, Jr., the introduction to Europe in the eighth century of the stirrup from India made it possible for the armed rider to become one with his horse and to deliver a blow, not with the strength of his own arm, but with the far greater power of the horse.[2] This power elevated the role of the mounted warrior from flanking and reconnaissance (as in Roman military traditions) to that of central player. Over time, the new military power of the mounted fighter was mirrored by economic and political power and by the formation of the elite knightly class at the top level of society.

People who see themselves as a special class quickly develop their own mythology and sense of self-importance. This was true of the European knightly class, which developed the elaborate cult of chivalry, with its rituals, literature of courtly love, and tradition of warrior values. Not surprisingly, chivalry reached its highest level among the French. It was the French, after all, who first demonstrated the value of the mounted horseman and developed his potential as a fighting machine. The Byzantine princess Anna Comena declared that "a Frank on horseback is invincible." They were clearly the best in Europe; therefore, when the pope appealed for a crusade against the infidels, he came first to the French. The knights of France had a long tradition to be proud of, and they embraced it tightly. Chivalry was the lens through which the feudal nobility perceived their world and, especially during the late Middle Ages, that lens effectively filtered out realities about society and technology that conflicted with their pride and worldview. The slaughter of French knights at Crécy by peasant archers was just that kind of unacceptable reality, and by all the evidence, they filtered it out.

There is little doubt that massed archery was the principal cause of France's disastrous defeat at Crécy—even greater than their own lack of strategy and coordination. England's tactical combination of archers with men-at-arms was an innovation that successfully challenged the military technology of the time in continental Europe. In the face of this challenge, how did the French respond? The evidence indicates that they did not adopt massed archery in the reform of their own forces. To do so would be to give ground to the idea that a peasant in a leather helmet with a bunch of slender arrows in his belt was in some way a match for his social superior. The cult of chivalry and the unbending pride of the nobleman would not open the door an inch to that idea. This corresponds with contemporary observations about the resistance to new technology in the industrial workplace. In what is now become a classic article in the *Harvard Business Review,* Paul Lawrence remarked that the resistance of workers to change was more due to the altered social arrangements that the technology would provoke than to the technology that would come into their lives. Downgrading the central role of the knight in favor of peasant archers and placing them in the front ranks as the English had done, would have altered social arrangements in feudal society, and the iron men of France would have none of it.

Instead of adopting the new military technology for themselves, the French merely invested more deeply in what they already had, and what had worked so well for them in the past. Over the ensuing decades, the French knight thus became more heavily armored. Chain mail was gradually eliminated in favor of armor plate; and armor plate was made thicker in critical areas. Open helmets were replaced with visored helmets. War horses received their own iron plating in vulnerable parts. Encouraged by their noble patrons, the armorers of Europe continued to make incremental advances in their art into the early sixteenth century— fully two hundred years after the Battle of Crécy—and well into the period when firearms had rendered armor totally obsolete. Their improvements in the old technology of shock warfare made the knight only slightly less vulnerable to archery, but they also made him slower and even more ungainly. No changes in tactics were established, reminding us of the comment of Robert Haas that "it's difficult to unlearn behavior that made us successful in the past." [3]

England and France had an opportunity to test each other again a decade after Crécy at the Battle of Poitier. Here, English forces under Edward's son, the Black Prince, again decimated the armored pride of France with a cloud of stinging arrows.

Fifty-nine years later, in October 1415, these rivals met in yet another major duel when Henry V, England's young and ambitious monarch, entered France to press his claims to territory and royal status. Like Edward almost seventy years earlier, Henry came with a small force and enjoyed initial success—taking the fortified coastal city of Harfleur—and proceeded into the interior of France before turning northward toward the safety of English-held Calais.

Each day of the long march to Calais, however, drained away some of the strength of Henry's band. Weakened by casualties, dwindling supplies, dysentery, and continuous chilling rains, the small English army found itself in a very tight spot. Its foragers found no provisions in the countryside along the line of march— cattle and foodstuffs were all removed to safety. Worse still, a large French army began shadowing its movements and grew larger and more menacing each day as new and enthusiastic recruits arrived. Before long the French force had grown to four times the size of Henry's dispirited band, and near the village of Agincourt it maneuvered into a position that effectively blocked Henry's line of march to the haven of Calais.

With the French host barring his route and with rations practically gone, Henry had no choice but to give battle. Exhausted, starving, and vastly outnumbered, few of Henry's men expected to see England again. The archers in particular dreaded what lay ahead as the French threatened to cut off the thumb, forefinger, and middle finger from the right hand of any captured bowman.

Henry took the initiative on the morning of the battle, moving his force out onto the rain-soaked field that divided the two armies, organizing formations of bowmen and men-at-arms behind bristling rows of sharpened poles so placed as to form a barrier to charging horsemen. The French host, already in ranks, observed this from a distance and anxiously awaited the signal to sweep their enemy from the field. Eager to be in the front ranks and to participate in the glory that the new day would bring, many had armed themselves before daybreak and mounted their war horses, which now sank ankle-deep into the mud. It must not have appeared to be much of a contest. As Shakespeare would say through the Constable of France to his bold companions: "Do but behold yon poor and starved band, and your fair show shall suck away their souls, leaving them but the shales and husks of men."

At last the signal spread among the host of France, and the first wave of ironclads moved forward across the mucky turf—first at a trot, then at full tilt. Following the example of their forebearers at Crécy and Poitiers, the English archers waited stoically and when the range was right released a succession of lofting volleys into the packed ranks of the advancing enemy.

> They triumpyd up full meryly,
> The grete batalle togder yede.
> Our achiers shotte full hertyly,
> And made Frensshmen faste to blede.
> There arwes wente full good sped,
> Our enemyes therwith doun gon falle,
> Thorugh brestplate, habirion, and bassonet yede.
> Slayne there were a thousand on a rowe alle.[4]

Horses and men tumbled under a blizzard of English missiles. Those who did not fall raced forward with leveled lances. As at Crécy, few of these succeeded in reaching the English line; and those who did were quickly isolated and dispatched by men-at-arms and pikemen. Each succeeding wave of horsemen followed the same script and met with the same disaster, often running squarely into the panicked retreat of the preceding wave.

Agincourt proved to be yet another grossly lopsided victory for the English. Henry lost less than 150 men to an estimated 6,000 of his enemies. The cream of French chivalry—the great grandsons of those who had fallen at Crécy—were piled up like cord wood in front of his line. In continuing the string of French disasters, Agincourt demonstrated the tenacity with which the nobility clung to the technologies and tactics that had accounted for past glories, even in the face of overwhelming evidence that their usefulness had long since faded. Their stubborn resistance to change brings to mind the modern warning, "When faced with a steam-rolling technology, you either become part of the technology or a part of the road."[5]

Innovation and Cycle of Institutional Rise and Decline

Even the most casual observer of everyday life must be struck by the ebb and flow of human energy, by the inexorable cycle of growth, maturity, and decline that is part and parcel of the organic world and human affairs. The military power of France—which had dominated Europe for two centuries—was first eclipsed by the more innovative English at the Battle of Crécy, and it would remain so for almost one hundred years. In the business world, success is likewise fleeting; longterm survivors are few and far between. In celebrating its seventieth year in circulation, *Forbes* magazine published a list of the one hundred largest U.S. companies at the time of its first issue in the early 1920s. These were the most powerful, the best financed, and most dynamic organizations of their day. Of the original one hundred, only twenty-one were recognizable seventy years later. In their place were firms that, for the most part, did not even exist at the time of the original listing. Many of the newcomer firms were based upon technologies and products beyond the imagination of thinkers seventy years before. What, then, will be the fate of these new and successful firms in future decades? Will the stock pages of the mid-twenty-first century contain the names of Hewlett-Packard, Sony, Xerox, IBM, Kodak, AT&T, 3M, or Boeing?

These questions suggest others about the vitality and energy that propels organizations toward dominance in the first place. What vital force energizes business organizations and other institutions? Where does it come from? Where does it go? What part does technological innovation play in the process?

Among historians, the focus of that question has traditionally been at the level of civilizations, and the most noted prober was Edward Gibbon, the eighteenth-century scholar whose *The Decline and Fall of the Roman Empire* was a great success when published and which remains widely known today, even if seldom read.

The history of the Roman world from its early days as a virtuous, quasi-democratic city-state, through the long period when the Roman Eagle spread its wings over an orderly and flourishing civilization of many nations, and ultimately through the wrenching centuries of dissipation and decline, has fascinated Westerners since Renaissance time. To Gibbon and his many readers the story was gripping—and relevant.

Like Rome, Gibbon's society had created its own empire. By 1776, the year of *The Decline*'s first publication, Britain was a modern maritime power. Like the youthful Roman republic, it was quasidemocratic and sure of its virtue. Whereas the Romans built roads to the far reaches of the known world, the British built ships and established sea-lanes to the last of the globe's hidden places. As Rome's legionnaires and administrators had done before them, the sons of Britannia carried their language, laws, and culture with them. To Gibbon and his contemporaries the parallels between the British Empire and Roman civilization in her glory were clear and disturbing. What was troubling, of course, was what might lie in store for Britain; hence, Gibbon's interest in the dynamics of Rome's decline and the great success of his book in the late eighteenth century.

In Gibbon's time Britain had come very far very fast. Through its victory in the Seven Years' War (1754–1760), it had established itself as a world power of the first order, largely at the expense of France and Spain. It found itself with vast colonies in North America, prospering plantation economies in the Caribbean, and trading posts scattered through Africa and Asia. This was heady stuff for a small island nation that for centuries had existed as a loose appendage to the main trunk of European power and culture. The question that must have puzzled Gibbon and other thinkers of his time was: Could Britain sustain this?

By the time of *The Decline*'s publication, cracks in the foundation of empire were already visible. The Seven Years' War had saddled Britain with enormous debts and the expense of maintaining the defense of farflung colonies. Its bungled attempts to have the American colonists pay their fair share had already resulted in rebellion and costly warfare. By all appearances, Britain's time of greatness would be short-lived.

Gibbon never developed a seamless theory for the rise and decline of Rome, but he did ascribe the fortunes of that great empire to a few intuitively appealing ideas. The first was that the greatness of Rome originated in its *esprit général* [6] (i.e., the faithfulness of its citizens to its institutions, to their sense of honor, and to each other). This was Rome's vital force. As long as it had this *esprit* it was strong. But Rome's *esprit,* according to Gibbon, was corrupted through immoderate growth, the debasement of its republican virtues, and by the infiltration of alien religions—especially Christianity. Its borders expanded outward to include peoples and religions that had no shared values with Rome, and "the victorious legions, who in distant wars acquired the vices of strangers and mercenaries, first oppressed the freedom of the republic, and afterwards violated the majesty of the purple." [7]

The British Experience

As it happened, Gibbon's contemporaries never had to come face to face with national decline in their lifetimes. The fortunes of their nation actually took a turn for the better. The Industrial Revolution just taking hold in Britain in the late 1700s gained in strength over the next century, adding immeasurably to the nation's wealth, and making it the leading manufacturer on earth. Industrialization gave the British Empire a whole new lease on life.

By the 1870s, however, it was observed that this new engine of vitality had begun to sputter. Between the 1870s and World War I, the lead of Britain over other nations was narrowed in some industries and eliminated in others. Prosperity continued in terms of national and per capita income, but Britain's share of world commerce slipped dramatically. Production of steel, coal, and manufactured goods all rose, but those of its rivals—Germany, the United States, France, and even Japan—rose at a much greater rate. Between 1890 and 1907, British steel output rose from 3.6 to 6.5 million tons. U.S. output, however, exploded from 4.3 to 23.4 million tons in the same period. Even German steel grew fivefold to almost double British steel production. [8]

More striking was the loss of world manufacturing market share during roughly the same period (Table 8.1).

Imports outstripped exports during this period, and many worried that the nation was living off its capital, financing its trade shortfall through the sale of securities.

Table 8.1.   Percentage of World
Manufacturing Market Share

	U.S.	Germany	Great Britain
1870	23.3	13.2	31.8
1913	35.8	15.7	14.0

Source: League of Nations, *Industrialization and
Foreign Trade* as cited in Aron Friedberg's *The
Weary Titan* (see note 3).

Princeton's Aron L. Friedberg gives us a inside look at the
mind and mood of British leaders during this era in his fine book,
The Weary Titan. The book explains how they first perceived that
the worm was turning, how they tried to understand their shifting
fortunes with the limited economic data then at their disposal, and
how they dealt with it. In 1882, we learn, a Cambridge professor
named John Seeley predicted that the giant land-mass states of
Russia and the United States would soon "surpass in power the
states now called great," just as the rising nation-states of the sixteenth century surpassed Renaissance Florence. In 1886 a government commission issued a report pointing out that Britain must
naturally decline relative to other nations because of its original
lead in industrialization. Economist Alfred Marshall saw the diffusion of technology to previously nonindustrialized nations and
Britain's own complacency with respect to new manufacturing
techniques as the principal villains.

It is clear from Friedberg's description of the times that the
British did not just wake up one morning to the fact that their
foreign competitors had edged them out. The progress of decline
was widely sensed even as it happened, it was measured with the
crude economic statistics of the time, and its causes and potential
cures were hotly debated. Books like Ernest William's *Made in
Germany* and F. McKenzie's *The American Invaders* sold well.

Joseph Chamberlain, a Conservative minister of Parliament, also
observed the advances of these nations and noted how they and
other countries, which had once been export markets, had systematically thrown up trade barriers (tariffs) to keep British goods
out. These countries, he complained, were now shipping their own
agricultural and manufactured products to Britain, where they
competed for domestic consumption. Passage of the Merchandise
Marks Act (1887), which required all foreign-made goods sold in
Britain to identify their origin, made clear to the person in the

street just how deeply these foreign products had penetrated the home market. In a 1904 speech, Chamberlain voiced a concern that would echo American sentiment near the end of the century:

> Whereas at one time England was the greatest manufacturing country, now its people are more and more employed in finance, in distribution, in domestic service. . . . I think it is worthwhile to consider—whatever its immediate effects may be—whether that state of things will not be the destruction ultimately of all that is best in England, all that has made us what we are, all that has given us prestige and power in the world.[9]

Chamberlain called for an economic federation tying the British world together. The British Isles, Australia, Canada, New Zealand, the Cape Colony, and other imperial holdings would form a scattered land mass, population, and common market large enough to maintain British prominence among nations. They would trade freely among themselves and retaliate against foreign trade barriers when necessary with barriers of their own. Like many of his contemporaries, Chamberlain understood that his nation was undergoing relative decline, but they saw its causes as external.

Britain, however, was a laissez-faire, free-trade nation—the land of Adam Smith and David Ricardo. The idea of trade barriers was as great an anathema to many of Chamberlain's contemporaries as was the idea of Queen Victoria doing housework. These antiprotectionists fought Chamberlain and his fellow-travelers tooth and claw. For them, the problem of relative decline had internal causes that could be remedied through better education, improved manufacturing methods, and the greater application of science to industry. "Above all," said one leading antiprotectionist, "we have to educate and encourage intelligence, adaptability, and diligence in all ranks of the commercial hierarchy."[10]

In the end, Britons concerned with the state of their once-mighty economy sorted themselves out into three groups: one that believed that the evidence of their relative decline was inconclusive; another that called for trade barriers against foreign competitors; and a still larger body that was not sure what to think. Not much was done, and time and events, and two great wars, led the nation on a long down hill slide from international power and prominence.

Had Britain lost its *esprit?* Or, as Marshall noted, had its competitors merely learned its techniques and practiced them more successfully?

We do know that British science and manufacturing technology was learned and widely copied throughout the eighteenth and nineteenth centuries. America's Industrial Revolution began in New England with the textile industry, which drew freely on British methods. It drew so freely, in fact, that twentieth-century Americans who complain about foreign competitors stealing their intellectual property and copying their manufacturing processes should know that their ancestors were themselves pioneers in the business of industrial shoplifting.

One of the founding spirits of American industrialism was Francis Cabot Lowell, who toured the mills of Scotland and England in 1811. Well educated, bright, and personable, Lowell made a good impression on his hosts, who were so flattered by his interest in their textile machines and methods of operations that they were only too pleased to explain everything to him. Every night in his hotel room, Lowell wrote down what he had learned that day and made sketches of the equipment and factory layouts he had seen. On returning to the United States, he and two partners formed the Boston Manufacturing Company. They opened their first plant in 1814 in Waltham, Massachusetts, based largely on his detailed notes.[11]

In the decades that followed, mechanics, artisans, and machine builders were lured from British mills by better opportunities and higher pay in America, despite laws prohibiting the export of textile machinery and the emigration of skilled workers. These émigrés formed a cadre around which the development of the American textile industry was organized. That industry made a number of important advances in manufacturing techniques, and by the 1860s New England textiles displaced British manufactures in the American market and enjoyed growing exports of their own.

Scientific knowledge, technology, and technical know-how are things we can have, but not things we can hold. The British experience makes that clear. A century later American industrialists learned the same lesson as world-class capabilities in automaking, steel, textiles, and electronics began springing up in Japan and a number of undeveloped Asian nations during the 1970s and 1980s. Today, Japan is discovering that its own revolutionary production processes and management methods can be duplicated elsewhere. Holding technologies and methods too tightly may not be a good idea in any case because these are eventually outmoded by newer technologies and methods.

Technological Innovation and Industrial Vitality

During the early 1980s James Utterback, a professor at MIT, completed a study for the National Science Foundation on the dynamics of industrial innovation. With advanced degrees in both engineering and management, and inspired by an association with Harvard's late William Abernathy, Utterback developed a curiosity about product and process innovations: in particular, how they first enter the competitive marketplace dominated by older technologies and how some survive and flourish, eventually displacing the dominant technologies.

Utterback's research took him into library stacks generally off the beaten path for engineers and management scholars. In examining industries dominated by technologies that had run their full cycle—from inception to dominance to decline—he found himself reading about such arcane subjects as the harvested ice business, the early typewriter, gas lighting, and the history of photography, among others. These represented industries that had completed the cycle of innovation, maturation, and, in most cases, decline. He found patterns that, for him, suggested a useful model for explaining how the technologies of today often end up in the dustbin of the future—along with the corporations that base their businesses on them. Professor Utterback's work helps us to think more deeply about this process, and provides a useful bridge between broader concerns of why civilizations and nations decline, and narrower curiosity about the fate of particular industries and firms. [12]

Utterback's work with William Abernathy led him to a model about how useful technological innovations enter the marketplace, how they perfect themselves and gain market adherence, and how their perfectability becomes marginal over time. He describes this in the form of the familiar S curve, shown in Figure 8.1. The new technology in this case appears as a crude innovation developed to meet some particular need. It enjoys little attention at first, perhaps because it is new, perhaps because it is a crudely fashioned solution to the need it serves. If it takes root, however, there is some likelihood that it will be perfected and more widely recognized and accepted. This leads to still greater performance improvement (the steeply sloping center of the curve) and a lowering of costs. The typewriter, the computer, and even the automobile provide good examples of this process. Early models of each were crude contraptions with many operational constraints, and each

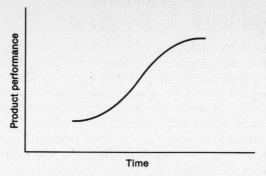

Figure 8.1 The Introduction and Improvement of
a New Technology. (*Source:* James M. Utterback
and Linsu Kim, "Invasion of a Stable Business by
Radical Innovation," in Paul Kleindorfer, ed., *The
Management of Productivity and Technology in
Manufacturing,* 1985. Used with permission.)

served a very limited market. Each rapidly became more service-
able, however, and addressed the needs of a broader market.

The idea of the *S* curve is that performance improvements in
a technology increase rapidly at first, but become marginal and
increasingly expensive over time. If you consider the technical history of the internal combusion engine, for example, an invention
of the late nineteenth century, you recognize that its days of rapid
performance improvements are well behind it—that current and
future tinkering with design and engineering will add fewer and
fewer increments of performance. On the other hand, the *S* curve
for personal computing through today's technology may be still in
its rapid growth phase. Logically it, too, will reach a point where
further progress slackens.

According to Utterback's model, and examples provided by
author-consultant Richard Foster,[13] new technologies are always
entering the marketplace, often in competition with mature technologies that serve the same need. Consider the piston aircraft engine. This engine technology underwent steady improvement from
the days of the Wright brothers through World War II; it only
encountered a serious challenge when jet engine technology was
introduced in the late 1940s. Both technologies existed to do the
same thing: to move airplanes through the sky. By the 1950s,
however, piston-powered technology had just about reached the
end of its rope while the potential of the new jet engine technology had decades of significant improvements ahead of it.

Utterback's insight into this *S* curve model of technology was his observation that those who embrace a mature technology—whose minds and fortunes are bound to it—usually react to a new competitive technology in predictable and disfunctional ways. Faced with a competing innovation, they seldom switch over to it; they are far too vested in the technology that made them successful in the first place. Like the knights of medieval France, they invest in efforts to enhance the performance of their current technology. By redoubling their efforts, the keepers of an established technology almost always increase the performance of that technology and continue enjoying market share and profits—at least for a while. Utterback cites the great performance improvements in gas lighting that occurred when the threat of Thomas Edison's incandescent electric lighting system spurred the gas industry to improve its own system. In this case, the innovation of a gas mantle improved the illuminating power of gas by a factor of five times in a single stroke. Unfortunately, each success in improving the performance of a mature technology merely convinces the firm that lives off that technology to hold its course—a course that leads to a dead end.

Meanwhile, new technologies have the potential to improve by great strides and, at the margin, relatively small costs. One can imagine the plight of the piston aircraft engine designers in the late 1940s, charged with making order of magnitude improvements in a technology that was already mature and near the limits of its inherent perfection. Figure 8.2 plots the life cycle of an older, established technology against that of an invading rival. As shown, the old technology increases its performance, even as the new technology is introduced. It cannot sustain rapid improvement, however, and the old gives way to the new, which is rapidly improving performance and lowering costs. In the long run, the new technology takes away market share and profits from the old. Firms that fail to make the bold leap from the old technology to the new ride the curve to obsolescence.

This may explain why so few successful technology-based enterprises survive over any great length of time. It is what management consultant Richard Pascale has called the "paradox of success." In an interview with *Industry Week* he remarked that "whether you're talking about a successful person or a successful company, there is an almost inescapable paradox that nothing fails like success."[14] Consider for only a moment the remarkable reversal of fortunes experienced by GM over the past two decades. In 1970,

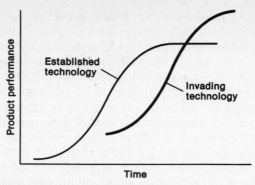

Figure 8.2 An established technology challenged, and then surpassed by an invading technology. (*Source:* James M. Utterback and Linsu Kim, "Invasion of a Stable Business by Radical Innovation," in Paul Kleindorfer, ed., *The Management of Productivity and Technology in Manufacturing*, 1985. Used with permission.)

GM enjoyed 50 percent of the rich and expanding North American auto market. Since the days of Alfred Sloan, it dominated its competitors and GM leaders could justifiably say that they truly defined the auto business: in design, distribution, pricing—all the rules of competitive engagement. Its competitors—all domestic firms—were weak followers of GM's lead. The company developed a mythology about itself and its know-how. This self-congratulatory mythology is typical among those who enjoy long-term institutional leadership. GM seldom brought in fresh blood from the outside, and it even established its own training institute to pass on the GM approach to business and auto making to promising employees. When the challenge to its dominance came in the 1970s, GM predictably failed to meet it with anything but "more of the same." When the driving public first demanded smaller, more advanced, and fuel-efficient cars, GM responded with downsized versions of its traditional vehicles. (To its credit, GM eventually made dramatic improvements and even launched a world-class small car company—Saturn—but it was fifteen year before these improvements were visible on the street.)

Decline Is Not Preordained

A number of prominent scholars have addressed the issue of rise and decline at different levels—some at the level of the nation, others at the level of the entire civilization. At the national level, economist Mancur Olson published *The Rise and Decline of Nations* in 1982, in which he argued that firms and interest groups in stable nations ultimately establish collusive, cartelistic, and lobbying organizations whose activities sap the efficiency and dynamism of their economies, causing them to lag behind other nations in economic growth. [15] This process, according to Olson, worsens over time unless some social upheaval (war, revolution, economic collapse, etc.) destroys these self-serving interests and the gridlock they impose upon the economic life of society.

The economic sclerosis that Olson described at the level of the national economy certainly has its parallel at the level of the individual firm where union work rules, white collar bureaucracies, and entrenched corporate nabobs collectively contribute to the kinds of inefficiencies and lost vitality that only a crisis or massive reorganization has a chance of reforming. This is just the sort of situation in which most mature American industrial firms found themselves in the 1980s and 1990s; the massive layoffs, plant closures, and restructurings of the past decade are the bitter medicine that will make it possible for these firms to regain their lost vitality and restart the engine of growth.

Oswald Spengler was among the scholars for whom the unit of analysis was the entire civilization. His two-volume work, *The Decline of the West,* published in the period 1918–1922, made a great impression on thoughtful readers numbed by the horrors of World War I. Spengler had a simple life-cycle model of growth, maturity, and decline. To him, civilization in the West had reached the apex of its growth and energy; it had achieved a mature stage of material well-being beyond which the only future was irreversible decline. Spengler's theory would apply as equally to a civilization as it would to a bowl of fruit: Both would inevitably ripen and rot. The theory had plenty of intuitive appeal to those who had lived through the first half of the twentieth century, and it was surely a great source of assurance to Marxists everywhere. The tragic spectacle of Europe weakened and torn asunder by two world wars and the gradual evaporation of European colonial empires seemed dramatic proof of Spengler's gloomy, deterministic hypothesis. Soviet and Asian Communists could confidently gloat that the future was theirs. Unfortunately for them, the dramatic economic resurgence of Europe in the post–World War II era and the disintegration of both Third World and Marxist states has been hard to square with the theory. Spengler's *Decline of the West* is read more today for its historical interest than as a guide to the present or the future. Only a handful of holdouts in lunatic asylums and on university campuses fail to recognize how the world has changed, and how Western values and the capability of its institutions for self-reform have demonstrated their resilience.

Arnold Toynbee, the late English historian, had a more dynamic view than did Spengler. In his six-volume *A Study of History,* Toynbee surveyed twenty-six civilizations that have risen and—except for our own—fallen into decline. In his *Study of History* he sought the common weakness, external force, or failure of internal spark that drove these civilizations into decline, but he found none. For Toynbee there was no spark, no force to account for this phenomenon, only a process of environmental challenge and response. In a growing civilization, Toynbee wrote, challenges are met with successful responses, which proceed to generate still different challenges and responses. If a civilization produces leaders who can creatively and appropriately respond to environmental challenge, he reasoned, then it will continue to flourish. If a challenge appears that is too great or if the response is weak or inappropriate, then the process of decline is set into motion.

Thus, the civilization that perceives threats to its integrity and that meets those threats with thoughtful and resourceful countermeasures need not be doomed to the scrapheap. Europe met that test more than once with regard to Islamic expansionism; and modern western Europe and America have successfully risen to the challenge of Soviet communism during our lifetime. Rome did the same in the second century A.D. when it produced a series of effective emperors. Japan, beginning in the 1860s, provides a striking example of how a society was seriously challenged—in this case, by the technologically advanced Western nations—and responded by adopting those Western scientific, industrial, and military forms that would put it on a competitive footing.

Survival at the Firm Level

Toynbee's theory has never been supported by scholars owing to the nonempirical approach he took to his sweeping study. Nevertheless, the concept of "challenge and response" has a great deal of intuitive appeal as well as a certain utility at the microlevel (i.e., as a way of explaining the longevity of individual enterprises). A good case in point is Motorola, the giant U.S. electronics firm, which has grown and prospered at a time when many other American firms in that industry are being soundly beaten by foreign competitors. Its vitality and success over long time periods is due to the effective management of change—in effect, challenge and response. Former Chairman Robert Galvin, in a speech to a Boston business gathering in 1990, related how his father, who preceded him as head of Motorola, had viewed fourteen other firms to be serious contenders in Motorola's business and markets in the 1940s. From the perspective of 1990, Galvin noted that none of those fourteen companies were any longer competitors. Many had gone out of business; others had lost their edge or had drifted into other markets. How has Motorola stayed off of the list of has-beens? Galvin explained that the firm has developed teams of forward scanners, groups of scientists and engineers who make it part of their daily business to look outward toward the firm's markets, its competitors, and the world of technology. It is their task to look for anything that could threaten their current businesses or that could identify the new directions their businesses should follow. With that knowledge, the organization is charged with making a credible response.

As early as 1970, James R. Bright advocated something quite similar, which he simply termed *monitoring*. His method called for more than simplistic scanning and accumulation of data; instead, he advocated consideration of alternative possibilities. "The feasibility of monitoring," Bright wrote, "rests on the fact that it takes a long time for a technology to emerge from the minds of men into an economic reality with its resulting societal impacts." [16] Bright's advice was to:

- search the environment for signals of the forerunners of significant technological change;
- assume that the signals are based on substance, and identify possible consequences;
- determine which aspects of the environment should be observed and measured to verify the speed and direction of the new technology; and
- report the information to management in a timely manner. [17]

The missing element in Bright's otherwise good advice is the requirement that management use this information to form an appropriate response.

Over the decades, Motorola has made the appropriate responses to change that have kept it current in technology and products. Since its founding in the late 1920s, the firm has regularly abandoned product markets in which it had created considerable success, jumping from car radios to two-way radios, to solid-state televisions, to microprocessers, to pagers, and to cellular phones. This willingness to abandon established positions is perhaps its best insurance for future survival. A younger member of the Galvin clan, Christopher Galvin, once remarked, "We know that change will shape our future, but adaptability to change will determine it. We expect unique technology surprises in the 1990s. We don't know what it *[sic]* will be, but somewhere out there is going to be a pony to ride." [18]

Motorola's most valuable survival tool, however, may be its tradition of open dissent, which allows workers, engineers, and managers to argue publicly with their bosses about products, processes, and new directions for the firm. Employees can file a minority report when ideas they consider valuable to the firm are unsupported by their colleagues and by their immediate superiors. These reports are read higher up in the Motorola chain of command, and many have resulted in major new and profitable product initiatives. [19]

Lessons for Leaders and Managers

"Challenge and response" is a useful way for leaders and managers of businesses and public institutions to think through the problems of vitality and survival. It begins with an assessment of the external challenges, moves to self-assessment and self-criticism, and logically ends with a resolution to develop effective responses to change. Every major firm that has lived a long and healthy life and every one that has struggled back from the slippery slope of decline has passed through these phases. Motorola, Hewlett-Packard, 3M, and Corning are firms that seem to have institutionalized some form of this process. Others, like Ford, Xerox, and Chrysler—giant firms that had lost their way—revitalized themselves by taking a hard look at their markets and competition, reexamining themselves, and coming back with vigorous plans for self-renewal under strong leadership. GM, Digital Equipment, IBM, Polaroid, most money-center banks, and public institutions, like universities and school districts, are in the early stages of this same vital process.

"Challenge and response" sits comfortably with Utterback's explanation of the dynamics of industrial innovation, and why market leaders who bind themselves too tightly to today's practices fail to respond properly to the challenge of radical innovations.

9

The Lessons and Limits of History

History repeats itself, but only in outline and in the large.

Will and Ariel Durant

The preceding chapters have presented episodes from the past that highlight one or another dimension of human experience from which leaders and managers may draw useful insights. These episodes were related to contemporary examples where possible so that their bearing on the problems experienced today might be more clearly seen.

We examined the contest between Cortés and Moctezuma. Cortés was bold and determined—he grasped the initiative from the moment he set foot upon the shores of Mexico, and he held it through the final resistance of the Aztecs along the causeways leading into Tenochtitlán. Throughout the conquest of Mexico, Cortés showed less concern for his life than with the great fame and fortune that the success of his venture would bring to him and his companions. Cortés's opponent during most of the story, the great and powerful Moctezuma, remained indecisive, fearful, and passive, and this posture surely contributed to the defeat of his people.

We saw how the weak but clever Louis XI turned the tables on the rich and powerful of his time. Louis was a great misfit, a man whose modes of thought and action did not fit the patterns of the day. This, of course, was his greatest strength. Where the barons were obvious and impulsive, Louis was subtle and patient. Like a guerrilla fighter, he learned to avoid their greater physical power and to strike at their weakest points. What he could not confront directly he would circumvent and undermine. He allowed his great rival, Charles of Burgundy, to impale himself upon his own aristocratic pigheadedness. Louis' story can be a model to the many underdogs in business and government who challenge powerful, entrenched rivals.

Chapter 4, on the power of ideas, considered the impact of new ideas in reshaping the quite different realms of Christianity and manufacturing. The stories of Luther and Deming—both successful reformers—make it clear that ideas are powerful catalysts in the process of change. Ideas in themselves, however, count for little; they must have effective messengers, and these must have an audience whose heart and mind is open. When they act in the capacity of change agents, business people need to develop a sense of when change is beneficial and when it is timely, knowing where and when to plant the seeds of change.

Chapter 5 considered Admiral Yamamoto's elaborate plan to deliver a knockout blow to the U.S. Navy at Midway, and the parts that overconfidence, overcomplexity, and bad luck played in his dramatic defeat. Yamamoto's elegant plan was based upon assumptions that proved false from the very start. Acting on good intelligence and blessed with equal doses of daring and good luck, the Americans were able to put their forces at just the right place at just the right time, and so they succeeded in turning the tide of the Pacific war.

Like the Japanese navy, every large organization has legions of staffers, planners, number-crunchers, and back-office analysts, and these play a major role in the development of strategy and competitive assessment. The story of Yamamoto's disaster may be of value to them, if only as a caution that the world is more complex than it seems and full of dangerous surprises.

Chapter 6, about Hadrian and the administration of the Roman Empire, was meant to stimulate thinking about the challenges to corporate institutions as they extend themselves beyond their domestic boundaries. The Roman world that Hadrian managed encompassed such a menagerie of different people that it is remarkable it held together for as long as it did. Celts, Germans, North Africans, Arabs, Jews, Slavs, Spaniards, and Italians were bound together in a political and cultural commonwealth for hundreds of years. Will today's corporate entities project them-

selves into the world as corporate *supra*states, for which nationality and political boundaries count for much less than they do today? Will those who lead and manage them succeed, as Hadrian
did, in drawing upon the human and innovative resources that are
now divided by language, statehood, and culture? This may be the
greatest business challenge of the next century, and Rome's commonwealth may provide many instructive lessons.

Chapter 7 dealt with the subject of generational leadership and
of one leader in particular who lacked the ability to transform himself
in the face of new thinking and shifting allegiences. In the character and career of Governor Thomas Hutchinson we found a leader
whose qualities of intelligence, integrity, and commitment had served
him well as a political leader and public servant during the twilight
years of British America. Hutchinson, however, lacked the personal dynamism to master the mood shift of his countrymen and
wrestle it in the direction he wanted it to go. A man of inflexible
nature, he was too brittle to adapt himself to changing circumstances and too cerebral to generate widespread support for his
views. His great misfortune was to not have been born twenty
years earlier. Which of us has not known such a person—as CEO
or political chief?

The influence of innovation on national and institutional vitality, and decline, was presented in Chapter 8. This subject must
certainly be on the minds of many readers today. We examined
the British experience with economic decline from their own point
of view—often in their own words—and considered the theories
of a number of historians that seek to explain this dynamic process. The repeated defeats of the French at the hands of English
archers in the fifteenth century were added to illustrate the role
that technological innovation plays in this process. The failure of
the French to adapt their military strategies to the devastatingly
successful English innovation of massed archery had less to do
with English technological superiority than it did with the impulse
of the French nobility to resist the adoption of military innovations that reduced their own importance and raised those of low-
born peasants. James Utterback's studies make it clear that innovation remains a powerful element in the dynamic cycle of industrial advancement and decline; if we look closely we can see the
heavy hand of human impulses here as well.

It was hoped that these historical episodes would enrich, or at
least stimulate, readers' perceptions with respect to analogous situations found in business and other forms of organizational life.

Historical Analogy for Better or Worse

Nikita Khruschev once remarked, "Historians are dangerous; they should be watched." The former Soviet premier did not elaborate, but we can infer that he understood the power of the past's image in shaping the public mind. Indeed, Soviet history prior to the age of *glasnost* is one of the most glaring examples of history as propaganda. There is always a bias in what we read or hear about the past, and it is inevitably the bias of the dominant group. In the United States, history books would have a different slant were they written by Native Americans or blacks, but it would be naïve to think that their books would be any less biased.

For all of its faults and despite the fact that most people loathed the history courses they took in school, history has a powerful effect on the human mind, taking unassembled information about the world—some of it very accurate and some of it much less so—and forming it into patterns invested with meaning. When similar patterns are encountered, analogies are naturally made. These analogies are often the bases of decisions, sometimes at the highest levels.

On the afternoon of June 25, 1950, President Harry S Truman was on an airplane rushing back to Washington to deal with the sudden invasion of South Korea by its Communist neighbor to the north. Truman later recalled:

> I had some time to think aboard the plane. In my generation, this was not the first occasion when the strong had attacked the weak. I recalled some earlier instances: Manchuria, Ethiopia, Austria. I remembered how each time that the democracies failed to act it had encouraged the aggressors to keep going ahead. Communism was acting in Korea just as Hitler, Mussolini, and the Japanese had acted ten, fifteen, and twenty years earlier. I felt certain that if South Korea was allowed to fall Communist leaders would be emboldened to override nations closer to our own shores. If the Communists were permitted to force their way into the Republic of Korea without opposition from the free world, no small nation would have the courage to resist threats and aggression by stronger Communist neighbors. If this was allowed to go unchallenged it would mean a third world war, just as similar incidents had brought on the second world war. [1]

Truman saw the invasion of South Korea as clearly analogous to the challenges faced by the Western democracies during the 1930s, and he acted quickly to support the South Koreans militarily. How deeply he reflected upon the unique facts in both cases is unclear.

His successor in the White House, Dwight D. Eisenhower, another man who had passed through the tempests of the 1930s and 1940s, likewise perceived Communist activities around the globe as analogous to the pre–World War II challenge, but that analogy was now refined into the famous domino theory. According to Eisenhower (and his secretary of state, John Foster Dulles), "You have rows of dominoes set up. You knock over the first one, and what will happen to the last one is that it will go over very quickly." Eisenhower tried to sell Winston Churchill on this theory in gaining his support for action against Communist insurgencies in southeast Asia: "If . . . Indochina passes into the hands of the communists, the ultimate effect on our and your global strategic position . . . could be disastrous . . . We failed to halt Hirohito, Mussolini, and Hitler by not acting in unity and in time." [2]

The domino theory was a popular construction or, as Arthur Schlesinger, Jr., called it, "a misconstruction," of the Munich analogy, and it was applied liberally during the middle Cold War period. According to the theory, if any single domino was tipped over, all the rest would fall; therefore, every domino was critical. None could be allowed to topple, no matter what the particular circumstances. The uncritical acceptance of the domino theory's iron law caused the United States all kinds of problems, compelling it to support all sorts of squalid dictators whose single virtue was their active anticommunism. By the time Lyndon B. Johnson occupied the White House, and before regular U.S. military forces had been assigned to combat duties in that area, the venerable Dean Acheson was advising him that Vietnam was the perfect analogy to Korea and another critical domino that the United States must prop up.

Johnson's predecessor in the Oval Office, John. F. Kennedy, found an analogy to the past at the moment of his gravest challenge. Kennedy, however, was well-versed in European and American history and had a keen sense of the past—perhaps more so than had any American president since Woodrow Wilson. In the dangerous days of the Cuban missile crisis, Kennedy recalled the carelessness with which the Germans, British, and French stumbled into World War I. Each side had misjudged the motives and intentions of the other; each overestimated its own strengths and underestimated the power and determination of the other. They drew themselves by degrees to the brink of war from which they found it impossibe to turn back.

Kennedy had read Barbara Tuchman's newly published, *The*

Guns of August, which recounted the events that led to the tragedy of World War I, and he saw similar dangers in his showdown with the Soviets. Several years later Arthur Schlesinger, Jr., wrote:

> What worried Kennedy particularly was the inconceivable way each super-power had lost hold of the reality of the other; the United States absolutely persuaded that the Soviet Union would never put nuclear weapons into Cuba; the Soviet Union absolutely persuaded that it could do so and the United State would not respond. Remembering Barbara Tuchman's enumeration . . . of the misjudgments which caused the First World War, he used to say that there should be a sequel entitled *The Missiles of October.*[3]

The analogy between 1914 and the two nuclear superpowers blundering closer and closer to war was clear to Kennedy, and he went to great lengths to assure that the missteps that led to the first of the great wars would not repeat themselves as a prelude to the third.

The use and misuse of historical analogy is nowhere better documented, and practical guidelines for *effective* use of historical analogy more fully elaborated than in a 1986 book by Richard Neustadt and Ernest May, *Thinking in Time: The Uses of History for Decision Makers.*[4] In the 1970s, as professors at Harvard's Kennedy School of Government, Neustadt and May began to teach the use of history in a graduate course of the same name to the school's clientele of midcareer government and military managers. "We saw," say the professors, "that despite themselves Washington decision-makers actually used history in their decisions, at least for advocacy or for comfort, whether they knew any or not."[5] This casual use (or misuse) of history to make points in the determination of important public policy or for purposes of self-assurance (or self-delusion) was disturbing to the two professors, and justifiably so: Washington policymakers were positioned to create either a great deal of good or a great deal of harm. They therefore developed a methodology for finding valid analogies and in steering clear of the knee-jerk variety so often passed around without scrutiny. Their methodology was to determine systematically the following when looking at an analogy:

1. What is known about the situation?
2. What is unclear?
3. What is presumed?
4. What are the likenesses to past events?
5. What are the differences?

Table 9.1.   The French–U.S. Anology on Vietnam

Likenesses	Differences
France fought to preserve a colony.	The U.S. was backing an independent nation.
France opposed reform and Vietnamese nationalism.	The U.S. supported non-Communist sociopolitical change.
The French fought against regular armies totaling 350,000 men, were taking high casualties, and were spending 8 percent of their national budget on the war.	A large South Vietnamese army was doing the fighting against a smaller guerrilla force. U.S. casualties were low, as was the costs in dollars.
The French Indochina war was very unpopular in France, and the French government was unstable.	Despite concern over U.S casualties, use of napalm, and instability in Saigon, most Americans supported the adminstration.

Source: Derived from Neustadt and May, *Thinking in Time,* p. 82.

Each question demands a factual answer, and these can only be obtained through reflection and investigation. If objective answers are obtained, then the decision maker is much less likely to contrive a false analogy or to confuse analogy with advocacy. To illustrate the point, Neustadt and May cite a nine-page memorandum developed in 1965 for President Lyndon Johnson by National Security Advisor McGeorge Bundy entitled "France in Vietnam, 1954, and the U.S. in Vietnam, 1965—A Useful Analogy."

Bundy's memorandum came at a crucial time in the process of deciding whether U.S. ground forces should be committed to Vietnam in a major way. General William Westmoreland—commander of U.S. ground forces in Vietnam at the time—had requested 150,000 men to seek out and engage the enemy. Granting his request would represent a major shift in the level and nature of U.S involvement in the conflict, from what had been a secondary role in advising and supporting South Vietnamese units to one of active combat. The French had made similar military commitments to their colony in the 1950s, but were forced to withdraw after their stinging defeat at Dien Bien Phu in March 1954.

As described by Neustadt and May, the memorandum failed to consider the first three criteria for valid analogy, but it did compare the likenesses and differences in the French situation of 1954 and that faced by the Americans in 1965. This comparison can be seen in Table 9.1.

According to Bundy's memorandum, the United States was

not in a situation analogous to the French and so had a much better prospect for success in Vietnam. The analogy was patently unsuitable for decision making, however, in that it compared the situation of France after four years of brutal warfare against the wily Vietnamese Communists to the case of the Americans, who in 1965 had only gotten their toes into the quicksand of Vietnam. The comparison was between apples and oranges, and it was probably made in advocacy of Westmoreland's troop request. Clearly, one would suspect that if a sincere evaluation of what was known, what was unclear, and what was presumed in this analogy had been made, the inadequacies of Bundy's comparison would have been more obvious, and perhaps Johnson's decision would have been different.

As everyone knows, Johnson decided in favor of sending major ground forces to Vietnam in 1965. He concluded, as did many of his advisors, that the Communists would come to terms once a high level of punishment had been inflicted on them by the U.S. military. A better sense of history would have reminded him that this same opponent had withstood the punishment dished out by the French army over many years without coming to terms.

The case of the Bundy memorandum underscores the way historical information can be misused in the decision-making process and reminds us of Carl Gustavson's warning that "any statement in which the prefatory 'history teaches us that . . .' is used as a springboard should be very carefully scrutinized."[6]

The Seers of Wall Street

Two days after Bill Clinton won the 1992 U.S. presidential election, the *Wall Street Journal* ran a front-page humor story by reporter Ron Suskind entitled "Incredible: Vikings Win Football Game, GOP Loses Election."[7] Suskind's story listed the many fanciful but once reliable election predictors that had missed the mark in this latest presidential contest. The Minnesota Viking football team had won a Monday night game the evening before the polls opened, and a Viking victory on election eve had always correlated with a Republican victory the following day. Likewise, grammar school children favored the Republican candidate in the annual poll conducted by the *Weekly Reader*—another sure-fire indicator of electoral success suddenly off target. In Crook County, Oregon, a majority of voters placed their bets on George Bush, breaking their uncanny record for picking winners in every presidential election since 1884.

Suskind's story went on to mention a handful of other once-reliable election indicators that had failed in this latest contest, among them the hemline indicator (long hemlines favor Republican victories), the baseball World Series winner (an American League victory coincides with a Republican being sent to the White House), and the tall man—short man indicator (taller candidates usually win). The story quoted Allen Lichtman, a professor at American University and a builder of forecasting models, saying, "For some of these predictors it's just a matter of time before the statistical probabilities catch up with them—and then they disappear."

Readers of the venerable *Journal* no doubt enjoyed the light-hearted spirit in which the article was written. No doubt many turned quickly to Section C, "Money and Investing," to whose pages humor seldom finds its way. The lead article there was "With Clinton Taking Over the White House, Here's What It Means for Your Finances."[8] A nationally known investment advisor counseled readers that "small [company] stocks have done better under Democrats," citing figures going back to 1928 to indicate that returns on big company stocks were about the same under Republican and Democratic presidents (5 percent and 5.8 percent, respectively), but that small company stocks had risen a whooping 12.7 percent per year under the Democrats while falling 2.6 percent during Republican administrations. "He and others suggest that investors tilt their portfolios to give a greater emphasis to stocks of smaller companies," the *Journal* reported. In fact, the small company stock play had been touted in the financial press by many investment managers as victory by the Democratic candidate seemed more and more certain.

Whether the editors of the *Wall Street Journal* noticed the similarity between its front-page story about unscientific indicators and the investment advice served up in "Money and Investing" is anyone's guess. There is obviously no causal link between victories by the Minnesota Vikings and the election of Republican presidents, and that is why it eventually failed as a predictive device: Statistical probabilities had indeed "caught up" with it. Nor was evidence given of any causal link between Democratic presidents and high returns for small company stocks. Neither the reporters who wrote the story nor the market advisers touting small company stock investments mentioned that more than a few events of importance took place during the period 1928–1992, the time frame over which the small company stock returns were calculated: the Great Depression, three major wars, the destruction and revitalization of America's major trading partners, one presidential assassination, the stock market crash of October 1987, and the birth of a half-dozen technology-based industries (aerospace, transistorized electronics, computers, microwave and fiber-optic communication, and biotechnology). Without controlling for these and other significant developments, any link between the party affiliation of presidents and small company stock performance can only be conjectural. This is what Gustavson called the "the single-cause explanation of a complex event [error]."

The market gurus quoted by the *Journal,* then, seriously misused history, and their advice on this matter is as dubious in its predictive value as the Minnesota Viking victory on the night of November 1, 1992.

Using Historical Information Effectively

Not everyone in the business world is as careless with historical information as implied by the example just given. Even on Wall Street, current methods for valuing securities rely on historical information and use this information as a caution against overly optimistic and overly pessimistic conclusions. For example, an accepted method for valuing any income-producing asset (a stock, a commerical office building, even an entire corporation) is twofold: first, determine the current or near-term earnings; second, estimate a "multiplier" for those earnings (i.e., what the market will pay for a dollar of those earnings). This second task requires the application of historical information and calls for greater judgment in that the fickleness, fear, and avarice of thousands of market participants over a period of years must be taken into account.

Earnings multipliers have fluctuated wildly over the past thirty years as the mood of investors have swung between the extremes of optimism and fear. Between 1960 and 1990, year-end earnings multipliers for the Standard & Poors 400 industrial stocks have fluctuated between the extremes of 22.4 and 7. Thus, investors have been willing to pay as much $22.40 for every dollar of current or near-term earnings of the S&P 400 stocks, or as little as $7, depending upon their mood and view of the future.[9] This is a remarkable divergence of valuation for the same assets over time, and it speaks volumes in favor of the contrarian investor's strategy of buying on pessimism and selling on optimism.

This phenomenon is mentioned here because most reputable market analysts have learned to use historical information to cast light onto current stock market conditions, viewing measures like price/earnings, price/book value, and dividend yield in the context of past experience. The movement of any of these measures from the mean to either extreme is thus a red flag signaling either danger or opportunity. Thus, an investment manager writing in *Barron's* in August 1991, when all of these measures were on the high side, could say, "The lesson of our entire investment history is that these value measures will revert to their means. . . . There is a huge price gap below this market just to reach historically normal levels." [10] (The stock market for large stocks did, indeed, move back toward historic levels in the year that followed; prices were anemic through 1992, whereas the underlying fundamentals of most companies improved.)

Reconstructing the Past to Improve Current Decisions

During World War II the U.S. Navy recruited Harvard's Samuel Eliot Morison, a reserve naval officer and respected scholar of American maritime history, to document the war in the Pacific as it happened. The top naval brass knew that they were involved in a struggle of historic proportions and that they and future generations of naval planners would have plenty to learn from the experience—but only if it was thoroughly and accurately recorded. Morison obliged with a multivolume work based upon his research and that of his team of assistants (which included a young college graduate named James Michener).

Few corporations have the resources to retain resident historians to chronicle activities as they happen, although quite a few commisson the writing of a company history to commemorate a fiftieth anniversary or other landmark event. Some do take the trouble to systematically reconstruct episodes from the recent past in order to search for lessons about success or failure. One that did is GM, which in 1981 organized a study of the development of its "X" and "J" platform cars. These new families of automobiles had been rushed through the development process during the late 1970s to give GM fuel-efficient products at a time when gasoline prices were high and volatile and when small foreign cars were successfully invading the U.S. domestic market.

Both "X" and "J" vehicle projects experienced severe quality, schedule, and cost problems. GM lost heavily during their first years of production, and the company's reputation for quality and reliability took a public beating. The intent of the study was to reconstruct the development process, determine what went wrong, and learn to avoid similar mistakes in future development projects. Almost eighty managers and engineers were involved, and the study was conducted by a group of outside consultants from the Sandy Company. In the short-run, important deficiencies in GM methods were uncovered. In the long-run, many participants of the study (a number of whom have since moved on to higher positions of authority in the firm) found their attitudes about project management and product quality transformed for the better, and the results are today visible in the high-quality rankings given to several GM models and manufacturing facilities.[11]

In a 1987 study with similar objectives, Hewlett-Packard conducted a systematic search for "best scheduling practices" within its corporate borders. Each of its fifty-six R&D centers was charged with doing postmortems on a number of recent development projects that had run the full cycle from project inception to new product introduction. Events and processes seen as contributing to project scheduling failures and successes were submitted by R&D centers to Corporate Engineering, which shared them among all units.[12]

Genuine efforts were made to systematically learn from the past and to transfer that learning into real-time activities, in both the GM and Hewlett-Packard cases.

Using Historical Analogy in Business

Most businesses change *incrementally* over time. This seems to be a survival trait in all but the most fast-paced industries. Firms anchor themselves in familar territory and only venture beyond current lines of business in measured steps, and then into analogous situations in which their current capabilities, product lines, and so forth, can contribute to their success. This makes the Neustadt and May methodology all the more useful since the ingredients for analogy are more abundant. As strategies and operational plans are developed, these can be examined in the light of parallel experiences from the past. This is done all of the time, but it proceeds more or less from intuition, and not necessarily in a systematic way.

As an example, consider that Company *X* is debating whether to open two new sales offices. Its archives (records) indicate that in the past each new sales office generated between $3 and $3.2 million in new revenue during its first twelve months of operations, with an average of $2.8 million in added expenses; revenues and margins typically improved after the first year. One group of executives favors moving ahead with the new sales offices, citing past successes; another group cautions that those successes were based on special conditions not likely to be repeated. The CEO wants full discussion of the issues before a decision is made.

Discussion within Company *X* would typically focus on real-time indicators of potential revenues and expenses for each sales office. Market research of current conditions and extrapolations into the future would be presented and debated. The record of the past would be brought up, with one group arguing that every new sales office had been profitable within a year and the other group firing back, "That was then, this is now."

Business people, for better or worse, are creatures of the present and the near-term future. As historian Allen Nevins once pointed out, "They think very little of the long past and the longer future [but] find safety in short views, and danger in guesses at future patterns." Real-time and forecasted business conditions should certainly be central to any decision by Company *X*, but the record of the past would add context to its deliberations. Plans to open a new sales offices could be examined through full discussion of May–Neustadt questions of what is known, what is unclear, what is presumed, and the differences and likenesses to the firm's past experience in opening sales offices. In this way the past would inform the present.

A Final Cautionary Tale

"This time it's different."

These words, according to legendary money manager John Templeton, are the most dangerous in the investor's phrase book. By extension, they should serve as a caution for anyone who must lead or manage. Over fifty years of experience in securities markets around the globe helped Templeton develop a keen sense of financial value and taught him how that value could be grossly inflated or depressed by the public mood. Like many others, he recognized that fear and greed often drive financial values to extremes; however, in company with a very few, he has been able to detach himself from the emotions that afflict the larger investment community at irregular intervals. For example, when stock values in Japan soared to levels that defied common sense in the late 1980s, Templeton's larger perspective kept him out of harm's way. It also kept him out of company with the crowd who justified their misguided enthusiasm with the notion, "This time it's different"— that somehow the normal measures of value did not apply.

Always generous in sharing his personal wealth and commonsense methods with the public, Templeton, in 1985, reprinted and circulated an obscure 1841 book by Charles Mackay, an English barrister, entitled *Extraordinary Popular Delusions and the Madness of Crowds*. [13] Mackay chronicled a number of mass manias, scams, and popular movements that had swept people up into bizarre and disfunctional behavior over the centuries. Among these were the traffic in relics, the Crusades, the practice of alchemy, the South Sea Bubble, the Mississippi Land Scheme, and an episode we recount here, the Great Tulip Mania of the 1630s.

Tulipomania. Mackay relates that the first tulip bulbs came into Western Europe via Constantinople sometime in the middle of the sixteenth century, and soon became popular among wealthy people in Germany and Holland. For some unrecorded reason, the fondness of the Dutch for this plant was so intense that not only the very wealthy, but even middle-class shopkeepers and merchants added to its rising demand by the early 1630s.

Before long, tulip bulbs commanded preposterous prices, and individuals were acquiring them less for the beauty they brought to Dutch gardens than for speculative purposes. Dealers became "market makers" for the many varieties of tulips, and normal pricing arrangements governed by supply and demand quickly gave way to various forms of manipulation.

Mackay demonstrated the stratospheric prices of the rarer tulip varieties through the case of a single bulb of the *Viceroy* variety, which sold for 2,500 florins. By comparison, a suit of clothes cost 80 florins, an ox cost 120 florins, and a silver drinking cup cost 60 florins at that time.

By 1636 demand for tulip bulbs was so intense that the stock exchanges of Amsterdam, Rotterdam, Leyden, and Haarlem became markets for their sale. In smaller towns, trading took place in public taverns. Some attempts were made to set up markets in London and Paris, and these met with limited success.

The upward trajectory of bulb prices created great fortunes for many in Holland. According to Mackay, "Everyone imagined that the passion for tulips would last for ever, and that the wealthy from every part of the world would send to Holland, and pay whatever prices were asked." All walks of Dutch society wanted to get aboard this great money machine, and many sold their homes and farms at ruinously low prices to raise the cash needed to do so.

Like all speculative bubbles, the tulip mania eventually deflated and prices cascaded downward. As Mackay told it:

> The more prudent began to see that this folly could not last for ever. Rich people no longer bought the flowers to keep them in their gardens, but to sell them again at a profit. It was seen that somebody must lose fearfully in the end. As this conviction spread, prices fell, and never rose again. Confidence was destroyed, and a universal panic seized upon dealers Many who, for a brief season, had emerged from the humbler walks of life, were cast back into their original obsurity. Substantial merchants were reduced almost to beggary, and many a representative of a noble line saw the fortunes of his house ruined beyond redemption.

The tulip mania was a classic of speculative excess, in which the inherent value of tulip bulbs was lost sight of in the greed-driven belief that their prices would continue to rise. The very purpose of the tulip, as a thing that brought pleasure and beauty to the garden, was likewise forgotten. In these respects Holland's tulip mania was no different than the U.S. stock market in the late 1920s, Wall Street's "go-go" years of the 1960s, the oil-patch boom of 1974–1981, the mania for owning real estate that drove the price of homes and office buildings on both U.S. coasts to ridiculous heights until 1989, and, more recently, the wild ride of the Tokyo Stock Exchange. In each case a sense of proportion, of historic perspective, was left on the shelf by the herd instinct to make money fast and easily. In each case, the mad rush to profits was supported by professionals, whose training and experience had taught them all about manias, bubbles, and the madness of crowds, but who believed nevertheless, "This time it's different."

Notes

Chapter 1

1. Joseph Strayer cited in Theodore S. Hamerow, *Reflections on History and Historians* (Madison: University of Wisconsin Press, 1987), p. 210.
2. Gary Yukl, *Leadership in Organizations* (Englewood Cliffs, NJ: Prentice-Hall, 1981), p. 70.
3. Warren Bennis and Burt Nanus, *Leaders: The Strategies for Taking Charge* (New York: Harper & Row, 1985), p. 4.
4. Yukl, *Leadership*, p. 70.

Chapter 2

1. Bernal Díaz de Castillo, *The True History of the Conquest of New Spain*, translated by J. M. Cohen (Harmondsworth: Penguin Books, Ltd., 1963), p. 38.
2. Many modern historians now use the spelling Moctezuma as closer to the emperors's name in the Nahuatl language of his people. This has been used here as well rather than Montezuma.
3. Bernardino de Sahagún, *The War of Conquest,* translated by Arthur J. O. Anderson and Charles E. Dibble (Salt Lake City: University of Utah Press, 1978), p. 12.
4. Díaz, *The True History of the Conquest.*
5. Francisco Lopez de Gomara, *Cortés: The Life of the Conqueror by His Secretary,* translated and edited by Lesley Byrd Simpson (Berkeley: University of California Press, 1964), pp. 25–26. It is not likely that these were the words used by Cortés, but they probably reflect his attitude. Gomara, who represents these as the conqueror's words, did not meet Cortés until two decades after the events.

183

6. R. C. Padden, *The Hummingbird and the Hawk: Conquest and Sovereignty in the Valley of Mexico, 1503–1541* (New York: Harper & Row, 1967), pp. 25–26.

7. The reader's instinct should be to discount these numbers, if not the entire notion, of massive human sacrifice by the Aztecs, given the source. The Spanish friars who recorded so much of what we know of the Aztec nation had plenty of reasons to portray the Aztecs as cruel and disgusting heathen; this would provide a justification for their destruction. Still, despite revisionist thinking that would like to make the Spaniards out to be perfectly cruel and the Aztecs to be unspoiled innocents in a state of of uncorrupted nature, the practice of human sacrifice was widely practiced in the Aztec world. Oppression of neighboring tribes was a matter of state policy.

8. Sahagún, *The War,* pp. 7–16.

9. Díaz, *The True History of the Conquest,* p. 131.

10. ibid., p. 150.

11. ibid., p. 214.

12. Hernán Cortés, *Five Letters to the Emperor,* translated by J. Bayard Morris (New York: W. W. Norton & Co., 1928), p. 87.

13. Díaz, *The True History of the Conquest,* p. 299.

14. Jeffry Timmons et al., *New Venture Creation* (Homewood, IL: Richard D. Irwin, Inc., 1985), pp. 103–4.

15. William Hickley Prescott, *History of the Conquest of Mexico,* Book 7, Ch. v. (New York: Harper Bros., 1843), p. 353.

16. Manfred Kets de Vries, Notes to case 9–484–081(Boston, MA: Harvard Business School, 1984).

17. William Bygrave and Jeffry Timmons, *Venture Capital at the Crossroads* (Boston: Harvard Business School Press, 1992).

18. Díaz, *The True History of the Conquest,* pp. 407–8.

19. Cortés, *Five Letters,* p. xvii.

Chapter 3

1. D. B. Wyndham Lewis, *King Spider* (New York and Hartford, CT: Coward McCann, Inc., 1929), p. 43.

2. Paul Murray Kendall, *Louis XI: The Universal Spider,* (New York: W. W. Norton & Co., 1971), p. 28.

3. Kendall, *Louis XI,* p. 28.

4. Johan Huizinga, *The Waning of the Middle Ages* (New York: St. Martin's Press, 1924), pp. 11–12.

5. André Maurois, *A History of France,* translated by Henry L. Binsse (New York: Farrar, Strauss and Cudahy, 1948), p. 42.

6. Abraham Zaleznik, "The Leadership Gap," *Academy of Management Executive,* 1990, Vol. 4, No. 1, p. 7.

7. Joseph M. Tyrrell, *Louis XI,* (New York: Twayne Publishers, 1989), p. 31.

8. Kendall, *Louis XI,* p. 168.

9. Pierre Champion, *Louis XI,* translated by Winifred Whales (New York: Dodd, Mead & Co., 1929), p. 223.

10. Henri Pirenne, *Historie de Belqique,* Vol. 2, translated by Jean Champion, p. 290.

11. A Breton messenger named Maurice Gourmel played a key role in Louis's spy net. Gourmel made copies of all correspondence carried between troublesome François II, duke of Brittany, and the king of England for 100 livres apiece. A Spanish envoy did the same with all letters passed between the king of Aragon and the king of England.

12. Kendall, *Louis XI,* p. 139.

13. Philippe de Commynes, *Memoirs of Philippe de Commynes* (London: W. B. Whittaker, 1823), p. 33.

14. Lewis, *King Spider,* p. 249.

15. Kendall, *Louis XI,* p. 118.

16. ibid., p. 249.

17. Commynes, *Memoirs,* p. 59.

18. See Roger Peters, *Practical Intelligences* (New York: Harper & Row, 1985).

19. Commynes, *Memoirs,* p. 276.

Chapter 4

1. Euan Cameron, *The European Reformation* (Oxford: The Clarendon Press, 1991), p. 1.

2. Roland N. Stromberg, *A History of Western Civilization,* rev. ed. (Homewood, IL: The Dorsey Press, 1969), p. 261.

3. Cameron, *Reformation,* p. 294.

4. Edwin O. Reischauer, *The United States and Japan,* 3rd. ed. (New York: Viking Press, 1964), p. 207.

5. ibid., p. 208.

6. Bruce Scott, John Rosenblum, and Audrey Sproat, *Case Studies in Political Economy: Japan 1854–1977* (Boston, MA: Harvard Business School, Division of Research, 1980), p. 112.

7. Herman Kahn, *The Emerging Japanese Superstate* (Englewood Cliffs, NJ: Prentice-Hall, 1970), p. 217.

8. Andrea Gabor, "The Man Who Changed the World of Quality," *International Management,* March 1988, p. 42.

9. Andrea Gabor, *The Man Who Invented Quality* (New York: Times Books, 1990), p. 82.

10. ibid., p. 103.

11. ibid., p. 55.

12. W. Edwards Deming, *Out of Crisis* (Cambridge: Massachusetts Institute of Technology/Center for Advanced Engineering Study, 1982), pp. 487–88.

13. Joseph Juran, *Juran on Leadership in Quality* (New York: The Free Press, 1985), pp. 6–8.

14. Robert H. Hayes, Steven C. Wheelwright, and Kim B. Clark, *Dynamic Manufacturing* (New York: The Free Press, 1988), p. 53.

15. "Report on Activity with the Occupation Forces in Japan 1948 to May 1950," cited in Kenneth Hopper's article, "Creating Japan's New Industrial Management: Americans as Teachers," *Human Resources Management,* Summer 1982, p. 15. This article is difficult to locate but well worth the effort for anyone wanting to gain insight into the early period of Japan's postwar recovery and the part that American advisors played in it. It is clear from Hopper's article that Polkinghorn, Protzman, and Sarasohn played a pivotal role in that recovery.

16. Deming, *Out of Crisis*, p. 487.

17. ibid., pp. 490–91.

18. Taichi Ohno and Setsuo Mita, *Just-in-Time for Today and Tomorrow*, translated by Joseph P. Schmelzus, Jr. (Cambridge, MA: Productivity Press, 1988), p. 123.

19. ibid., pp. 1–2.

20. Kiichiro Toyoda, quoted in Ohno and Mita, pp. 26–27.

21. Kiyoski Suzaki, *The New Manufacturing Challenge* (New York: The Free Press, 1987), p. 12.

22. Robert H. Hayes, "Why Japanese Factories Work," *Harvard Business Review*, July–August 1981, p. 56.

23. "Future Perfect," *Economist*, January 4, 1992, p. 61.

24. V. Daniel Hunt, *Quality in America* (Homewood, IL: BusinessOne-Irwin, 1992), p. 29.

25. Everett M. Rogers, *Diffusion of Innovation*, 3rd. ed. (New York: The Free Press, 1983), p. 5

26. ibid., pp. 14–16.

27. Carl G. Gustavson, *A Preface to History* (New York: McGraw-Hill Book Co., Inc., 1955), p. 152.

28. ibid., pp. 315–16.

29. Everett M. Rogers, "Social Structure and Social Change." In Gerald Zaltman, ed., *Processes and Phenomena of Social Change* (New York: John Wiley & Sons, 1973), pp. 75–92.

30. For complete case studies of these two institutions, see Gregory Watson, *Strategic Benchmarking* (New York: John Wiley & Sons, 1993).

Chapter 5

1. H. P. Willmont, *Pearl Harbor* (Engelwood Cliffs, NJ: Prentice-Hall, 1983), p. 8.

2. John Deane Potter, *Yamamoto: The Man Who Menaced America* (New York: Viking Press, 1965), pp. 75–41.

3. Samuel Eliot Morison, *History of United States Naval Operations in World War II*, Vol. 4, (Boston: Little, Brown & Co., 1950), pp. 75–78.

4. Gordon W. Prange, *Miracle at Midway* (New York: McGraw Hill, 1982), p. 51.

5. Cynthia A. Montgomery and Michael E. Porter, eds., *Strategy* (Boston: Harvard Business School Press, 1991), p. xii.

6. Kenneth R. Andrews, *The Concept of the Corporation*, 3rd ed. (Homewood, IL: Dow Jones-Irwin, 1978), p. 50.

7. Nimitz, quoted in Samuel Eliot Morison, *History*, p. 84.

8. Mitsuo Fuchida and Masatake Okumiya, *Midway: The Battle That Doomed Japan* (New York: Ballantine Books, 1955), pp. 91–92.

9. Prange, *Miracle at Midway*, p. 181.

10. Fuchida and Okumiya, *Midway*, p. 139.

11. Prange, *Miracle at Midway*, p. 102.

12. George Gay, *Sole Survivor: The Battle of Midway and Its Effects on His Life* (Naples, FL: Naples Ad/Graphic, 1979), p. 121.

13. Fuchida and Okumiya, *Midway*, p. 156.

14. Prange, *Miracle at Midway*, p. 374.

15. Fuchida and Okumiya, *Midway,* p. 7.

16. John Winton, *War in the Pacific: From Pearl Harbor to Tokyo Bay* (London: Sedwick & Jackson, 1978), p. 40.

17. "For Better Products, Use Fewer Parts," *New York Times,* June 26, 1988, p. 31.

18. Ralph E. Gomory, "From the Ladder of Science to the Product Development Cycle," *Harvard Business Review,* November–December 1989, p. 103.

19. R. N. Paul, N. B. Donavan, and J. W. Taylor, "The Reality Gap in Strategic Planning," *Harvard Business Review,* May–June 1978, p. 126.

20. See Herbert Simon, *Models of Man: Social and Rational* (New York: John Wiley & Sons, 1970).

21. Translated by John Deane Porter in *Yamamoto,* p. 318.

Chapter 6

1. From *Aelii Spartiani de Vita Hadriani,* as translated by Bernard W. Henderson in *The Life and Principate of the Emperor Hadrian* (Rome: L'Erma di-Bretschneider, 1968), p. 34. Henderson's work was originally published in 1923. The *Vita* is one of the few ancient sources of biographical information about Hadrian. It was part of a series of biographies of Roman emperors in a larger work called the *Augustan History,* which attempted to follow on the tradition of Suetonius's *Lives of the Caesars.* According to Henderson, the biographies offered by the *Vita* are "hopelessly inferior to their model. They are . . . incredibly stupid and verbose; and lack almost completely Suetonius' wit and interest." Hadrian himself is said to have composed an autobiography, that, like much else from the ancient world, has been lost to time and human carelessness.

2. Edward N. Luttwak, *The Grand Strategy of the Roman Empire* (Baltimore: Johns Hopkins University Press, 1976), pp. 82–83.

3. Company data as reported in "The Stateless Corporation," *Business Week,* May 14, 1990, p. 103.

4. Robert Reich, "Who Is Us?" *Harvard Business Review,* January–February, 1990, p. 55.

5. Raymond Vernon and Louis T. Wells, *The Manager in the International Economy,* 6th ed. (Englewood Cliffs, NJ: Prentice-Hall, 1991), p. 18.

6. "The Stateless Corporation," p. 101.

7. Robert Reich, "Who Is Them?" *Harvard Business Review,* March–April, 1991, p. 79.

8. "The Logic of Global Business: An Interview with ABB's Percy Barnevik," *Harvard Business Review,* March–April 1991, pp. 91–93.

9. M. P. Charlesworth, *The Roman Empire* (London: Oxford University Press, 1951), p. 121.

10. This wise advice was not apparently followed in Egypt, where the native population and their fields were heavily worked to produce the grain crops on which the city of Rome depended. The result was periodic work stoppages and threats of revolt.

11. G. H. Stevenson, *Roman Provincial Administration* (Oxford: Basil Blackwell, 1939), pp. 92–93.

12. Charlesworth, *The Roman Empire,* p. 50.

13. Translations of ancient sources in Henderson, *The Life and Principate of the Emperor Hadrian,* p. 75.

14. Michael Grant, *The Army of the Caesars* (New York: Charles Scribner's Sons, 1974), pp. 237–38.

15. Richard Mansfield Haywood, *The Myth of Rome's Fall* (New York: Thomas Y. Crowell Co., Inc., 1958), pp. 26–27.

16. Many point to the sack of Rome by the Visigoths in A.D. 410 as the effective end of the Western Roman Empire. The Eastern Roman Empire maintained a credible state until the fall of its capital, Constantinople, to the Turks in A.D. 1453.

17. *Business Week,* November 11, 1991, p. 68.

18. See Jeremiah J. Sullivan, *Invasion of the Salarymen: The Japanese Business Presence in America* (Westport, CT: Praeger, 1992).

19. Sullivan, ibid., p. 84.

20. Dennis Laurie, *Yankee Samurai* (New York: HarperBusiness, 1992), pp. 141–76.

21. Deborah Jacobs, "Suing Japanese Employers," *Across the Board,* October 1991, pp. 30–37.

22. "United Technologies: Like Japan, but Different," *Economist,* November 3, 1990, pp. 76–77.

Chapter 7

1. Cited in Amanda Bennet, "Many of Today's Top Corporate Officers Are the Right People for the Wrong Time," *Wall Street Journal,* October 27, 1992, pp. B1, B4.

2. For more on NCR, see Richard Foster, *Innovation: The Attacker's Advantage* (New York: Summit Books, 1986), pp. 139–41.

3. E. James Ferguson, *The American Revolution: A General History, 1763–1790* (Homewood, IL: Dorsey Press, 1974), p. 13.

4. John R. Galvin, *Three Men of Boston* (New York: Thomas Y. Crowell Co., Inc., 1976), p. 11.

5. Bernard Bailyn, *The Ordeal of Thomas Hutchinson* (Cambridge: Harvard University Press, 1974), p. 23.

6. Galvin, *Three Men of Boston,* p. 18.

7. Janice Potter, *The Liberties We Seek: Loyalist Ideology in Colonial New York and Massachusetts* (Cambridge: Harvard University Press, 1983), p. 12.

8. Robert McCluer Calhoon, *The Loyalists in Revolutionary America, 1760–1780* (New York: Harcourt Brace Jovanovich, Inc., 1973), p. 52.

9. Galvin, *Three Men of Boston,* p. 69.

10. Bailyn, *Ordeal of Thomas Hutchinson,* p. 35.

11. Galvin, *Three Men of Boston,* p. 64.

12. Ralph Volmey Harlow, *Samuel Adams: Promoter of the American Revolution* (New York: Macmillan, 1923), p. 36.

13. Joseph A. Schumpeter, *Capitalism, Socialism and Democracy* (New York: Harper & Row, 1947), p. 145.

14. Galvin, *Three Men of Boston,* p. 114.

15. Bailyn, *Ordeal of Thomas Hutchinson,* p. 25.

16. Bennet, "Many of Today's Top Corporate Officers Are the Right People for the Wrong Time," p. B4.

Chapter 8

1. Henri de Wailly, *Crécy 1346: Anatomy of a Battle* (London: Poole, Dorset, Blandford Press, 1987), p. 12.

2. Lynn White, Jr., "The Medieval Roots of Modern Technology." In Kathleen Drew and Floyd Lear, eds. *Perspective in Medieval History* (Chicago, IL: University of Chicago Press, 1963), pp. 20–21.

3. Interviewed in "Harvard Business Review," September–October, 1990, p. 139.

4. Anonymous poem, from Chistopher Hibbert, *Agincourt* (London, B. T. Batsford Ltd., 1964), p. 107.

5. Unascribed remark cited by Lowell Bryan in "The Role of Top Management," *McKinsey Quarterly*, Fall 1991.

6. An idea borrowed from Montesquieu.

7. Edward Gibbon, *The History of the Decline and Fall of the Roman Empire*, Vol. 37, pp. 162–63.

8. Aron L. Friedberg, *The Weary Titan: Britain and the Experience of Relative Decline, 1895–1905* (Princeton, NJ: Princeton University Press, 1988), p. 25.

9. Charles W. Boyd, ed., *Mr. Chamberlain's Speeches*, Vol. 2 (London: Constable, 1914), p. 267, as cited in Friedberg.

10. Friedberg, *The Weary Titan*, p. 76.

11. James A. Henretta, W. Elliot Brownlee, David Brody, and Susan Ware, *America's History* (Homewood, IL: The Dorsey Press, 1987), p. 312.

12. Until recently, James Utterback's works have been published only in scholarly journals. Fortunately, thoughtful managers will have access to his ideas about the management of innovation in an excellent forthcoming book, *Mastering the Dynamics of Innovation* (Boston: Harvard Business School Press, 1994).

13. See Richard Foster, *Innovation: The Attacker's Advantage* (New York: Summit Books, 1986).

14. *Industry Week*, January 7, 1991, p. 13.

15. Mancur Olson, *The Rise and Decline of Nations: Economic Growth, Stagflation, and Social Rigidities* (New Haven, CT, and London: Yale University Press, 1982).

16. James R. Bright, "Evaluating Signals of Technological Change," *Harvard Business Review*, January–February, 1970, p. 64. My thanks to James Utterback for bringing this article to my attention, as well as his related article with James W. Brown, "Monitoring for Technological Change," *Business Horizons*, Vol. 15, October 1972, pp. 5–15.

17. ibid., p. 64.

18. "A Third Generation Galvin Moves Up," *Forbes*, April 30, 1990, p. 57.

19. G. Christian Hill and Ken Yamada, "Staying Power: Motorola Illustrates How an Aged Giant Can Remain Vibrant," *Wall Street Journal*, December 9, 1992, pp. A1, A18.

Chapter 9

1. Harry S Truman, *Memoirs, Volume 2: Years of Trial and Hope* (Garden City, NY: Doubleday & Co., Inc., 1956), pp. 332–33.

2. Eisenhower quoted in Arthur M. Scheshinger, Jr., *A Thousand Days: John F. Kennedy in the White House* (Boston: Houghton Mifflin Co., Inc., 1965), p. 536.

3. Arthur M. Schlesinger, Jr., *A Thousand Days: John F. Kennedy in the White House* (Boston: Houghton Mifflin Co., Inc., 1965), pp. 831–32.

4. Richard E. Neustadt and Ernest R. May, *Thinking in Time: The Uses of History for Decision Makers* (New York: The Free Press, 1986).

5. ibid., p. xii.

6. Carl G. Gustavson, *A Preface to History* (McGraw-Hill Book Co., Inc., 1956), p. 5.

7. *Wall Street Journal,* November 5, 1992, pp. A1, A18.

8. John R. Dorfman and Karen Slater Damato, *Wall Street Journal,* November 5, 1992, p. C1.

9. Similar wide swings exist in the capitalization of income-producing real estate.

10. Thomas J. Feeney, "Is History Bunk? By Past Standards, the Market Is Hugely Overvalued," *Barron's,* August 12, 1991, p. 18.

11. Based on conversations with Stephen Wells and Bruce Pince of Sandy Company. Implications of this study are developed by Gregory Watson in *Strategic Benchmarking* (New York: John Wiley & Sons, Inc., 1993).

12. ibid.

13. My thanks to John M. Templeton for sending me a copy of this interesting volume, reprinted by Templeton Publications in 1985 by arrangement with Dorset Press, a division of Marboro Books Corp.

A Guide to Further Reading

The following list of books is intended for those readers who wish to learn more about the individuals and events upon which the historical episodes in these chapters are based. The notes for each chapter would normally suffice for this purpose, but many of the sources cited there are too esoteric to be of interest to the general reader; others are difficult to find for anyone lacking access to a world-class university library. Nevertheless, a number of books can be suggested that are both rich in detail and engrossing in the way they get their stories across; these are listed by chapter and subject. As one would expect, these books are also the ones most likely to be available in public libraries and retail bookstores. All are listed as in print as of 1992–1993, which means that any reputable bookstore can order them if they are not already on the shelf.

Chapter 2

In contrast to the paucity of books available on Louix XI, there are plenty available, many in paperback, on the conquest of Mexico. From these books the reader, once hooked on this fascinating period, can fan out to dozens of other books about pre-Columbian civilizations and exploration of the New World.

If only one book were to be read, it would have to be that of Bernal Díaz del Castillo, *The True History of the Conquest of New Spain,* which is available in the Penguin classics series. Díaz was born in the year Columbus sailed from Palos on his first voyage of discovery, and he died eighty-nine years later in Guatelmala, the last survivor of the men who fought their way into the heart of Tenochtitlán. His vivid descriptions of Cortés, Moctezuma, and the native people makes for exciting reading. Unlike the writings of Cortés, which were always contrived to win favor at court, Díaz writes from the heart—as a common soldier who only hoped to leave a clear record of an uncommon set of events.

Díaz, of course, saw the conquest through the eyes of a European invader who knew little of the larger world he had come into. For a broader perspective, R. C. Padden's *The Hummingbird and the Hawk: Conquest and Sovereignty in the Valley of Mexico, 1503–1541* (New York: Harper Torchbooks, 1975) is recommended. Padden offers background in the early history of the Aztec nation, the religious beliefs that governed its life, and how the appearance of Spanish invaders led to a duel for sovereignty at the cosmic level. It is a terrific read.

Chapter 3

Paul Murray Kendall's *Louis XI: The Universal Spider* (New York: W. W. Norton: 1971) is accountably the best book on this subject for the English-speaking reader. Kendall covers the Spider King's life in full, and in the telling provides layers of interesting detail about statecraft in western Europe at the time. Charles the Bold is also a major subject here. Keeping track of who's who among the Burgundians, the English, the Italians, and the French noble houses can be difficult in this book, yet Kendall's biography brings Louis and the important people of his time very much to life.

For a full picture of late medieval France, the chaotic world Louis inherited, one could not do better than to read *A Distant Mirror: The Calamitous Fourteenth Century,* by the late Barbara Tuchman (New York: Alfred A. Knopf, 1978; paperback edition by Ballantine, 1989). Tuchman was one of the best writers of narrative history in the postwar era, and *A Distant Mirror* is a tale of honor, venality, courage, and human folly that is so well told that the book is difficult to put down.

Chapter 4

Thousands of volumes have been written about Martin Luther and the Protestant Reformation over the years; the one by Euan Cameron, *The European Reformation* (Oxford: The Clarendon Press, 1991) is perhaps the best of the current crop. It does a fine job on Luther and his fellow reformers, and it provides a solid picture of what European societies were like in the fifteenth and sixteenth centuries.

Innovations in printing resulted in Martin Luther's tracts and oratory being spread widely during his ministry. Books about the great reformer soon followed. Today, word processors deluge us with books and articles about the quality reform movement and several books, most of them gushy and uncritical, have appeared lately about W. Edwards Deming . One worth reading is Andrea Gabor's, *The Man Who Invented Quality* (New York: Times Books, 1990). The man's own epistles can always be read. Deming's *Out of Crisis* (Cambridge: Massachusetts Institute of Technology/Center for Advanced Engineering Study, 1982) is widely available and contains the quality *meister*'s thoughts on the problems facing modern managers and his own set of sensible solutions.

Chapter 5

Because the tide of war in the Pacific turned at Midway, there were bound to be plenty of books about this battle and those who fought it. The most complete of the lot is Gordon W. Prange's *Miracle at Midway* (New York: Penguin Books, 1983, paperback). Prange is a master of the Pacific war chronicles and like all effective historians tells the story through War Department documents as well as through many eyewitnesses. The book is remarkably unchauvinistic: Prange finds plenty of heroism and stupidity on both sides. The same virtue applies to *Midway: The Battle That Doomed Japan,* by Mitsuo Fuchida and Masatake Okumiya, which is still generally available in a Ballantine paperback edition. Okumiya was a participant in the Midway campaign, but aboard the carrier *Ryujo* in the Aleutian Task Force. Fuchida was a flight officer aboard the *Akagi,* Admiral Nagumo's Midway flagship. In addition to a full description of the battle from the Japanese perspective, these authors provide a useful discussion of Japan's evolving naval strategy.

For a broader discussion of the Pacific war, John Toland's *Ris-*

ing Sun (New York: Bantam, 1982, paperback) on the rise and fall of the Japanese Empire is very engrossing reading.

Chapter 6

Attempts to find a single, solid source on the life and times of Emperor Hadrian were unsuccessful, and so the historical material in chapter 6 on his administration has been drawn from a number of more specialized sources. Likewise, little exists in print on methods of Roman management; what does exist—books like G. H. Stevenson's *Roman Provincial Administration* (Oxford: Basil Blackwell, 1939)—is only available in research libraries and fails to speak to the issues the modern manager would find particularly relevant.

What the typical bookstore or library browser finds on the subject of ancient Rome are the classic histories in various editions: *The Twelve Caesars,* by Suetonius; *The Histories* and other works of Tacitus; and Julius Caesar's *Conquest of Gaul.* Works of modern scholarship tend to focus on Roman literature, art, or—most often—on the Roman army. Of the latter, Michael Grant's *The Army of the Caesars* (New York: Charles Scribner's Sons, 1974) is highly recommended, as is his *History of Rome* (New York: Macmillan, 1978, paperback).

Chapter 7

The very best source on the life and public career of Thomas Hutchinson is Bernard Bailyn's *The Ordeal of Thomas Hutchinson* (Cambridge: Belknap/Harvard University Press, 1974). As a neo-Puritan ascetic of limited emotional range, however, Hutchinson is not the most engaging subject for the general reader—especially 420 pages of him—and so Bailyn's more recent book, *Faces of Revolution: Personalities and Themes in the Struggle for American Independence* (New York: Alfred A. Knopf, 1990; Vintage, 1992, paperback) may be more satisfying. Also worth reading is *Patriots: The Men Who Started the American Revolution,* by A. J. Langguth (New York: Simon & Schuster, 1988; Touchstone Books, 1989, paperback). This is engagingly written and widely available.

Chapter 8

Chapter 8 contained an extended passage on the innovative use of massed archery by the English at the battles of Crécy, Poitier, and

Agincourt. Once again, Tuchman's *A Distant Mirror: The Calamitous Fourteenth Century* provides extensive information about prevailing military practices during this period. Readers will quickly see how the social position of the French nobility blinded them to the need to make their own changes.

Several references were made to Aron L. Friedberg's *The Weary Titan: Britain and the Experience of Relative Decline, 1895–1905* (Princeton, NJ: Princeton University Press, 1988). This is a scholarly book that deserves a broader audience. For American readers in particular, it provides prospective on the position of their own economy in a time of rapid change.

Finally, James Utterback's forthcoming book *Mastering the Dynamics of Innovation* (Boston: Harvard Business School Press, 1994) provides a practical model that describes how product and process innovations invade and transform industries. His book contains a number of extended cases (on harvested ice, incandescent lighting, photography, the typewriter, and plate glass) that bring this model to life, helping readers to see their own industries with new eyes, and showing ways in which firms can revitalize their capabilities.

Chapter 9

An important source for chapter 9 is *Thinking in Time,* by Richard E. Neustadt and Ernest R. May (New York: The Free Press, 1986, paperback). Their methodology for making valid analogies to past events is described in this very readable book, which is aimed at decision makers, public and private.

Index